Advance Praise for
Petrodollar Warfare

William R. Clark's *Petrodollar Warfare* is an oracle of our times, exposing the hidden geopolitical strategies of the power elite and the interlocking agendas of big oil and the neoconservatives in power today. Clark is a winner of two Project Censored awards for publishing important news stories ignored by the corporate media in the US.

— Peter Phillips, Professor of Sociology, Sonoma State University, and Director of Project Censored

Petrodollar Warfare by William R. Clark is an important contribution to the question of what the Iraq war was and is all about. Clark links the emerging Euro currency to Iraq's pricing of its oil as one significant factor leading to Washington's decision to topple Saddam Hussein. It might be open for argument whether a "petroeuro" as a replacement for the "petrodollar" is likely or not, given the many divisions within the European Union. But Clark's thorough documentation of the discussion, notably plans for an Iranian Oil Bourse to counter NYMEX and the London IPE, provides a useful basis for further thinking about one of the vital strategic issues of today. Clark also extensively treats the issue of Peak Oil, or global depletion, as a major unspoken factor in the US oil agenda. This book is definitely worth careful reading.

— F. William Engdahl, author of
A Century of War: Anglo-American Oil Politics and the New World Order'

If you think you understand the headlines, think again: current events can only be understood when we follow the money. In *Petrodollar Warfare*, William Clark guides us through the hidden history of the petrodollar era and deftly uncovers the basis of current US strategy in the Middle East.

This sobering book not only elucidates our past and present, but shows the way toward global monetary reform. As Clark makes clear, America's founding ideals can only be fulfilled if the people of the US are willing to confront the twin demons of proto-fascism and kleptocracy.

— Richard Heinberg, author of
The Party's Over: Oil , War and the Fate of Industrial Societies,
and *Powerdown: Options and Actions for a Post-Carbon World*

Not only does *Petrodollar Warfare* give you the big picture of the intertwined world of war, oil, and money, but William Clark also provides ideas for change. This book helps to fuel the grassroots engine for progress in America.

— Jim Hightower, author of *Let's Stop Beating Around the Bush*
and *Thieves in High Places: They've Stolen
Our Country and it's Time to Take it Back*

Back in 1997, when I wrote about M. King Hubbert and Peak Oil in the first edition of *The Last Hours of Ancient Sunlight*, not many people were aware that we were fast approaching a worldwide energy crisis. Now we're in the middle of two wars over it, as William Clark so brilliantly documents in *Petrodollar Warfare*. Oil in euros, deceptions from the White House, wars for profits and political power; it reads like a Ludlum novel. Unfortunately, it may well be altogether too true.

— Thom Hartmann, author of *The Last Hours of Ancient Sunlight*

With *Petrodollar Warfare*, William Clark provides a badly needed, carefully researched explanation of the deep and dark mechanisms underlying international movements of money and military forces. Clark tells the fascinating and distressing story of how America achieved world dominance and looks with tough honesty and realism at what the future might hold. If *Petrodollar Warfare's* bold analysis can help more Americans to understand the current pathology of their own extraordinary country, then it will assist both the world and America to find a better path into a less violent and energy-addicted future.

— Julian Darley, author of *High Noon for Natural Gas: The New Energy Crisis* and coauthor of *Relocalize Now! Getting Ready for Climate Change and the End of Cheap Oil*, and cofounder of the Post Carbon Institute

I first became aware of William Clark's writings in the latter part of 2004. I was amazed by his clarity and almost intuitive grasp of economic issues as well as his ability to relate those to everyday life across several disciplines. Watch what this man says. In *Petrodollar Warfare*, he may be telling us things that we will need to hear for our own survival.

— Michael C. Ruppert, author of *Crossing the Rubicon: The Decline of the American Empire at the End of the Age of Oil*
and publisher of *From the Wilderness*

PETRODOLLAR WARFARE

OIL, IRAQ AND THE FUTURE OF THE DOLLAR

PETRODOLLAR WARFARE

OIL, IRAQ AND THE
FUTURE OF THE DOLLAR

WILLIAM R. CLARK

NEW SOCIETY PUBLISHERS

Cataloging in Publication Data:

A catalog record for this publication is available from the National Library of Canada.

Cover design and composite illustration by Diane McIntosh.
Comstock Images / Alamy Image.

Printed in Canada. First printing June 2005.

Paperback ISBN: 0-86571-514-9.

Inquiries regarding requests to reprint all or part of *Petrodollar Warfare* should be addressed to New Society Publishers at the address below.

To order directly from the publishers, please call toll-free (North America) 1-800-567-6772, or order online at www.newsociety.com

Any other inquiries can be directed by mail to:
New Society Publishers
P.O. Box 189, Gabriola Island,
BC V0R 1X0, Canada
1-800-567-6772

New Society Publishers' mission is to publish books that contribute in fundamental ways to building an ecologically sustainable and just society, and to do so with the least possible impact on the environment, in a manner that models this vision. We are committed to doing this not just through education, but through action. We are acting on our commitment to the world's remaining ancient forests by phasing out our paper supply from ancient forests worldwide. This book is one step toward ending global deforestation and climate change. It is printed on acid-free paper that is **100% old growth forest-free** (100% post-consumer recycled), processed chlorine free, and printed with vegetable-based, low-VOC inks. For further information, or to browse our full list of books and purchase securely, visit our website at: www.newsociety.com

NEW SOCIETY PUBLISHERS   www.newsociety.com

This study is dedicated to the citizens of the United States,
our soldiers, and to the Iraqi people,
all of whom have suffered under grave injustice.

"We owe respect to the living; to the dead we owe only truth."
— *Voltaire, 1785*

Contents

Acknowledgments

I am grateful to Chris Plant of New Society Publishers who helped transform my original online essay into a full-length book. In addition, I am deeply thankful for the patience and persistence afforded to me by the staff at New Society Publishers, especially the editors, who included Ingrid Witvoet and Judith Brand. Likewise I am immensely gratified for the ingenious and powerful cover artwork created by Diane McIntosh.

In no particular order I must thank many other individuals who helped bring this project to fruition. I owe much gratitude to Dr. Peter Phillips of Project Censored at the University of California at Sonoma, along with the faculty and students who voted my original Internet essay as one of the most important but "censored" news stories of 2003. Additionally, I commend F. William Engdahl for recently updating his fascinating book, *A Century of War*. Engdahl's analysis of the American Century and division of the post-World War II period into three distinct economic paradigms was used liberally in the first chapter of this book.

I must also thank Richard Heinberg whose two books, *The Party's Over: Oil, War and the Fate of Industrial Societies* and *Powerdown: Options and Actions for A Post-Carbon World*, offered a meticulous analysis of Peak Oil and realistic appraisals of alternative energy technologies. Furthermore, my appreciation of the challenges surrounding Peak Oil have been broadened by the writings of Colin Campbell, founder of the Association for the Study of Peak Oil and Gas(ASPO), and author of numerous books, including *The Truth about Oil and the Looming Energy Crisis*, and *The Essence of Oil and Gas Depletion*. Another resource who has deepened my appreciation of current events is Michael Ruppert. The tireless research conducted by Ruppert and the writers at From the Wilderness Publications regarding Peak Oil and global political economy is always very thought provoking.

Most of all, I am sincerely thankful to the hundreds of readers from around the world who contacted me throughout 2003–2005 with comments, questions, critiques, and even a few graduate thesis's based on my research. Your quest for awareness and clear concern for humanity was the principal motivating factor that encouraged me to write *Petrodollar Warfare*. I offer this book as a humble gesture to those who continually seek knowledge in a effort to gain a better understanding of our complex world.

This volume is an effort to ultimately enhance the long-term national security of the United States, as well as the world community. While this book critiques numerous policies of the George W. Bush administration, especially with regard to neoconservative doctrine and the resulting Iraq War, it is important to realize that US politicians of all stripes have become excessively shortsighted in their policy-making roles. More than 30 years of US political administrations have placed the country in a situation with both severe economic and energy challenges that must immediately be addressed with new and alternative solutions. As the author, I bear sole responsibility for the contents of this text.

— William R. Clark, March 2005

Foreword

BY JEFF WRIGHT

The Lost American Century?

The world changed forever on September 11, 2001. It could have changed for America in ways that would have assured she remained in the ranks of the truly enlightened, liberated nations of Western civilization. Instead, it seems, that promise has largely been squandered with a vengeance.

The world changed again on March 19, 2003, with the US-led invasion of Iraq. It is almost assured, unless quick action is taken, that this century will become one of fear, oppression, and economic decline for our nation. Our leaders, of both the Republican and Democratic parties, have continued the pattern of self-destructive behavior practiced with increasing disregard of our original purpose and promise as a nation.

The 20th century has often been called "The American Century." To be sure, America has much to be proud of from the last century. Our efforts to stabilize and advance the world in two world wars have no equal. Our development of the majority of modern technology and infrastructure driving the world to increasing wealth realization has no equal. And, until recently, our system of distributing the wealth provided by that infrastructure has been the most advanced model ever provided. We are about to throw it all away.

Our increasing tendency to push our model rigidly into other societies of the world is in fact the sign of an authoritarian state. That is coupled with a foreign policy that seeks to protect that state's corporate interests through manipulation and intimidation of other governments, directly or through surrogates, backed with both overt and covert projections of military power and intelligence capability. This face of the American presence in the world is too little talked about or analyzed by the citizens of the United States and especially the general media. Most of it is shielded from view through the system of government security classification measures.

From the late 1940s to the 1980s, for good or ill, many of these force projections were driven by Cold War politics. Our ongoing shoving match with the Soviet Union protected some countries but trampled many smaller countries underfoot. In addition, the adventurism and empires of some of our closest allies have contributed, part and parcel, to our involvement in attempts to control other parts of the globe where our interests are not vital. These are facts, not judgments.

Even a cursory examination of the current situation is helpful as an example. The boundaries of the current state of Iraq, and by definition the surrounding nations, were arbitrarily drawn by the British and the US at the end of WW I. Further, throughout the region, many nations have been controlled and manipulated by western and eastern European interests after WW II and in the subsequent Cold War.

Why is Iran today run by Ayatollahs? Because the US and UK covertly overthrew Iran's fledgling democracy in 1953 and installed Mohammed Reza Shah Pahlavi in power. The CIA also created and supported Osama bin Laden and his organization in Afghanistan throughout the 1980s as "freedom fighters." The US is also currently supporting the overthrow of the democratically elected government of Venezuela. We control and manipulate governments throughout Central and South America directly against our supposed "values" and in a way that is leading to their people's ever-increasing hatred of our country through our meddling in their internal affairs — including Argentina, Colombia, Chile, Ecuador, Haiti, Nicaragua, Panama, Peru and Venezuela.

We have created these despots and dictators all over the world, thereby creating today's "anti-American" attitudes. In fact, any lengthy research will reveal that our covert and overt operations over the decades have created most of our current enemies. The CIA has coined a term for this outcome: "blowback." Blowback is now coming at us from all directions. At some point the American public must realize that we are not hated simply because we exist. I would suggest that the reader do an Internet Google search on almost any country using such search criteria as Country X + CIA + weapons + military. You will be shocked by the results.

The war coverage of Operation Iraqi Freedom was overwhelming. US military planners termed the assault "shock and awe." What the rest of the world saw on their TVs was reported and perceived as nothing less than "sick and awful." We have destroyed a nation of 24 million people in what was possibly the most expensive "hit" in history. The US has now notified our allies, enemies, and sometime adversaries that unilaterally, when we choose, we can pick anyone apart that we deem necessary, and we can do it in a pre-emptive fashion.

We are currently embroiled in the occupation of Iraq in an attempt to clean up one of the many messes largely of our own making. We will fail. We will fail by the evidence of our own eyes on 24-hour news channels. We have entered into the Never-ending War. Look at what is happening in Iraq through the billions of other eyes in the world. We have forfeited the "moral high ground."

In addition, on March 19, 2003, we finally and completely discarded the US Constitution and adherence to the rule of international law. What mere "law" can withstand the awesome power the government must adopt as "necessary" to enforce internal and worldwide order as our government now views it?

We have entered into the endless degradation of our own rights and liberties as a free people. Each escalating terrorist attack against us will engender a new level of "security" to protect the hapless masses. Yet we will become less secure. The early part of the 21st century will likely be recorded in history as the closing stages of personal rights and liberties, the decline of US international stature, and the end of the once-noble "American experiment."

As a direct result of our government's actions, our economy has been placed in serious jeopardy — our apparent power is illusory. Since the late 1980s, we have been the world's largest debtor nation. We fund our balance of payments deficit, our governmental fiscal deficit, and our public debt through more than $3 trillion of foreign purchase of that debt. That has been enabled in the past only because the dollar has been the World Reserve Currency, principally maintained by petrodollar recycling. The government, corporations, and individuals now live off their credit cards.

The fact that governments around the world are briskly adding euros to their central bank reserve funds is indicative of the lost faith — both in the US dollar and in our fiscal policies regarding debt. Since 2002 the euro has become a more stable currency than the dollar. Undeniably, before the Iraq War the euro had begun making serious inroads in the dollar's ability to remain the World Reserve Currency, directly affecting our ability to continue to fund our deficits and debt.

It is logical to suggest that one of the reasons Germany and France opposed the war in Iraq was that they knew Saddam Hussein's switch to the euro as Iraq's oil transaction currency enhanced the movement worldwide to the euro as a major reserve currency. Although never effectively reported or discussed in the US media, the Iraq War was waged in part to thwart this momentum within OPEC, which portends dire consequences for the US economy. This is particularly so later this decade as we enter a period of enormous deficits and unfunded liabilities in public programs.

The Iraq War has also adversely affected our trading relations with other nations, especially the European Union. This, coupled with a euro that continues to increase in strength and the conscious movement of economic interests away from the US, will directly impact our domestic economy. Much of our infrastructure is already in dire straits without the Never-ending War. Manufacturing is declining and moving overseas at an incredible rate, and there are significant signs that the consumer economy is "over bought" evidenced by the enormous $2 trillion of consumer debt. Americans can only buy ahead or refinance so much before even the credit cards run out.

All in all, the American people have let themselves be lead down the garden path too far, too often by successive administrations. This, combined with increasing levels of the subtle indoctrination that allows many in our society to remain "fat, dumb, and happy," contributes to the sheep syndrome we are experiencing and is in fact exploited by our increasingly clever politicians.

Unfortunately much of the "anti-war" crowd is often misguided and uninformed. Some of them incorrectly place blame on members of the US military. The far left has often failed to understand the difference between a tool and how it is used, whether the issue is gun ownership or the military. That makes it very easy for the authoritarians and those opposed to the true republican form of government to counter and misdirect the issues to their advantage. This will only end when informed republicans enter the debate and stop the rhetoric of the authoritarians.

Only severe "shock and awe" to the citizens of the United States will shake the complacency and misguided support seen across the land for continuing the policies of George W. Bush and previous administrations. From many indicators it is about to happen. However, the only thing we may have left to fear at this point is the reaction of our government to Americans' desire to return to the path laid out by the founders of this nation. Our leaders seem to have decided they like the power more than a two-century-old model for freedom.

Many will argue that the view contained in this paper is cynically opposed to the view that ultimately the government is good. A long list of quotes from the founders that directly dispute that claim will probably be viewed as irrelevant. Even against the noted trend of the last 30 years or the documented evidence of our government's behavior on the dark side would fail to convince as well. It is natural for the citizens of any dominant empire to believe that they are doing what they are doing for all the "right" reasons, whether true or not.

The best proof is simply in more closely analyzing current and coming events. Listen and watch closely for the signposts as indicated in this book. Draw your own conclusions from actual evidence. But then, once the trend is clear, do not fail to act. Or don't act. However, if the reader comes to agree with the viewpoint in this book, at minimum do not continue to give aid and support to policies and decisions that are realized to be heavily flawed and detrimental to our true national security interests. The "conventional wisdom" is hard to buck, and the truth hardest of all to swallow if realized later rather than sooner.

We may have few opportunities to correct events in a way that's much more satisfactory to the real long-term survival and security of the United States and the world. Even talking with your friends and neighbors about the obvious nature of what is happening is extremely important.

Most Americans seem to live in a complacent paradise, ignorant of geography, geopolitics, and the dangers that are brewing all around them. This will prove to be highly injurious to our civilization. We are allowing our leadership to make decisions affecting our grandchildren without true and open debate, without following our fundamental laws, and without telling us what is really known. Under these conditions it cannot reasonably be expected that America will remain a free and prosperous nation for much longer.

America needs your support in whatever form it can be brought to bear, for we have likely entered the most dangerous decade of our history. The challenges analyzed in this text are not conservative/liberal or Republican/Democrat issues, but rather *American issues.* This text offers what many people think are better solutions to the problems we face, and what is in our best long-term national security interest.

Some readers will disagree with this book. However, I hope it will not be said that something contained in this text is anti-American. The author and contributors to this book do not believe that the current or any past US administration that contributed to these problems was anti-American. They may be un-American in certain behaviors and policies, but they are certainly not anti-American.

In *Petrodollar Warfare*, William Clark makes clear that our most important task is to face these challenges, working together with the global community to create a more sustainable and peaceful world in the new century.

Jeff Wright is a former Naval Security Group (NSG) Cryptologic Tech, NAVSEEACT Technical Liaison/System Analyst, Area of Operations: Pacific Rim and Far East (1976–1980) He currently is a Network and Software Development Entrepreneur focused on Model Driven Architecture.

Introduction

Hegemony, \He*gem`o*ny\, noun \Greek *hegemonia*, fr. *Hegemonia* leader, fr. *Hegeisthai* to lead] – preponderant influence or authority especially of one nation over others

— Webster's Ninth New Collegiate Dictionary, 1990

If a nation expects to be ignorant and free, in a state of civilization, it expects what never was and never will be...The People cannot be safe without information. When the press is free, and every man is able to read, all is safe.

— Thomas Jefferson, US President 1801–1809

Thomas Jefferson's words foreshadowed the unfortunate state of affairs facing the United States today. As a proud American whose family ancestry traces back to the American Revolutionary period, I found this book difficult to write. I have little doubt that *Petrodollar Warfare* will prove to be controversial, perhaps unpopular within certain groups, and that some will attempt to dismiss out of hand the facts presented and seek to relegate this analysis to conspiracy theory rather than evaluate this research from an objective perspective. It is this head-in-the-sand position that maintains the status quo and places the United States in great jeopardy.

Some readers will conclude that challenges surrounding US economic and energy problems provided a legitimate rationale for applying unilateral military force against Iraq. Indeed, many will also advocate similar US military operations in the near future. Ultimately such beliefs reflect individual value judgments, and as such, I doubt this book will sway readers who ascribe to that particular moral framework. Of course other readers will subscribe to a different ethical perspective regarding these issues.

Perhaps most critical to the survival of any functional democracy is that the citizenry be sufficiently informed of real challenges facing their nation, so they might rationally discuss and publicly debate such issues. Furthermore, the framers of the Constitution were acutely aware that the absence of an informed citizenry will ultimately jeopardize the liberty of all citizens and facilitate the dangerous concentration of centralized government power. History has shown that society is prone to manipulation, oppression, and tyranny without an open press.

Above all else, the founders were most concerned with building checks and balances into our system of government and sought to contain the tendency of political power to flow unheeded to the executive branch during times of war. The almost complete lack of critical debate within the US media and society in general regarding the recent Iraq War motivated this book. After my original online essay was voted in 2003 as one of the most important but censored news stories by Project Censored,[1] I became fully cognizant of how extensive the information flow is filtered by the US mass media. Although regrettable, it is not surprising that in the past 15 years these sources of broadcast news — TV, radio, and print — have been reduced to only five major corporate conglomerates.

As Thomas Jefferson eloquently warned, *liberty depends on the freedom of the press, and that cannot be limited without being lost.* It was the eternal inspiration of Jefferson with which this book was written. My own sense of patriotic duty compelled me to express dissent and inform others that our current military-centric geostrategy will ultimately result in massive US economic failure. Such an event will be compounded if our national energy policies are not overhauled and restructured to both reduce consumption and rapidly implement alternative energy technologies.

It is imperative that the US citizenry become cognizant that monetary maneuvers away from the dollar by the international community indicate a manifest intolerance of a unilateralist United States employing militant imperialism that seeks to gain control over the world's energy supply and denies the self-determination of sovereign nations regarding their chosen oil export currency. The 2003 Iraq War and its subsequent occupation has pushed the US further along the precarious path of imperial overstretch and economic decline.

Despite the toppling of Saddam Hussein's regime and chaotic US occupation, the original rationales voiced in favor of disarming Saddam Hussein's Iraq with its supposed reconstituted weapons of mass destruction (WMD) program have disappeared. Despite the swift military victory and toppling of the oppressive regime, it is irrefutable that this conflict's stated objectives were at best deceptive and at worst outright fraudulent. Many questions remain unanswered.

For example, the earlier 1990–1991 war against Iraq involved a broad coalition of nations backed by a UN mandate, but why did the vast majority of the previous coalition fail to join the US and UK during this recent conflict? If Iraq's old WMD program truly possessed the threat level repeatedly purported by the Bush and Blair administrations throughout 2002 and into 2003, surely our historic allies would have lined up militarily to disarm Saddam Hussein if he posed any semblance of this alleged threat level?

Why did the UN Security Council fail to provide a second resolution in 2003 authorizing the use of force? Clearly this lack of authorization reflected the UN's deep misgivings and resulted in a markedly unilateral war in which America fielded an army of 255,000 in Iraq and surrounding nations, while the British contributed 45,000, and the Australians committed a paltry 2,000 troops.[2] The lack of UN authorization, lack of NATO support, and the global community's protests against the war were all unprecedented events.

Moreover, despite over 400 unfettered prewar UN inspections, no substantive evidence was ever reported to the Security Council that Iraq was reconstituting its WMD program. In fact, the Bush administration's claims citing Iraq's WMD capability were highly improbable considering the severity of the ongoing UN sanctions against Iraq. Lastly, and despite the Bush administration's repeated implications to the contrary, neither the CIA, DIA or the UK's MI6 ever produced any viable links between Saddam Hussein and the Al Qaeda terrorist network, nor has any evidence ever materialized suggesting Saddam Hussein was involved in the September 11th attacks.

On the contrary, suggesting a relationship between Saddam Hussein, a secular despot who oppressed the religious Shi'ite majority in Iraq, and Al Qaeda terrorists who endorse a fanatical form of fundamentalist Islamic Whabbism defies both logic and that region's history. Numerous WMD and counterterrorism experts warned that the publicly stated prewar justifications were highly implausible. They were right.

What motivated the Bush administration to invade Iraq? The simplistic answer is an effort to preserve US global dominance. Moreover, a little-known fact belies the deeper reasons for the invasion: in order to prop up the US' declining economic status as the sole superpower, its military force was required to gain strategic control of Iraq's oil supply and oil currency for both macroeconomic and geostrategic considerations.

More specifically, this was a war to gain control over Iraq's hydrocarbon reserves and, in doing so, maintain the US dollar as the monopoly currency for the critical international oil market. It was, and is, about retaining the dollar as the world's reserve currency, and it is also about securing its continued use as a mechanism for effortless US credit expansion and global supremacy. It is also about the installation of numerous US military bases in Iraq to gain strategic dominance of the region with the largest remaining hydrocarbon reserves on the planet. As the reader will witness, these assertions are based on a rigorous analysis of the facts, backed with stated US strategic goals.

Although completely unreported by our government and the US corporate media, one of the answers to the enigma surrounding the Iraq War was the simple yet shocking realization that it was partly an oil currency war waged by the US against the euro, currency of the European Union (EU). The calculated goal of regime change in Baghdad was designed to prevent further momentum within the Organization of the Petroleum Exporting Countries (OPEC) toward the euro as an alternative oil transaction currency. In order to preempt OPEC, the US government needed to gain control of Iraq along with its oil reserves. Iraq was really no different than any other imperial war; it was a war over power.

The purpose of this book is to stimulate much needed debate in our society, our government, and hopefully in the international policy-making arena. Only informed and motivated citizens compel changes within the decision-making apparatus of their governments. I hope that US citizens and the world community will begin an open dialogue regarding the complex issues discussed in this book.

Chapter 1 of *Petrodollar Warfare* illustrates that in the post-WWII era, hegemonic power was, and is, derived principally via channeling oil wealth and the issuance of World Reserve Currency. Attempting to maintain these two essential aspects of US hegemony provided motivation for the Iraq War

Chapter 2 outlines how the 2003 Iraq War was also an attempt to fulfill the long-term US geostrategic objective of securing US bases in the center of the Persian Gulf before the onset of global Peak Oil. Chapter 3 discusses the implications of the geological phenomenon referred to as global Peak Oil, which ASPO projected will occur around 2008.[3] US and UK domestic energy supplies are in permanent decline, whereas Iraq and Saudi Arabia are predicted to be the last to reach peak oil production.[4]

Chapter 4 outlines the macroeconomics of petrodollar recycling and the unpublicized, but real, challenge to US economic hegemony from the euro as an alternative oil transaction currency. Chapter 5 discusses the apparent broad global movement away from the dollar. This development is due not only to macroeconomic factors, which most likely were inevitable, but also to recent geopolitical tensions following the invasion of Iraq. Unfortunately, it is hard to argue that this movement would have been more containable if current US foreign and defense policies were not seen as unilateral strategies designed to obtain monopoly control over the world's primary energy supply. Our trading partners and other affected nations would have been much more inclined to help convert the dollar hegemony system into a new global monetary and financial system in enlightened ways.

Chapters 6 and 7 end with a reflection and critique of past and present US fiscal and foreign policies regarding oil and energy issues and propose various policy alternatives utilizing a multilateral framework. These comprehensive reforms are predicated on domestic reform of the US media conglomerates, political campaign finance systems, and associated corporate sponsorship.

General readers should find the petrodollar recycling process and effects relatively straightforward once the basics are understood. Academic readers seeking a technical analysis of this phenomenon from a purely economic perspective should read David E. Spiro's book, *The Hidden Hand of American Hegemony: Petrodollar Recycling and International Markets*.

A comprehensive analysis of Peak Oil and various alternative energy technologies is regretfully beyond the scope of this book. For readers interested in a thorough review of those issues, two references by Richard Heinberg provide an in-depth exploration of these subjects, *The Party's Over: Oil, War and the Fate of Industrial Societies* and his profound follow-up book *Powerdown: Options and Actions for A Post-Carbon World*. Despite these two caveats relating to *Petrodollar Warfare*, the reader does not need a PhD in economics or geology in order to recognize that the status quo of petrodollar recycling and energy consumption is untenable considering the unsustainable structural imbalances in the global economy and the vast implications of the impending global Peak Oil phenomenon.

I advocate immediate reform of the global monetary system to include a dollar/euro currency trading band with reserve status parity, a dual-OPEC oil transaction standard, and a UN-sponsored multilateral project regarding broad-based energy reform in alignment with the Upsalla Protocol. These could potentially restore the damaged international stature of the US, while providing new mechanisms to create a more balanced global monetary system. Most importantly, given the imminent peaking of global oil production, monetary and energy reforms are required if we are to avoid the devastating outcome of global warfare over oil currency and oil depletion.

An analysis of current US geostrategic, monetary, and energy policies suggests that the 21st century will be much different from the previous era, with one possible exception. The first half of the 20th century was filled with unprecedented levels of violence and warfare on a global scale (15 million killed in WW I, 55 million in WW II). The first two decades of the 21st century present challenges that could also result in the unleashing of another period of catastrophic human suffering and destruction. In the post-nuclear age, this must *not* be allowed to transpire. In order to avoid such a terrible fate in this new century, American citizens, more than any others, must accept and undertake sacrifices for the betterment of humanity; we must once again begin living within our means relative to both fiscal and energy policies.

The United States' founding fathers declared that the most fundamental and patriotic duty was to be an informed citizenry. As such, this book was written from my sense of patriotic duty in an effort to inform readers in the US and abroad. While some may find the analysis presented in *Petrodollar Warfare* controversial or perhaps disconcerting, it is presented in the hope that the beginning of the 21st century may be crafted by the international community into a more economically stable, energy sustainable, and less violent period than the opening decades of the previous century. Humanity and morality demand nothing less.

> Whenever the people are well-informed, they can be trusted with their own government. Whenever things get so far wrong as to attract their notice, they may be relied on to set them to rights.

> — Thomas Jefferson, Author of the Declaration of Independence, US President, 1801–1809

One

The American Century:
Post-World War II Period

Overview of US Economic and Military Hegemony:
A Contrast in Strengths and Weaknesses

> We, I hope, shall adhere to our republican government and keep
> it to its original principles by narrowly watching it.
> The price of freedom is eternal vigilance.

> — Thomas Jefferson, US President 1801–1809

At the dawning of the 21st century, the United States is generally acknowledged as the most powerful economic and military nation since the Roman Empire. It is in fact the most absolute global power ever seen for its reach, influence, and control. The US is rightly regarded as the unchallenged superpower. Europe describes the US as the world's "hyperpower," while academics describe the US as the global hegemonic power. Indeed, the US economy is the world's largest, with a Gross Domestic Product (GDP) of approximately $10.5 trillion compared to an annual world GDP of $32 trillion. Since the 1980s the US GDP per capita has grown much faster than that of Japan and Europe. US economic growth is boosted by a high capital investment rate from both domestic and foreign sources, and rising labor productivity associated with its flexible labor markets. New York remains the premier financial center of global banking and commerce, and the US is generally regarded as the leader in globalization.

Since 2001 the general consensus is that tax cuts, cheap credit, and fiscal priming on an unprecedented scale provided a tremendous stimulus to consumer spending in the US economy. For the bullish consensus, this policy stance has been most successful, as measured by recent GDP growth rates of four percent and higher. However, this is a simplistic view that is based on unfounded assertions. Most commentators have not sufficiently discussed the long-term costs of this "recovery" as manifested in the ever-mounting structural imbalances in both the domestic and global economy. Specifically, each of these years has resulted in record US trade gaps, record levels of financial leveraging, record levels of personal indebtedness, record levels of bankruptcies, record levels of budget deficits, and abysmal national savings rates.

The budget deficit for fiscal year 2004 was a record $413 billion, which is $38 billion more than in 2003 and over $70 billion more than originally estimated by the Bush administration. Projected deficits of $5.9 trillion or more over the next ten years will almost certainly drag down economic growth, reduce job and wage opportunities.[1] The US trade deficit also continues to set new records. The trade gap for 2004 soared to a staggering $665.9 billion, nearly six percent of GDP, and in far excess of the previous record set in 2003 of $496.5 billion. The cumulative US trade deficit since 1990 now totals well over $3.5 trillion. To finance these deficits, the US must borrow an equivalent amount, meaning everyday the American government is spending billions borrowed from central banks in China, Japan, Taiwan, and from other foreign entities and individuals, who now own 40 percent of the total current US debt of $7.6 trillion.

Given these imbalances, the US trade deficits suggest our economy is currently not effectively able to compete with the Japanese and European economies in our "post-industrial" society, but instead we are addicted to borrowing prodigious amounts of money without providing goods and services in return. The reasons are simple; most US investment in sustainable markets such as manufacturing has become foreign rather than domestic, while most of our domestic investment is now in non-sustainable markets, commonly referred to as the service-based industry. This pattern of US investment in foreign manufacturing with a growing domestic service sector has produced unprecedented imbalances in the US trade position that is not sustainable.

An analysis of the domestic economy indicates a deteriorating situation, albeit more gradual than the external account position. Foremost is the very mixed picture of job creation that is unlike any previous "recovery period." For example, the US has lost approximately 1.1 million jobs since 2001, according to Labor Department statistics. On the other hand, the economy's growth in the second half of 2003 was reported to be a very healthy 6.1 percent, the fastest six-month growth period in 20 years. In contrast, in 2003 the average duration of unemployment between jobs had risen to 20 weeks, again the longest period since 1984.[2] These disparities between "economic growth" and lack of job creation are unique to the historical post-recovery pattern of the US economy and reflect intrinsic contradictions in our so-called post-industrial economy.

In a controversial admission, one of the top economic advisors in the Bush administration publicly stated that these trends will somehow be helpful to the US economy over the long term. In early 2004 President Bush's chief economic adviser, Greg Mankiw, implied that outsourcing white-collar service jobs abroad where labor is cheaper is a benefit to the US economy, or "just a new way of doing international trade .... It's something that we should realize is probably a plus for the economy in the long run."[3] This seems contradictory given that the reduction in the net US tax base is now at its lowest level since the 1950s. In fact, many of these recently displaced workers were formerly earning sustainable manufacturing incomes, but are now faced with lower-paying service-related jobs and, in some cases, personal bankruptcy due to increasing debt levels. The recent data reflects the disconcerting realization that the so-called service-based economy does not appear to be a feasible long-term model for US economic viability or job growth, even for those with first-rate technical skills.

In fact, the US employment figures have become exceptionally misleading. At the time of writing, unemployment is listed at 5.5 percent, but these highly politicized statistics are fundamentally flawed, as they do not include individuals who are eligible to work but have simply given up finding a job due to the lack of domestic job creation. Under the current methodology, the US could continue to lose hundreds of thousands of workers each month, but the unemployment rate could remain the same or fall even lower.

For example, the Labor Department stated in July 2004 that the economy added a paltry 32,000 jobs, compared to the estimated 150,000 new jobs per month that are required to keep up with population growth. Despite the fact that only one fifth of the required job growth was created for those entering the workforce, the unemployment figure dropped by 0.1 percent to 5.5 percent.[4] This "low" unemployment statistic is spun and proclaimed by politicians as a sign of an "improving economy" that is "adding jobs," when in fact since 2001 US population growth has far exceeded job creation.

In reality the US economy lost a net of at least 1.1 million jobs between 2001 and 2004, and over double that amount in lost manufacturing jobs during the same period. This job market is in its longest slump since the Labor Department began recording statistics in 1939. To illustrate the misleading statistics, the real unemployment data for the first quarter of 2004, including part-time employees who were seeking full-time work, was estimated to be 7.4 percent, rather than the reported 5.6 percent.[5]

Moreover, when underemployment is included — as defined by involuntary part-time work, discouraged workers, and other marginally attached workers (i.e., those who have looked for work in the last year but are not counted as unemployed) — the job picture is much different. According to Job Watch at the Economic Policy Institute, the total underemployment rate in June 2004 was 9.6 percent, which is far higher than the 7.3 percent in March 2001 when the recession officially began.[6] Despite optimistic claims of the economy entering into a "recovery stage" as of November 2001, the real unemployment rate reveals that jobs are being lost and are simply not being replaced — at least not in the United States. This is one of many contradictions in statistical reporting of the US economy. In general, the ability to produce jobs in the US is deteriorating.

Unfortunately these trends are not likely to dissipate in the near future, partly due to overseas outsourcing of manufacturing and skilled information technology-related positions, and partly due to generalized downsizing of US-based employers. White-collar service jobs, such as engineering and even US tax return preparation, have been suggested as new opportunities for outsourcing. Skilled information technology-enabled jobs are rapidly moving to cheaper English-speaking labor markets such as India. The obvious deduction is that the current US job market is contracting under the pressures that Morgan Stanley economist Stephen Roach termed the "global labor arbitrage."[7] There are no indicators that outsourcing of US jobs will abate in the near future.

The domestic imbalances are significant given the unprecedented chasm that has grown between income levels of workers in the US. Kevin Phillips, author of *Wealth and Democracy: A Political History of the American Rich*, vividly illustrated the disparity in production worker versus corporate CEO compensation.[8] In 1988 the ratio of CEO wages to the hourly wages of production workers was 93 times that of workers but increased to a massive 419 times by 1999. While the incomes of workers barely kept up with inflation, the incomes of top executives went up 481 percent, despite corporate profits rising by only 108 percent during the same period.[9] Clearly, these changes are not due simply to market forces.

Phillips deftly argued that perhaps the most important cause of today's wealth inequality in the US is a circular relationship between wealth and political influence. The ultrarich, he explains, use their money to buy political influence and then employ their resulting influence to accumulate more money. Regardless of that assertion, Phillips is quite correct; the current upward retribution of wealth does not bode well for our societal structure and political system.

The present reality is a disconcerting picture of the middle class shrinking as it goes further into debt, while the top one percent of income earners continue to consolidate more of the nation's wealth. Despite statistics of four percent economic growth, the main factor sustaining the economy is increased personal debt through mortgage refinancing — courtesy of ultracheap credit. What is currently unknown is the impact of higher interest rates as the Federal Reserve begins to earnestly increase the overnight lending rate, given the absence of any real growth in personal incomes. Obtaining middle-class status in America is becoming increasingly difficult due to negligible growth in wages and increasing debt levels. This pattern has contributed to personal bankruptcies reaching historic highs in 2002, 2003, and 2004.[10, 11]

Some economists, such as Stephen Roach and former World Bank analyst Richard Duncan, see the US economy as *fundamentally unbalanced*. The reasons specified relate to the widening disparities in the world's external accounts, with the US as the main culprit. As Stephen Roach stated, "The United States squanders its already depleted national saving [while the] rest of the world remains on a subpar consumption path."[12] Duncan argued that the global economy is in a "state of extreme disequilibrium," and an evitable "unwinding" of the global disequilibrium will soon occur, in which he predicted the current US-centric economy will experience major dislocations as the global economy rebalances.[13]

Both of these economic commentators claim that the situation in the US economy can only get worse. In November 2004, during a private lecture on the economy, Roach suggested the US would eventually experience an "Economic Armageddon."[14] Such alarming predictions have been wrong before, but it is quite clear the trade and budget deficits have made the US economy much more vulnerable to external shocks that could be triggered by an interruption of the oil supply, a large stock market/currency decline, or perhaps a terrorist attack.

In summary, the US economy, as it is currently structured, has no mechanism to reverse the massive trade imbalances, which are causing our nation to sink deeper into debt and into an unfavorable power relationship of dependency

> The US economy, as it is currently structured, has no mechanism to reverse the massive trade imbalances, which are causing our nation to sink deeper into debt and into an unfavorable power relationship of dependency with other nations.

with other nations, especially China and Japan. In 2003, the prestigious Bank of International Settlements (BIS) warned, "The global economy faces a fundamental dilemma, which is becoming more acute with time. How can imbalances in growth and external accounts across the major economic regions be resolved while maintaining robust global growth overall?"[15] The BIS suggested that the rest of the world has been far too dependent on the US economy and that deflationary pressures would build unless "expansionary demand management policies" were implemented in both Europe and Asia.

In other words, the world's most prestigious bank publicly stated its concerns about the declining dollar due to US structural imbalances, and that the real test for the rest of the world was to become less dependent on the US economy by creating additional engines for global growth. Without a doubt, further increases in US trade deficits, budget deficits, consumer and corporate debt creation, along with a corresponding disparity between domestic savings is clearly unsustainable. Compounding these problems are the ideologically driven tax cuts in 2001 and 2003. Current levels of US consumption instead of production are not a sustainable model for wealth creation in any nation, including the United States.

Despite these significant economic imbalances and subsequent concerns, US military power is regarded as essentially omnipotent, with unrivaled ability to project military power to almost anywhere on the globe. While Russia had the second-largest annual military expenditures of approximately $91 billion in 2003,the US defense spending of $417 billion that year not only dwarfed that of Russia, but exceeded the next 20 nations' defense spending combined.[16] To put this into perspective regarding the latest armed conflict, Iraq's estimated annual military expenditures in 2002 were only $1.4 billion, equivalent to less than two days' expenditures in annual US military spending. That year Iraq held the 38th position in total annual military expenditures worldwide, tied with the Philippines, and just below the Czech Republic with $1.6 billion.[17] Although stateside commentary sometimes claims that China is a potential challenger to US military power, with 2003 expenditures of only $33 billion, this is unsubstantiated. In 2003 Japan ($47B), France ($37B), and the UK ($35B) each had higher military expenses than did China.[18]

Technologically the US defense establishment is also the most broadly advanced. A few nations have highly specific military capabilities that exceed it, but none come anywhere close to the size, breadth, and depth of the US defense superstructure. This is to be expected as we spend more on national defense per capita than any nation, and by a *very large margin*. For example, per capita military expenditures in the US and Israel are the highest in the world, $1419 and $1551 respectively.[19] Third-highest is Saudi Arabia at $789, while Japan and various European countries spend between $362 and $627 per capita; China spends $25. In 2003 US military expenditures represented *47 percent of the entire world's share.*[20] This defies any meaningful comparison.

Additionally, no nation or alliance possesses basing that approaches the global network of US military bases that have been continually constructed over the past five decades. Using the terminology coined by Chalmers Johnson, the US truly is "The American Empire of Bases."[21] The Department of Defense currently lists 725 military installations in 120 countries, operating or training in 130 of the 189 nations in the United Nations, from Iceland to Australia, from Greenland to New Zealand. Johnson made the somewhat startling observation that the US has 38 separate bases on the Japanese island of Okinawa alone, covering the "choicest 20% of the island."[22] US naval power, with its ability to project force from its fleet of aircraft carriers, has a unique military capability. Even at its height, the Soviet Union had no comparable navy or military basing structure.

This vast empire of bases gives the US an unrivaled ability to roam the world, virtually unchallenged, to do as it pleases seemingly unconstrained by international convention. With the implosion of the old Soviet Union, now over a decade ago, the semblance of a military competitor has disappeared. Unknown to most Americans, CIA briefings given to Congress after the breakup of the Soviet Union made it clear that the Soviets never had, or ever funded, anything but a small fraction of what the US consistently spent throughout the Cold War period.

Paradoxically, Americans find themselves in an unusual dilemma. Despite its omnipotent military power and current position as the largest economy in the world, the US has become an increasingly fearful and isolated nation. We have been instilled with a belief that America is so vulnerable to a small rogue group of terrorists that it must engage in a worldwide "war on terror" that according to Vice President Cheney may last "beyond our lifetimes." According to former National Security Advisor Zbigniew Brzezinski, the US has acquired a somewhat "paranoiac" view of the world.[23]

The question is, how could we as Americans think that our country would be anything more than minimally vulnerable to isolated but specific terrorist-type threats? The most recent evidence of a "paranoiac" worldview at the highest levels of US government was relayed in retired General Wesley Clark's book, *Winning Modern War.* According to Clark, during a visit to the Pentagon two months after the September 11, 2001, attack, he became alarmed when informed of

> Despite its omnipotent military power and current position as the largest economy in the world, the US has become an increasingly fearful and isolated nation. ... instilled with a belief that America is so vulnerable to a small rogue group of terrorists that it must engage in a worldwide "war on terror".

US military planners working on a five-year, seven-war campaign against nations that were deemed to be "state-sponsors" of terrorists groups.[24] At the time, Clark considered such a military strategy to be unfathomable, and regretfully dismissed the plausibility that US leaders would actually advocate such policies.

With the exception of the Taliban regime in Afghanistan, what other governments were actively supporting Al Qaeda? Much evidence suggests that Saudi Arabia and Pakistan were sympathetic to the Taliban, and likely supporting Osama bin Laden. Neither of these two countries were included as part of the "axis of evil."

Perhaps the ultimate illustration of this irrational paranoia in America's national sentiments was the amount of public support for the March 2003 invasion against Iraq — a nation that had over the previous 12 years become reduced to a nearly de-industrialized country with a feeble military unable to protect its borders or even its capital. Never before has the US openly defied the international community and discarded international law in order to wage an unprovoked "preventative war" against another country. That historical event should be instructive of some underlying forces.

Although the majority of governments worldwide and the UN did not agree with President Bush and Prime Minister Blair's justifications for the Iraq War, many Americans became convinced that Saddam Hussein posed an imminent threat to the US, and as such, an immediate invasion of Iraq was warranted. However, subsequent to the invasion, none of the originally stated threats against the US have been proven to be true. During 2004 notable evidence was provided by former members of the Bush administration stating that the Iraq War was a predetermined decision when Bush was sworn in as president in January 2001.

These assertions were verified in *The Price of Loyalty*, a book that detailed the recollections of former US Treasury Secretary O'Neill. He was surprised to learn during the very first National Security Council meeting in January 2001 that Bush sought to "find a way" to topple Saddam Hussein.[25] A subsequent book by former terrorism czar Richard Clarke, *Against All Enemies*, further confirmed the Bush administration's desire to invade Iraq after the September 11th attacks. According to Clarke, when he informed President Bush the next day, that Saddam Hussein had no ties to Al Qaeda, Bush "testily" ordered him to "Look into Saddam, Iraq," while Donald Rumsfeld stated his desire, "getting Iraq."[26]

Paradoxically, at the beginning of the Bush administration, former Secretary of State Powell declared that the UN sanctions were effective and that Iraq did not pose any threat to its neighbors or to the US. On February 24, 2001, Powell stated: "[Saddam Hussein] has not developed any significant capability with respect to weapons of mass destruction. He is unable to project conventional power against his neighbors. So in effect, our policies have strengthened the security of the neighbors of Iraq."[27] In 2005 the final report from the chief US weapons inspector Charles Duelfer concluded that Iraq had not produced any WMD since 1991 and that the "former regime had no formal written strategy or plan for the revival of WMD."[28]

Additionally, neither the Central Intelligence Agency (CIA) nor the Defense Intelligence Agency (DIA) was able to find any credible links between Saddam Hussein and the Al Qaeda 9/11 terrorist attacks despite an intensive analysis.[29] Considering that Saddam Hussein's debilitated military force was unable to challenge its immediate neighbors or the US, he was unable to rebuild his WMD program, and there was no evidence of Iraqi involvement in the 9/11 attack, or even tacit support of Al Qaeda, what was driving the Bush administration to preemptively invade Iraq?

This book attempts to explain from an analytical perspective the non-publicly disclosed, but major, economic and strategic forces that drove President Bush's desire to topple Saddam Hussein from the very beginning of his administration, well before 9/11. The actual threat to the US was not based on violence or terrorism, but something different, yet not altogether surprising — declining economic power and depleting hydrocarbons.

Throughout history, the rationales provided by various political leaders to undertake wars usually turned out to be quite different from the real underlying reasons. Typically, in retrospective analysis the "simple reasons" stated in public often obfuscate the much broader and complex issues that were never publicly stated. Of course different constituents may draw different conclusions from the historical analysis of contemporary warfare, but in either case the objectives as publicly stated at the time are usually confounded with underlying strategic issues.

Military historians have often observed that the vast majority of modern warfare has usually been based upon underlying issues regarding access to resources and related economic issues. Michael Klare, international energy expert and author of *Resource Wars: The New Landscape of Global Conflict*, noted that even so-called religious wars are often driven by underlying strategies to gain control over natural resources.[30] Throughout history, political leaders have often exploited race or religion as mechanisms to create generalized hatred and draw popular support for campaigns of warfare.

This book presents facts that will refute the publicly stated reasons for the 2003 Iraq War, and offers an alternative hypothesis based primarily on well-established US strategy regarding control of oil, and a unique analysis regarding the macroeconomics of the US dollar.

While some Americans may not accept the conclusion offered in this text, the majority of objective US readers and international observers will find this analysis informative, convincing, and perhaps disconcerting. It is intended to stimulate some level of debate within US and EU societies and at the policy-making level regarding these crucial, yet essentially unreported, issues.

Although the US invasion of Iraq was a quick military success, for which we are grateful, the US dollar has not regained its traditional safe-harbor status following the war, but has continued its downward trajectory relative to most other major currencies. Currency traders had expected the dollar to strengthen following a successful US military campaign, as was witnessed after the 1991 Operation Desert Storm. Despite the appearances of a stock market rally in 2003–2004, the dollar's continued deterioration suggests that the US economy is not exactly healthy. The dollar is the symbol of US economic power, the center of the world's financial markets, and the foundation upon which the American Century was built.

> Since early 2002 the international capital markets have developed a notable preference for the euro. Washington appears to have abandoned a strong dollar policy and allowed the dollar to fall without intervention.

However, since early 2002 the international capital markets have developed a notable preference for the euro. Washington appears to have abandoned a strong dollar policy and allowed the dollar to fall without intervention, other than that of the Japanese. The public comments from Washington are that the markets should decide the value of the dollar.

A careful analysis of the nuances of international finance reveals that what is actually taking place is a high-stakes game for geopolitical influence. We are witnessing a struggle between two competing global currencies: the euro and the dollar. The emergence of the euro has provided the first viable challenger to US dollar's supremacy since the end of World War II.

The Bush administration's drive toward a war in Iraq was represented not only by the highly visible neoconservative hawks — such as Donald Rumsfeld, Paul Wolfowitz, and Richard Perle — but also by the more powerful, veiled interests whose global role depends upon the dollar's status as the World Reserve Currency. These influential groups are well represented by the cabinet members of the Bush administration and include large transnational energy companies, such as Halliburton, Exxon Mobil, and ChevronTexaco. The other half of these influential interests are the Big Five American defense conglomerates of Boeing, Lockheed-Martin, Raytheon, Northrop-Grumman, and TRW, as well as numerous other military-industrial contractors.

These giant energy and military firms wield enormous political clout in Washington, often hiring former Washington insiders to enhance their political power. Cheney's tenure as CEO of Halliburton between the two Bush administrations is the most well-known example of the powerful government-energy nexus. This is the same corporate–military–industrial–petroleum network of conglomerates that preferred a puppet government in Iraq, for reasons that will become apparent later in this chapter.

In the high-stakes power game of geostrategy, maintaining the dollar as the World Reserve Currency was a major component in the Bush administration's push for the Iraq War. Once this fundamental concept is known, the strategic and political divisions between the US and the EU/Franco-German alliance in both the prewar and postwar periods become understandable.

America's dominant position as the sole superpower ultimately rests upon two pillars: its overwhelming military superiority and its control of the global economic system by the unique role of the dollar as the World Reserve Currency. An analysis of the facts before, during, and especially after the Iraq War strongly suggests it was designed to preserve the second pillar of US domination — the dollar and its unique role regarding international oil sales.

The American Century: Three Phases

A historical review of the American Century can be traced back through distinct economic periods in the post-World War II period. F. William Engdahl offered an exemplary model in which he divides this postwar period of US supremacy into three separate phases. The following constructs including the three phases of US dominance is liberally borrowed from Engdahl's online essay, "The American Century? Iraq and the Hidden Euro-dollar Wars,"[31] also chronicled in his updated book, *The Century of War: Anglo-American Oil Politics and the New World Order.*[32]

Even before WW II and America's emergence as a superpower, the US had the largest economy, but at the time it was not a leading factor in global management. In 1929, before the Great Depression, the US produced a prodigious 44.5 percent of global industrial production, compared to Germany's 11.6 percent, Great Britain's 9.3 percent, France's 7 percent, the Soviet Union's 4.6 percent, and Japan's 2.4 percent.[33]

However, the aftermath of WW II dramatically reinforced this dynamic, and the US emerged as a superpower. During the war its economy was transformed into a semi-command economy in which industrial production almost quadrupled. Women entered the workforce in vast numbers, while the American citizens made significant sacrifices in lifestyle and consumption for the war effort. By the end of the war the US had not only gained economic dominance, but also enjoyed greatly enhanced security in the northern and southern hemispheres.

Following the successful D-Day invasion of June 1944, the Allies realized the war would probably end within a few years, and it was obvious the world would be in dire need of economic and diplomatic stabilization. This led to the famous Bretton Woods Monetary Conferences of 1944–1945 that established a new international monetary system based on the US dollar. A plaque erected at the original conference site in Carroll, New Hampshire, states:

In 1944 the United States government chose the Mount Washington Hotel as the site for a gathering of representatives of 44 countries. This was to be the famed Bretton Woods Monetary Conference. The Conference established the World Bank, set the gold standard at $35 an ounce, and chose the American dollar as the backbone of international exchange. The meeting provided the world with badly needed post war currency stability.

For a time the US performed its new hegemonic role rather admirably. The economies of Europe and Asia were literally bombed-out and desperately needed to be reconstructed in the postwar period. Hence, it was the Bretton Woods Conferences that created the World Bank and the International Monetary Fund (IMF) to facilitate this noble goal. These two organizations were later instrumental in rebuilding both the European and Japanese infrastructures. The first phase of the American Century began in the immediate postwar period from 1945 and 1948 when the Cold War officially began. Engdahl and many other contemporary commentators refer to this period as the "Bretton Woods Gold Exchange system."[34]

Under the Bretton Woods system in the immediate aftermath of the war, the international order was relatively tranquil. The United States emerged as the sole superpower, with a strong industrial base and the largest gold reserves of any nation. The initial task was to rebuild Western Europe, and in 1949 it was decided to create the NATO (North Atlantic Treaty Organization) alliance against possible Soviet Union military incursions into Western Europe. The role of the US dollar was directly tied to that of gold. So long as America enjoyed the largest gold reserves, and the US economy was in large measure the most productive and efficient producer, the entire Bretton Woods currency structure from French franc to British pound sterling and German mark was stable. Dollar credits were extended along with the Marshall Plan to financially assist the rebuilding of wartorn Europe and Asia.

American companies, including oil multinationals, gained nicely from their dominant positions in European trade at the onset of the 1950s. Washington even encouraged the creation of the Treaty of Rome in 1958 in order to boost European economic stability and generate larger US export markets in the bargain. For the most part, this initial phase of what *TIME* magazine publisher Henry Luce termed "the American Century" was a period of enlightened US leadership. To be sure, in terms of economic gains this immediate postwar period was relatively benign for both the US and Europe.[35] The US enjoyed healthy trade and fiscal positions, which allowed subsequent economic flexibility.

Likewise, this was the era of American liberal foreign policy, such as the Marshall Plan and the Berlin Airlift. The United States was welcomed as the dominant power in the Western community of nations. As it commanded overwhelming gold and economic resources compared with Western Europe, Japan, and South Korea, the US could well afford to be open to European and Japanese trade and exports. The tradeoff was European and Japanese support for the role of the US during the Cold War. American leadership was based during the 1950s and early 1960s less on direct coercion and more on arriving at consensus, whether in trade rounds regarding the General Agreement on Tariffs and Trade (GATT) or other issues. Elites, such as the Bilderberg group, were organized to share the evolving consensus between Europe and the United States.[36]

The first most benign and prosperous phase of the American Century came to an end by the early 1970s. This, due in part to the escalating expenses of the Vietnam War and the growing economic strength of Europe and Japan, was greatly exacerbated by the unexpected arrival of domestic peak oil production in the lower 48 US states in 1970. By the mid-1960s, the Bretton Woods Gold Exchange began to break down, as Europe had rebuilt its manufacturing base and had become a strong exporter. One visible example of renewed economic power was Volkswagen automobile sales in the US.

This growing economic strength in Western Europe coincided with soaring US public deficits as President Johnson escalated the tragic war in Vietnam. Given the huge debt being created by the military operations in Southeast Asia, several European countries became concerned about the dollar's value and began redeeming their dollars for gold. The most notable was Charles de Gaulle of France, the first of the major European countries to take its dollar export earnings and claim gold from the US Federal Reserve, which was legal under the Bretton Woods Conference.

However, by November 1967 withdrawals of gold bullion from the US Treasury had become extensive. The weak link in the Bretton Woods Gold Exchange arrangement was Britain, often referred to as the "sick man of Europe."[37] It broke the first link in the Bretton Woods monetary system in 1967, when the pound sterling was devalued. As Engdahl noted,

> [This] accelerated the pressure on the US dollar, as French and other central banks increased their call for US gold in exchange for their dollar reserves. They calculated with the soaring war deficits from Vietnam, it was only a matter of months before the United States itself would be forced to devalue against gold, so better to get their gold out at a high price.[38]

By the summer of 1971 the drain on the Federal Reserve's gold stocks had become critical, and even the Bank of England joined the French in demanding US gold bullion for their dollars. In August 1971 the British ambassador showed up at the Treasury Department to redeem $3 billion for its fixed exchange value in gold of $35 per ounce (approximately 5.3 million ounces, or 2600 tons of gold).[39] At this time the Nixon administration opted to abandon the dollar-gold link entirely, thereby going to a system of floating currencies on August 11, 1971. Otherwise Nixon would have risked the collapse of the gold reserves of the US. Rather than risk damaging US credit, he changed the rules, or more accurately, he abandoned the rules.

The break with gold effectively ended the Bretton Woods Agreement and opened the door to an entirely new phase of the American Century. In this phase, large international banks, such as Citibank, Chase Manhattan, or Barclays Bank, in effect privatized control over monetary policy. These institutions assumed the role that central banks held under the Bretton Woods gold system, but of course without any ability to redeem dollars for gold. In this phase, market forces determined the dollar's value, which resulted in substantial inflation during the early 1970s. In an effort to stem this inflation, the Nixon administration adopted wage-price freezes in late 1971, but inflation continued to increase significantly during the 1970s.

The combined forces of a free-floating dollar, a growing US trade deficit, and massive debt associated with the ongoing Vietnam War contributed to both the volatility and devaluation of the dollar in the 1970s. According to research outlined in David Spiro's book, *The Hidden Hand of American Hegemony*, it was during this time that OPEC began discussing the viability of pricing oil trades in several currencies. This unpublished proposal involved a basket of currencies from the Group of Ten nations, or G–10.[40] These members of the Bank of International Settlements (BIS), plus Austria and Switzerland, included the major European countries and their currencies, such as Germany (mark), France (franc), and the UK (pound sterling), as well other industrialized nations, such as Japan (yen), Canada (Canadian dollar), and of course the US (US dollar). It should be noted the powerful G–10/BIS also has one unofficial member, the governor of the Saudi Arabian Monetary Authority (SAMA).

In order to prevent this monetary transition to a basket of currencies, the Nixon administration began high-level talks with Saudi Arabia to unilaterally price international oil sales in dollars only — despite US assurances to its European and Japanese allies that such a unique monetary/geopolitical arrangement would *not* transpire. In 1974 an agreement was reached with New York and London banking interests that established what became known as "petrodollar recycling." That year the Saudi government secretly purchased $2.5 billion in US Treasury bills with their oil surplus funds, and a few years later Treasury Secretary Blumenthal cut a secret deal with the Saudis to ensure that OPEC would continue to price oil in dollars only.[41]

In typical understatement Spiro noted that, "clearly something more than the laws of supply and demand ... resulted in 70 percent of all Saudi assets in the United States being held in a New York Fed account."[42] Naturally, this arrangement with the Saudi government prevented a market-based adjustment and was the basis for the second phase of the American Century, the petrodollar phase. What follows is the extraordinary history in which petrodollar recycling was vigorously implemented during the 1970s.

Recycling Petrodollars

In May 1973, with the dramatic fall of the dollar still vivid, a group of 84 of the world's top financial and political insiders met at Saltsjobaden, Sweden, the secluded island resort of the Swedish Wallenberg banking family. This gathering of [the] Bilderberg group heard an American participant, Walter Levy, outline a 'scenario' for an imminent 400 percent increase in OPEC petroleum revenues. The purpose of the secret Saltsjobaden meeting *was not to prevent the expected oil price shock, but rather to plan how to manage the about-to-be-created flood of oil dollars*, a process US Secretary of State Kissinger later called 'recycling the petrodollar flows.' [emphasis added]

— F. William Engdahl, *A Century of War*[43]

Beginning in the mid-1970s the American Century system of global economic dominance underwent a dramatic change. The oil price shocks of 1973–1974 and 1979 suddenly created enormous demand for the floating dollar. Oil-importing countries from Germany to Argentina to Japan all were faced with how to acquire export-based dollars to pay their expensive new oil-import bills. The rise in the price of oil flooded OPEC members with dollars that far exceeded domestic investment needs and were therefore categorized as "surplus petrodollars." A major share of these came to London and New York banks where the new process of monetary petrodollar recycling was initiated.

Engdahl's remarkable book, *A Century of War*, chronicled how certain geopolitical events mirrored a "scenario" discussed during a May 1973 Bilderberg meeting. Apparently powerful banking interests sought to "manage" the monetary dollar flows that were premised upon what the group envisioned as "huge increases" in the price of oil from the Middle East. The minutes of this Bilderberg meeting included projections of OPEC oil prices increasing by 400 percent.[44]

In 1974 US Assistant Treasury Secretary Bennett and David Mulford of the London-based Eurobond firm of White Weld & Co. set about the mechanism to handle the surplus OPEC petrodollars.[45] Kissinger, Bennett, and Mulford helped orchestrate the secret financial arrangement with SAMA that creatively transformed the high oil prices of 1973–1974 to the direct benefit of the US Federal Reserve Banks and the Bank of England.

Despite the financial windfall enjoyed by the US/UK banking and petroleum conglomerates who "managed the recycling of petrodollar flows," most Americans regard the 1973–1974 oil shocks as a particularly painful time of high inflation and long lines at every gas station. In the developing countries these high oil prices created huge loans from the International Monetary Fund — debts to be repaid entirely in dollars.

Saudi Arabia and the other OPEC producers deposited their surplus dollars in US and UK banks, which then took these OPEC petrodollars and re-lent them as Eurodollar bonds or loans, to goverments of developing countries desperate to borrow dollars to finance their oil imports. While beneficial to the US- and UK-based financial centers, the buildup of these petrodollar debts by the late 1970s facilitated the basis for the developing world's debt crisis of the early 1980s. Hundreds of billions of dollars were recycled between OPEC, the London and New York banks, and back to developing countries.

Also, following the collapse of the Bretton Woods Agreement, a massive shift from gold to dollar reserve assets quickly took place. In 1971 gold represented approximately 50 percent of the International Reserve assets, but after 1971 gold was rapidly replaced by foreign exchange currencies, which now represent about 95 percent of Central Bank Reserve assets. Dollars became the major reserve currency for most nations. Since then the net effect of petrodollar recycling has provided the Federal Reserve with an unparalleled ability to create credit and expand the money supply in such a manner that was impossible under the previous Bretton Woods Agreement.

In *The Dollar Crisis*, Richard Duncan attributed the 1974 petrodollar recycling mechanism to the "first boom-and-bust crisis of the post-Bretton Woods era."[46] In fact this transitional period created an unbalanced system replete with unforeseen and undesirable artifacts, mainly a massive developing world debt as a result of the high oil prices. In August 1982 Mexico announced it would likely default on repaying Eurodollar loans, breaking another chain in the global monetary system. The developing world debt crisis was set in motion when Paul Volcker and the US Federal Reserve had to unilaterally increase US interest rates in 1979 in an effort to save the failing dollar.

After three years of record high US interest rates, the dollar was "saved" by 1981, but most of the developing nations were drowning in what they perceived as rather usurious US interest rates on their petrodollar loans. The IMF enforced debt repayment to the London and New York banks by acting as debt policeman in implementing the dreaded "austerity" programs.[47] As a result, public spending for health, education, and welfare decreased as the IMF required banks to provide timely debt service on their petrodollar loans. These austerity programs were often perceived as draconian measures by the local populations and may have contributed to the contemporary anti-globalization movement.

The petrodollar supremacy phase was a successful attempt by the US' ruling establishment to slow down its geopolitical decline as the hegemonic power of the postwar system. The IMF Washington Consensus enforced draconian debt collection on developing countries, forcing them to repay dollar debts despite the social upheavals and lack of funds for domestic growth.[48] Moreover, this system prevented economic independence from developing nations in our hemisphere, and kept the US banks and the dollar afloat.

In the 1970s Japan became the US' largest trade partner, but with no indigenous oil supply and yet a major industrial nation, it was, and still is, a significant importer of oil. Japanese trade surpluses have been facilitated by the export of cars, electronics, and other goods that are then used to buy oil in dollars. The remaining surpluses are invested in US Treasury bonds to earn interest. It has been suggested that the G–7 was founded in an effort to keep Japan and Western Europe inside the orbit of the US dollar system. However, from time to time into the 1980s and again after the 1997 monetary crisis, various voices in Japan would call for three major currencies — dollar, German mark, and yen — to share the World Reserve role. These reforms aimed at balancing the global monetary system never transpired, while the dollar continued its role as the official World Reserve Currency.

From a narrow standpoint, the petrodollar phase of US domination seemed to work as it provided a level of stability regarding global oil prices. However, as Engdahl noted, this situation has created unsustainable debt levels in many developing nations, and some have suggested an ever-worsening economic decline in living standards.[49] The IMF "austerity" policies often damaged national economic growth, while transferring the wealth out of the host country and into areas for reinvestment that did not benefit the nation that sold off its natural resources.

Despite the economic power gained from this artificial alliance with Saudi Arabia, even in the petrodollar phase US geostrategists were basically of the realist tradition and were able to construct a liberal consensus for American foreign policy and military policy. To use a term coined by Joseph Nye, American's "soft power" was still used to negotiate periodic new trade arrangements or other issues with its allies in Europe, Japan, and East Asia.[50]

Neoconservatives and the "Petroeuro" Challenge

The end of the Cold War in the early 1990s allowed the natural emergence of a newly unified Europe and the European Monetary Union. As far back as 1997 it was recognized that a unified Europe could begin to present an entirely new challenge to the American Century. It took one decade after the 1991 Gulf War for this new dynamic to emerge into a full-blown challenge, resulting in one of the underlying economic reasons for the 2003 Iraq War. The present conflict stemming from the 2003 invasion of Iraq is the first major proxy battle in the new, third phase of securing American dominance.

Several slogans have been offered to justify the Iraq War, but certainly one of the most peculiar is the idea proffered by Stanley Kurtz, Max Boot, and other neoconservative commentators who advocate military action and regime change as part of their bold plan for "democratic imperialism."[51] However, this neoconservative proclivity for Orwellian-like sophistry does not resemble any useful model for geostrategic planning. The ongoing guerilla war in Iraq suggests that "democratic imperialism" is likely viewed by vast swaths of Iraqi society as militant imperialism. A more direct appraisal of the situation requires a review of statements made by George Kennan, head of policy planning in the US State Department. Kennan is often regarded as one of the key architects of US global strategy in the postwar period. In 1948 he advocated the following candid advice to US leadership:

> We have about 50 percent of the world's wealth, but only 6.3 percent of its population. In this situation, we cannot fail to be the object of envy and resentment. Our real task in the coming period is to devise a pattern of relationships which will permit us to maintain this position of disparity. To do so, we will have to dispense with all sentimentality and day-dreaming; and our attention will have to be concentrated everywhere on our immediate national objectives. We should cease to talk about vague and unreal objectives such as human rights, the raising of the living standards, and democratization. The day is not far off when we are going to have to deal in straight power concepts. The less we are then hampered by idealistic slogans, the better.[52]

The "idealistic slogans" that Kennan recommended US policy makers *discard* are the very ideas that our government is *supposed* to represent, such as: "human rights," "raising living standards," and "democratization." While the US has largely been able to avoid "straight power concepts" for five decades, it has now become the only vehicle for which it can maintain its dominance. Indeed, Kennan's term "straight power" is the appropriate description of current US geopolitical unilateralism. Unfortunately, the basis for the broad proliferation of global anti-American sentiments is a tragic result of the Bush administration's insistence on *hard power* diplomacy.

The foundations for aggressive, overt US foreign polices are evident from various interviews and policy papers provided by neoconservative thinkers, such as Dick Cheney, Donald Rumsfeld, Paul Wolfowitz, Richard Perle, David Frum, and William Kristol. The origin of these polices can be traced to a controversial defense policy paper written by Wolfowitz in February 1992 for then Secretary of Defense Cheney. In this paper Wolfowitz advocated that the US seek to dominate the world community in the aftermath of the Cold War.

These policy documents specifically stated that no nation or group of nations should be allowed to compete or even "play a larger role" in the world. The potential challengers to US dominance as referenced in this document included US allies such as Europe, Japan, and India.[53] In March 1992 when this paper was leaked, it created much controversy and thus was subsequently toned down in a later version. Nonetheless, the idealistic goal of a US global power enforcing its role of domination remained alive throughout the 1990s.

In September 2000, during the presidential election between Al Gore and George W. Bush, a small Washington think-tank, the Project for a New American Century (PNAC), released a major policy study, "Rebuilding America's Defenses: Strategies, Forces and Resources for a New Century."[54] This 90-page report gives a better understanding of the Bush administration's foreign policies. This manifesto revolved around a geostrategy of US dominance — stating that no other nations will be allowed to "challenge" US hegemony.

On Iraq, it stated, "The United States has sought for decades to play a more permanent role in Gulf regional security. While the unresolved conflict with Iraq provides *the immediate justification*, the need for a substantial American force presence in the Gulf *transcends the issue of the regime of Saddam Hussein*."[55] [emphasis added] The PNAC authors acknowledged that for decades US geostrategists have sought to introduce *permanent* military basing in Iraq, regardless of whether Saddam Hussein remained in power. With the neoconservatives firmly in power, components of both the 1992 and 2000 policy papers were incorporated into formal US policy, the 2002 US National Security Strategy (NSS).

For decades the US has been successful in employing a combination of both economic and military power to pursue neoliberal globalization, while retaining its global military superstructure even after the demise of the Soviet Union. However, these historical trends that facilitated multilateral policies were largely abandoned under the neoconservative doctrine that advocates *overt* projection of US military force to pursue global domination. Not surprisingly, this radical US unilateralism has altered geopolitical alignments and created tension around the world. Rather than work out areas of agreement with European partners, Washington increasingly sees a united European Union as the major strategic threat to American hegemony, especially the "Old Europe" of Germany and France.

This strategy is unfortunately the historical pattern witnessed from a declining economic power. The British Empire began its decline around 1870, at which time the British

> For decades the US has been successful in employing a combination of both economic and military power to pursue neoliberal globalization, while retaining its global military superstructure even after the demise of the Soviet Union.

government often resorted to increasingly desperate imperial wars in South Africa and elsewhere. So too is the US using its military might in an effort to advance what it can no longer achieve by economic means.[56] While no nation or group of nations seeks to challenge its military superiority, the broad momentum toward the euro presents a real, but unspoken, economic challenge to US hegemony. At present, the US dollar has become its Achilles heel.

The successful introduction of the euro in January 1999 added an entirely new element to the global monetary system and ushered in what may be called the third phase of the American Century, in which the latest Iraq War plays a major role. This phase, according to Engdahl, threatens to bring a new "malignant or imperial phase" to replace the earlier phases of American hegemony.[57] Certainly, the neoconservatives are quite open about their imperial agenda, while more traditional US policy-makers attempt to either deny these policies or obfuscate their motives by promoting ideals such as "spreading democracy" through force of arms. Regardless, the economic imbalances in the current US economy and the reality of a challenger to the dollar's role in the global economy define this new phase of the American Century.

Third Stage of the American Century: Petrodollar Warfare

This new emerging phase appears to be unfolding with a manifest difference from the two initial phases of the American Century — 1945 to 1971, and 1971 to 1999.[58] This new phase of unbridled *unilateralism* and *hard power* is an attempt to continue US domination in the aftermath of 9/11 and the Iraq War. American power from 1945 to 1999 can be described as predominately that of an accepted global hegemon, based on its vast economic and military capabilities. While a global hegemon dominates power in an unequal distribution of international power, its influence is based more on consent among its allies, and not generated solely by coercion.

During the first five decades after WW II, American dominance was largely based on an understanding that the US would provide certain services to its allies, such as military security or regulating world markets, that would benefit both the larger group and itself. This period was marked with a sufficient degree of American multilateralism within the UN framework and international cooperation between the US and Europe regarding NATO military operations.

However, unlike a dominant power that enjoys some level of acquiescence from other nation states, an imperial power has no obligations to allies, nor does it have the freedom for such policies, as the only raw dictate becomes how to hold on to its declining power, often referred to as "imperial overstretch." This is the worldview that neoconservatives such as Cheney and Rumsfeld advocate, nothing less than US domination of the international order. This requires the doctrine of "preventative warfare," military control over the world's primary energy supply, along with military enforcement of the dollar — and only the dollar — as the international currency standard for oil transactions. Unlike the previous periods of US domination, forward-leaning military unilateralism is the underlying posture.

An unspoken war between the dollar and the euro for global supremacy is at the heart of this new phase of the American Century, referred to in this text as the petrodollar warfare stage. It will be vastly unlike the earlier period from 1945 to 1999. In this new era, the US freedom to grant economic concessions to the G–7 industrialized nations is rather diminished.[59] (This also applies to Russia, the eighth member of the G–8).

The prewar diplomatic conflicts and ongoing reluctance of the world community to broadly internationalize the postwar Iraq situation were the opening acts in this new conflict. The ultimate prize in this game of strategy is the currency that OPEC uses as their international standard for oil transactions. It has traditionally been the dollar, but the euro is now challenging this arrangement. In other words, we are witnessing an unspoken oil-currency war between the US and EU.

The petrodollar warfare stage was ushered in on March 19, 2003, with the unprovoked military invasion of Iraq by the US, UK, and a small contingent of Australian soldiers. This stage will be based on two primary factors: using the US military to secure physical control over the planet's remaining hydrocarbon deposits, and using the US military and its various intelligence agencies to enforce the petrodollar arrangement. Iraq was the first overt conflict in this third stage.

Bluntly stated, the petrodollar warfare stage unfortunately represents the application of violence by the US intelligence agencies or military in an effort to enforce the dollar standard as the monopoly currency for international oil transactions. Iran, Venezuela, Russia, and potentially even Saudi Arabia may move away from the petrodollar arrangement in the near to immediate term, thereby becoming the targets of US antagonism. While the Russian political apparatus is fairly immune to direct US interventions, the plausibility of regime change in various less-powerful oil-producing states in the Middle East, Caspian Sea region, West Africa, and Latin America remains ever present.

To understand the importance of this unspoken battle for currency supremacy, we should review the events that facilitated the emergence of the US as the dominant global superpower after 1945. It is obvious that US hegemony has traditionally rested on two formidable pillars. Foremost is its overwhelming military superiority over all other global rivals. In 2003 the US' defense spending was more than three times the total of the twelve-state EU, approximately $417 billion versus $120 billion, with the US spending more than the 20 next-largest nations combined. If this disparity were not enough, Washington plans additional defense spending of $2.1 trillion over the next five years (through 2009).

The US figure does not include the annual expenditures of its vast intelligence network, totaling at least $30 billion. No nation or group of nations comes close in defense or intelligence-related spending. China is most interested in economic development and is at least two decades away from becoming a military power that could potentially challenge the US. Certainly no other nations have any interest in challenging the formidable pillar of US military dominance in the near term.

The second pillar of American dominance in the world is the role played by the US dollar as the international World Reserve Currency. Until the advent of the euro in 1999, there was simply no potential challenge to dollar supremacy in world trade. Maintaining this is a strategic imperative if America seeks global dominance. It should be noted that dollar hegemony is in many respects more important than US military superiority. Indeed, removing the dollar pillar will naturally result in the diminishment of the military pillar.

> On September 24, 2000, Saddam Hussein emerged from a meeting of his government and proclaimed that Iraq would soon transition its oil export transactions to the euro currency.

On September 24, 2000, Saddam Hussein emerged from a meeting of his government and proclaimed that Iraq would soon transition its oil export transactions to the euro currency.[60] Why would Saddam Hussein's currency switch be such a strategic threat to the bankers in London and New York? Why would the US president risk 50 years of carefully crafted global alliances with various European allies and advocate a military attack that could not be justified to the world community?

The answer is simple: the dollar's unique role as a petrodollar has been the foundation of its supremacy since the mid 1970s. The process of petrodollar recycling underpins the US' economic domination that funds its military supremacy. Dollar/petrodollar supremacy allows the US a unique ability to sustain yearly current account deficits, pass huge tax cuts, build a massive military empire of bases worldwide, and still have others accept its currency as medium of exchange for their imported good and services. The origins of this history are not found in textbooks on international economics, but rather in the minutes of meetings held by various banking and petroleum elites who have quietly sought unhindered power.

US Dollar: Fiat Currency or Oil-Backed Currency?

> What the powerful men grouped around the Bilderberg had evidently decided that May [1973] was to launch a colossal assault against industrial growth in the world, in order to tilt the balance of power back to the advantage of Anglo-American financial interests and the dollar. In order to do this, they determined to use their most prized weapon — control of the world's oil flows.

Bilderberg policy was to trigger a global oil embargo in order to force a dramatic increase in world oil prices. Since 1945, world oil had by international custom been priced in dollars .... A sudden sharp increase in the world price of oil, therefore, meant an equally dramatic increase in world demand for US dollars to pay for that necessary oil.

Never in history had such a small circle of interests, centered in London and New York, controlled so much of the entire world's economic destiny. The Anglo-American financial establishment had resolved to use their oil power in a manner no one could have imagined possible. The very outrageousness of their scheme was to their advantage, they clearly reckoned.

— F. William Engdahl, *A Century of War*, 2004[61]

At this point he makes an extraordinary claim: '*I am 100 percent sure that the Americans were behind the increase in the price of oil. The oil companies were in real trouble at that time, they had borrowed a lot of money and they needed a high oil price to save them.*'

'He says he was convinced of this by the attitude of the Shah of Iran, who in one crucial day in 1974 moved from the Saudi view' ... 'to advocating higher prices.'

'*King Faisal sent me to the Shah of Iran, who said: "Why are you against the increase in the price of oil? That is what they want? Ask Henry Kissinger — he is the one who wants a higher price."*' [emphasis added]

Yamani contends that proof of his long-held belief has recently emerged in the minutes of a secret meeting on a Swedish island, where UK and US officials determined to orchestrate a 400 per cent increase in the oil price.

— *Observer* (UK) interview with Sheikh Yaki Yamani (Saudi Arabian Oil Minister from 1962–1986) at the Royal Institute of International Affairs, January 14, 2001[62]

As previously noted, the crucial shift to an oil-backed currency took place in the early 1970s when President Nixon closed the so-called gold window at the Federal Treasury. This removed the dollar's redemption value from a fixed amount of gold to a fiat currency that floated against other currencies. This was done so the federal government would have no restraints on printing new dollars, thereby able to pursue undisciplined fiscal policies to maintain the US' superpower status. The only limit was how many dollars the rest of the world would be willing to accept on the full faith and credit of the US government. The result was rapid inflation and a falling dollar.

Although rarely debated outside arcane discussions of the global political economy, it is easy to grasp that if oil can be purchased on the international markets *only with US dollars*, the *demand* and *liquidity value* will be solidified, given that oil is the essential natural resource for *every industrialized nation*. Oil trades are the basic enablers of a manufacturing infrastructure, the basis of global transportation, and the primary energy source for 40 percent of the industrial economy.

During the 1970s a two-pronged strategy was pursued by the US and UK banking elites to exploit the unique role of oil in an effort to maintain dollar hegemony. One component was the requirement that OPEC agree to price and conduct all of its oil transactions in the dollar only, and the second was to use these surplus petrodollars as the instrument to dramatically reverse the dollar's falling international value via high oil prices. The net effect solidified industrialized and developing nations under the sphere of the dollar. No longer backed by gold, the dollar became backed by *black gold*.

Throughout this time President Nixon was increasingly embroiled in what became known as the Watergate Scandal. Consequently he named Henry Kissinger both Secretary of State and head of the White House's National Security Council. In these highly empowered roles, Kissinger promptly pursued the monetary strategy as outlined in the Bilderberg plan. During 1973–1974 US Treasury Secretary William Simon began secret negotiations with the government of Saudi Arabia in an attempt to buttress global oil sales in dollars only, and thereby thwart discussions at that time of transitioning oil trades to a basket of currencies. Saudi Arabia, as the largest OPEC oil producer, was the natural choice. Neither Congress nor the CIA was informed of these agreements until Saudi Arabia had completed their purchases of $2.5 billion in US Treasury bills. By the time Congress was informed of this "add-on arrangement," it was a fait accompli.[63]

Engdahl contended that Kissinger, acting as Nixon's intelligence czar, was able to "misrepresent to each party [Israelis, Syrians and Egyptians] the critical elements of the other, ensuring the [October 1973 Yom Kippur] war and its subsequent Arab oil embargo." He reasoned that once the oil embargo began, "the Arab oil-producing nations were to be the scapegoat for the coming rage of the world, while the Anglo-American interests responsible stood quietly in the background."[64]

Regardless of whether subsequent events unfolded as envisioned by the Bilderberg group, it is obvious their prophetic "scenario" of oil prices escalating by 400 percent, along with dramatic increases in dollar liquidity, did in fact occur seven months later. By January 1974 the price of OPEC's benchmark oil stood at $11.65 per barrel (up from $3.01 in early 1973). Furthermore, it is also a matter of historical record that, during this time, the US had engaged in secret negotiations with the Saudi Arabia Monetary

Authority to establish a petrodollar recycling system via New York and London banks.

This brilliant, if somewhat nefarious, act of monetary jujitsu enormously benefited not only the US/UK banking interests, but also the Seven Sisters of the US/UK petroleum conglomerate (Exxon, Texaco, Mobil, Chevron, Gulf, British Petroleum, and Royal Dutch/Shell). These major oil interests had incurred tremendous debts from the capital requirements in their large, new oil platforms in the inhospitable areas of the North Sea and Prudhoe Bay, Alaska. However, following the 1974 oil price shocks, their profitability was secure. Engdahl candidly noted that "while Kissinger's 1973 oil shock had a devastating impact on world industrial growth, it had an enormous benefit for certain established interests — the major New York and London banks, and the Seven Sisters oil multinational of the United States and Britain."[65]

The unique monetary arrangement was formalized in June 1974 by Secretary of State Kissinger, establishing the US-Saudi Arabian Joint Commission on Economic Cooperation. The US Treasury and the New York Federal Reserve would "allow" the Saudi central bank to buy US Treasury bonds with Saudi petrodollars.[66]

Likewise, London banks would handle eurozone-based international oil transactions, loaning these revenues via Eurobonds to oil-importing countries. The debt and interest from these loans would then flow to the dollar-denominated payments to the IMF, thereby completing the recycling of surplus petrodollars to the Federal Reserve.

Until November 2000, no OPEC country violated the petrodollar oil price arrangement. As long as the dollar was the strongest international currency, there was little reason to consider other options. However, in the autumn of 2000, Saddam Hussein emerged from a meeting of his government and announced that Iraq would soon transition its oil-export transactions to the euro. Saddam Hussein referred to the US dollar as currency of the "enemy state."[67] It is not clear if Saddam Hussein initiated the idea of transitioning to a petroeuro or if the EU approached him with this idea. Regardless, Iraq opened up a euro-based bank account with the leading French bank, BNP Paribas. Shortly thereafter, Iraqi oil proceeds went into a special UN account for the Oil for Food program and were then deposited in BNP Paribas.[68]

At the time of the transition, Iraq's UN Oil for Food account held $10 billion. A short news story detailing this development appeared on November 1, 2000, on the Radio Liberty website of the US State Department.[69] CNN ran a very short article on its website on October 30, 2000, but after this one-day news cycle, the issue of Iraq's switch to a petroeuro essentially disappeared from all five of the corporate-owned US media outlets.[70] (Note: These five conglomerates collectively control 90 percent of the information flow within the United States.)

Although this little-noted Iraqi move to defy the dollar in favor of the euro, in itself, did not have a huge impact, the ramifications regarding further OPEC momentum toward a petroeuro were quite profound. If invoicing oil in euros were to spread, especially against an already weak dollar, it could create a panic sell-off of dollars by foreign central banks and OPEC oil producers. In the months before the latest Iraq War, hints in this direction were heard from Russia, Iran, Indonesia, and even Venezuela. There are indicators that the Iraq War was a forceful way to deliver a message to OPEC and other oil producers: Do not transition from the petrodollar to a petroeuro system. Engdahl's conversation with a forthright London-based banker is rather enlightening:

> Informed banking circles in the City of London and elsewhere in Europe privately confirm the significance of that little-noted Iraq move from petrodollar to petroeuro. 'The Iraq move was a declaration of war against the dollar,' one senior London banker told me recently. 'As soon as it was clear that Britain and the US had taken Iraq, a great sigh of relief was heard in London City banks. They said privately, "now we don't have to worry about that damn euro threat."'[71]

Petrodollar recycling works quite simply because oil is an essential commodity for every nation, and the petrodollar system demands the buildup of huge trade surpluses in order to accumulate dollar surpluses. This is the case for every country but the US, which controls the dollar and prints it at will or fiat. Because the majority of all international trade today is conducted in dollars, other countries must engage in active trade relations with the US to get the means of payment they cannot themselves issue. The entire global trade structure today has formed around this dynamic, from Russia to China, from Brazil to South Korea and Japan. Every nation aims to maximize dollar surpluses from their export trade because almost every nation needs to import oil.

This insures the dollar's liquidity value and helps explain why almost 70 percent of world trade is conducted in dollars, even though US exports are about one third of that total. The dollar is the currency that central banks accumulate as reserves, but whether it is China, Japan, Brazil, or Russia, they simply do not stack all these dollars in their vaults. Currencies have one advantage over gold. A central bank can use it to buy the state bonds of the issuer, the United States. Most countries around the world are forced to control trade deficits or face currency collapse.[72]

Such is not the case in the United States, whose number one export product is the *dollar itself*. This unique arrangement is largely due to the dollar's

World Reserve Currency role, which is underpinned by its petrodollar role. Every nation needs to obtain dollars to purchase oil, some more than others. This means their trade targets are countries that use the dollar, with the US consumer as the main target for export products of the nation seeking to build dollar reserves.

To keep this process going, the United States has agreed to be importer/ consumer of last resort because its entire monetary supremacy depends on dollar recycling. The central banks of Japan, China, South Korea, and numerous others all buy US Treasury securities with their dollars. That in turn allows the US to have a stable dollar, far lower interest rates, and a $500–$600 billion annual balance of payments deficit with the rest of the world. The Federal Reserve controls the dollar printing presses, and the world needs its dollars.

Another benefit in this process for the US is that when oil is priced in a monopoly currency, the nation that prints that currency greatly minimizes its exposure to "currency risk" for their oil/energy prices. In other words, as long as OPEC prices a barrel of oil in the $22–$28 range, US consumers have very steady oil prices regardless of whether the dollar is highly valued or highly devalued against other major currencies. Until the dollar's devaluation relative to the euro in 2002, OPEC's pricing band generally reflected the price of international oil trades, and the US enjoyed a stable "oil bill." Under the OPEC pricing band established in 2000, a US petrodollar would be worth between 1.5 and 1.9 gallons of sweet crude, when the price of the barrel of oil was between $22 and $28 respectively (42-gallon production barrel).

No other hard currency in the world *guarantees access* to the most valuable "commodity" on earth — oil and gas. (Note: I do not consider oil to be a mere *commodity*. As writer/commentator/veteran Stan Goff noted: "Oil is not a normal commodity. No other commodity has five US navy battle groups patrolling the sea lanes to secure it."[73]) Furthermore, no other hard currency possesses this unique "storage of wealth" that is realized as the monopoly currency for international oil purchases.

After August 1971 when the dollar lost its "gold backing" and became a floating currency, the following three years were periods of volatile dollar devaluation with escalating inflationary pressures. Subsequently, elite US and UK banking interests, in conjunction with Saudi Arabia, created an oil-backed dollar. By 1975 all of OPEC adopted a petrodollar recycling system in which the dollar transitioned from being — "as good as gold" — to being "as good as *black* gold." For better or worse, this also meant that the printing on US Federal Reserve notes could have been changed from "In God We Trust" to the more accurate descriptor "In OPEC We Trust," or most specifically, "In Saudi Arabia We Trust." Despite the lack of discussion in mainstream economic commentary regarding this unique geopolitical arrangement, in essence US dollar hegemony is strongly underpinned by petrodollar recycling.

The old rules for valuation of the US dollar and economic power were based on its flexible market, free flow of trade goods, high per-worker productivity, manufacturing output, trade surpluses, government oversight of accounting methodologies by the Securities and Exchange Commission (SEC), developed infrastructure, education system, and, of course, total cash flow and profitability. Superior US military power afforded some additional confidence in the dollar. While many of these factors remain present, over the last two decades the US has diluted many of the safe-harbor economic fundamentals. Since the mid-1970s the petrodollar created new rules for the dollar and essentially eliminated US *currency risk* for oil consumption.

The lack of currency risk is one of the reasons that taxes on oil and gas are much lower in the United States. The average world price for a gallon of gasoline in 2004 was about $5, nearly 60 percent higher than typical US prices.[74] Higher petrol taxes in the EU and elsewhere provide a cushion for other countries' currency risks for imported oil and energy purchases. Without this, a particular country could experience wild swings in daily prices at the gas pump due to fluctuations in its domestic currency's valuation relative to the dollar on the international currency market.

The US has traditionally been immune to oil price risk and has enjoyed relatively stable gasoline prices for this same reason. However, chapters 4 and 5 present evidence that the US dollar's immunity to currency risk regarding international oil pricing is diminishing. A stable oil bill is likely one of the reasons why the EU would prefer a euro-based oil transaction option. One interesting development in the US presidential campaign in the autumn of 2000 was a small spike in global oil prices. In order to ease prices, the Clinton/Gore administration released 30 million barrels of oil from the US Strategic Petroleum Reserve, for which candidate Bush criticized candidate Gore.[75]

What most Americans failed to realize were the dramatic effects of higher gas (or petrol, as it is commonly known) prices in Europe. These high fuel prices in the autumn of 2000 occurred when the euro was at its historic low point compared to the US dollar, valued at about 82 cents, or 18 percent less than the dollar. The French, Germans, Spanish, Greeks, and related eurozone nations not only experienced an increase in fuel prices due to a dip in oil production, but also felt the brutal effects of currency risk due to the euro's relative low valuation.

The situation in Western Europe during September 2000 in many ways appeared reminiscent of the fuel crisis in the US of 1973–1974 and 1979.

Indeed, that autumn the entire European economy basically ground to a halt with near-violent protests due to high petrol prices. Considering the euro's susceptibility to currency risk regarding energy prices and its low relative valuation in 2000, an unwelcome crisis unfolded with soaring petrol prices within the EU.

The crisis lasted only a few days but was so acute that French fishermen blockaded the Channel ports because their fuel costs had doubled, even though their fuel was already tax-free. Schools were closed, hospitals were put on red alert, and supermarkets started rationing bread. Transportation came to a near standstill in much of Western Europe. The EU's currency risk for their imported oil was dramatic.

> Thousands of truckers from across Germany clogged the streets around the capital's center Tuesday demanding relief from higher gas prices. And they got some when the government offered low-interest loans to some trucking companies.
>
> The protest is the biggest so far in Germany, on the heels of demonstrations that halted traffic in France, Britain and Spain before easing in recent days. Elsewhere Tuesday, minor blockages continued in Spain, where markets ran out of fish, and Greek motorists fearing for shortages due to trucker strikes lined up for gas.[76]

At the time, the euro was beginning its widespread use, but its lower valuation relative to the US dollar that autumn appears to have not only adversely impacted oil prices in Western Europe, but also facilitated societal discord. Protests erupted in France where thousands of farmers drove their tractors into Paris as a sign of their displeasure at the rapid increase in fuel prices. This resulted in the deployment of French riot police. News reports of the economic fallout also included disruptions in the UK, Spain, and Greece.[77]

European governments likely sought strategies to mitigate further crises stemming from oil currency risk. In June 2001, both France and Russia proposed in the UN Security Council that the 1991 UN sanctions against Iraq be lifted, thereby allowing foreign investment to flow into Iraq in an effort to repair its deteriorating oil infrastructure. However, this proposal was predictably killed by the US and UK. In a situation similar to in present-day Iran, American companies were barred from investing in Iraq's vital oil industry. If Iraq had been determined to be disarmed, the UN sanctions would had been lifted, and oil-lease contracts awarded to France, Russia, China, and Italy would have been initiated.[78]

Of course, two years later a US military invasion toppled Saddam Hussein, and postwar oil contracts were strictly limited to the war's coalition partners, which in this case included several US oil companies, British Petroleum (BP), and the Worley Group, an Australian oil-engineering firm. Subsequent chapters elaborate on the significance of what Vice President Cheney's Energy Task Force termed "foreign suitors of Iraqi oil."[79]

US Structural Imbalances: Twin Deficits

The position of the dollar today is similar to that of sterling in the 1920s and 1930s, when sterling ceased to be the automatic global reserve currency and started to face competition from other currencies, notably the dollar.

— Paul Donovan, economist at the global investment bank UBS, 2003[80]

The dollar has been the leading international currency for as long as most people can remember. But its dominant role can no longer be taken for granted. If America keeps on spending and borrowing at the present pace, the dollar will eventually lose its mighty status in international finance. And that would hurt: the privilege of being able to print the World Reserve Currency, a privilege which is now at risk, allows America to borrow cheaply, and thus spend much more than it earns, on far better terms than are available to others.

— "The Disappearing Dollar," the *Economist*, December 2004[81]

The US ruling establishment has to date been rather successful in diverting the country's attention from its growing economic crisis. We have heard that an economic recovery has finally arrived and that real job creation will ultimately occur. In late 2004 the Federal Reserve finally began increasing the overnight lending rate in an effort to stem inflationary pressures supposedly created by a "growing economy." Only time will tell if the Federal Reserve will be able to restore the overnight lending rates between banks to normal levels without creating economic stagnation as the era of cheap credit in the US returns to a more sustainable level.

Regardless, without a significant increase in the number of jobs *and increased wages*, individual debt cannot be serviced by personal income. As the Federal Reserve increases the lending rate, the increase in asset prices will diminish, but the high debt levels will remain. Indeed, not only will the debt remain, but the cost of servicing it will go up noticeably. As interest rates rise in 2005, wages and salaries must increase or massive debt defaults will follow.

The structural problems are beginning to expose themselves, most notably in the dollar's multi-year decline, along with significantly unbalanced domestic fiscal policies. In this highly unstable system US trade deficits and net debt/ liabilities to foreign accounts are now well over 25 percent of GDP and climbing rapidly. Since the 2000 stock market decline and the re-emergence of budget deficits in Washington, the net debt position almost doubled.[82] The net foreign indebtedness of the US has become an ominous sign of an unbalanced global economy.

In 1999, the peak of the dot.com bubble mania, US net debt to foreigners was some $1.4 trillion. By the end of 2004, it was projected to exceed $3.7 trillion.[83] Before 1985 the United States had been a net creditor, gaining more from its foreign investments than it paid to them in interest on Treasury bonds or other US assets. However, since the end of the Cold War, the US has become the world's largest debtor nation.

> Before 1985 the United States had been a net creditor, gaining more from its foreign investments than it paid to them in interest on Treasury bonds or other US assets. However, since the end of the Cold War, the US has become the world's largest debtor nation.

In comparison, the EU traditionally has a small but positive net trade surplus, with an aggregate current account of one percent. As a percent of its GDP, during 2002 the US exported 9.3 percent, while the EU exported 19.7 percent. While the economic growth of the US economy far outpaced that of the EU since 1999, when the euro was launched, this was partly due to the dollar's reserve role and the unique privileges derived from that designation. Most notably, the dollar's role has allowed the Federal Reserve and the US government to inject an unprecedented amount of liquidity into the US economy. During the 1960s France's Charles de Gaulle complained about the exorbitant privilege that accrued to the United States by virtue of the dollar's role in the post–WW II international monetary system.

Following the collapse of the Bretton Woods Agreement in 1971, all restraints of proper fiscal discipline were lifted, resulting in excessive credit and debt creation. Some have argued that this process, when combined with the dollar-denominated debts from the IMF and World Bank, amounted to "super hegemony." Economist Michael Hudson famously titled his groundbreaking 1972 book *Super Imperialism: The Origin and Fundamentals of US World Dominance.*[84]

It does not require much foresight to see the strategic threat of these deficits to the role of the United States. With a stunning trade deficit of $665 billion, the US must import or attract, at a minimum, $1.8 billion every day, to avoid a dollar collapse and keep its interest rates low enough to support the debt-burdened corporate economy.

Euro Challenges US Dollar Hegemony

> The monetary integration of Europe could alter 'the political character of Europe in ways that could lead to confrontation with the United States' .... and could lead to a world that was 'very different and not necessarily a safer place.'
>
> — Martin Feldstein, former head of the President's Council of Economic Advisors, 1997[85]

> Americans do not yet understand the significance of the euro, but when they do it could set up a monumental conflict, it will change the whole world situation so that the United States can no longer call all the shots.
>
> — Helmut Schmidt, former German Chancellor, 1997[86]

The introduction of the euro heralded not only a new stage in European economic integration, but also an important potential challenge to the dominance of the US dollar as the international reserve currency. Indeed, it presaged the only real macroeconomic challenge to US global primacy. When the euro was launched in 1999, leading EU government figures, bankers from Deutsche Bank, and French President Chirac went to major holders of dollar reserves — China, Japan, Russia — and tried to convince them to shift some of their reserves from dollars into euros.[87] However, that proposal was perhaps premature at the time and clashed with the need to devalue the highly appreciated euro so German exports could stabilize growth within the newly integrated eurozone. A falling euro was the case until 2002.

With the debacle of the US dot-com bubble bursting, the Enron and Worldcom finance scandals, and the recession in the US, the dollar began to lose its attraction for foreign investors. The euro gained steadily until the end of 2002. Then, as France and Germany prepared their diplomatic strategy to block war in the UN Security Council, the central banks of Russia and China quietly began to unload dollars and buy euros. The result was severe dollar devaluation in the few months just before the war. Perhaps central banks were hedging their investment risks due to war. Iraq is just one pawn in this high-stakes strategic game of chess.

However, in Washington and New York, the upper echelons of the US political and banking establishment knew what was at stake. The Iraq War was not about Saddam Hussein's old WMD program or the "war on terrorism." It was the threat that other members of OPEC would follow Iraq and shift to a petroeuro system, thereby eroding the dollar's dominant role in the global economy. Engdahl forewarned that if France, Germany, Russia, or OPEC oil exporting countries were to shift "even a small portion of their dollar reserves into euro to buy bonds of Germany or France or the like, the United States would face a strategic crisis beyond any of the postwar period."[88]

As one economist termed it, an end to the dollar's World Reserve role would be a catastrophe for the United States. To stem a sudden divestiture of dollar assets, US interest rates from the Federal Reserve would have to be pushed higher than in 1979 when Paul Volcker raised rates above 17 percent to stop the collapse of the dollar's valuation.[89]

The global community is currently witnessing a clash between Wall Street and competing Franco-German financial interests, with London and the pound sterling caught in the middle. In 2002 Canadian economist Michel Chossudovsky eloquently described the significance of these economic and strategic developments in his book *War and Globalization*. Well before the Iraq War, he noted the unfolding global monetary movements regarding the dollar and the euro.

> The European common currency system has a direct bearing on strategic and political divisions. London's decision not to adopt the common currency is consistent with the integration of British financial and banking interests with those of Wall Street, not to mention the Anglo-American alliance in the oil industry (BP, Exxon-Mobil, Texaco Chevron, Shell) and weapons production (by the "Big Five" US weapons producers plus British Aerospace Systems). This shaky relationship between the British pound and the US dollar is an integral part of the Anglo-American military axis.
>
> What is at stake is the rivalry between two competing global currencies: the euro and the US dollar, with Britain's pound being torn between the European and the US-dominated currency systems. In other words, two rival financial and monetary systems are competing worldwide for the control over money creation and credit .... What we are dealing with is an 'imperial' scramble for control over national economies and currency systems.[90]

Eurasia versus the Anglo-American Alliance

> Oil and gas are not the ultimate aims of the US [in Iraq]. It's about control. If the US controls the sources of energy of its rivals — Europe, Japan, China, and other nations aspiring to be more independent — they win.
> — Pepe Escobar, *Asia Times*, January 2002[91]

The current clash of petrodollars versus petroeuros, which began in Iraq, is by no means over. Despite the initial US military victory in Iraq, the aftermath of the war has not effectively thwarted other oil producers from stating their interest in converting their export currency to the euro. During 2003 and 2004, numerous public statements by the Iranian and Russian governments illustrated momentum toward a petroeuro system.[92] Naturally, these developments appeared in the foreign media but not in the US media.

To be sure, the euro was created by European geopolitical strategists to establish a multipolar world after the collapse of the Soviet Union. The aim was to balance the overwhelming economic dominance of the US in world affairs. If the euro succeeds in becoming an established international oil transaction currency, this will indeed facilitate the creation of a bipolar world, with the US and EU serving as two powerful engines for global economic growth.

Regarding the Iraq invasion, it should be noted that neither the American nor the French and German governments was primarily concerned with the deplorable humanitarian condition and fate of Iraq's people. The German and French opposition to the US drive to war was recognition that America's rush to create absolute global domination posed a serious threat to the political, economic, and strategic interests of the German and French ruling classes; the goal of the opposition was to forestall the US' ability to enhance its global projection of power. In essence, the Iraq War was about dollars, euros, oil, and geostrategic power in the 21st century.

In February 2003, a French intelligence-connected newsletter, *Intelligence Online*, presented an interesting analysis, "The Strategy Behind Paris-Berlin-Moscow Tie."[93] This article referred to the emergence of a France-Germany-Russia bloc that prevented the US and UK from gaining UN Security Council authorization for the Iraq War. This Paris-based intelligence report noted the recent geostrategic shift of European and Russian political alliances in an effort to create a counter power to the United States. Referring to these new ties between France and Germany, and more recently with Russia, it observed, "a new logic, and even dynamic seems to have emerged. An alliance between Paris, Moscow, and Berlin running from the Atlantic to Asia could foreshadow a limit to US power."[94]

In his classic 1998 book, *The Grand Chessboard*, former US National Security Adviser Zbigniew Brzezinski recognized that control over Eurasia was a geostrategic imperative in order to maintain US hegemony. His candid comments about a US empire may prove prophetic, as current events suggest "collusion" between the "vassals" is forming in opposition to the neoconservative doctrine of global domination:

> Eurasian geostrategy involves the purposeful management of geostrategically dynamic states and the careful handling of geopolitically catalytic states, in keeping with the twin interests of America in the short-term preservation of its unique global power and in the long-run transformation of it into increasingly institutionalized cooperation. To put it in a terminology that hearkens back to the more brutal age of ancient empires, the three grand imperatives of imperial geostrategy are to prevent collusion and maintain security dependence among the vassals, to keep tributaries pliant and protected, and to keep the barbarians from coming together.[95]

As reiterated by Engdahl, this basic "strategic approach of creating a Eurasian heartland is the historical origin of many clashes between

Continental powers and maritime powers over the past century."[96] During the 1990s this emerging strategic challenge from a French-German-EU policy regarding Iraq and other countries likely fostered some members in the US policy establishment to begin contemplating preemptive strategies to enforce the petrodollar system before Bush became president. Leading neoconservatives were developing a bold strategy to preserve the faltering US economic system. This strategy was detailed in policy papers written by members of PNAC.[97] Major proponents of this consensus included Cold War veterans, such as Donald Rumsfeld and Dick Cheney.

Although many Americans are not familiar with the imperial goals outlined by PNAC, foreign media reports suggest that traditional US allies are alarmed at the implications of its global domination. In September 2000 PNAC's major policy document, "Rebuilding America's Defense: Strategy, Forces and Resources for the New Century," *"The challenge of this coming century is to preserve and enhance this 'American peace,'"* and in order to preserve this "peace," the US must be able to *"fight and decisively win multiple, simultaneous major-theater wars."*[98] [emphasis added]

One of the most severe public critiques of neoconservative policies before the Iraq War was offered by Tam Dalvell, a British Labour MP. In 2002 he delivered the following polemical remarks regarding PNAC's policy document that called for large increases in defense spending in an effort to gain control over numerous areas of "US strategic interest."

> This is a blueprint for US world domination — a new world order of their making. These are the thought processes of fantasist Americans who want to control the world. I am appalled that a British Labour Prime Minister should have got into bed with a crew which has this moral standing.[99]

In the week following the invasion of Iraq, Pat Rabbitte, leader of the Labour Party in Northern Ireland, wrote in an opinion piece for the *Irish Times*, "These men are intent on world domination or, as they put it themselves, 'American global leadership.' They have an imperial agenda, which they have been pursuing for more than five years." As Rabbitte candidly noted, "In the eyes of international law, this is an illegitimate war. But that does not concern these policy-makers."[100]

Unfortunately, the majority of nations that have traditionally been our allies share unfavorable views such as those expressed by Dalvell and Rabbitte. According to international polls conducted one year after the Iraq War, the majority of people in allied nations, such as Canada, Mexico, Britain, France, Italy, Germany, and Spain, had an unfavorable view of President Bush's role in world affairs.[101] In addition, according to a poll conducted by the Pew Global Attitudes Project, the majority of people living in Jordan, Morocco,

Pakistan, Turkey, France, Germany, and Russia also held negative views toward the US. The majority of respondents — including countries that have historically been allied with the US — believed "the US is conducting its campaign against terror *to control Mid East oil and to dominate the world.*"[102] [emphasis added]

Only in the United States and Britain did the majority of people indicate that the campaign against terror was a sincere effort to reduce international terrorism. It is clear much of the global community has lost confidence in US leadership and is suspicious of its intentions regarding the war on terror. In addition, astute observers and writers have become cognizant of the fact that the 2003 Iraq War was initiated from a defensive posture — in an effort to preserve a faltering system of American economic hegemony. Unfortunately, without a major change in US strategy, the Iraq War will not be the last imperial war over the oil reserves in the Persian Gulf and elsewhere.

> Only in the United States and Britain did the majority of people indicate that the campaign against terror was a sincere effort to reduce international terrorism.

The global community has reached a critical moment in history, with two foreseeable outcomes: an attempt at multilateralism and the preservation of peace, economic prosperity, and security; or a unilateralist world plagued with increasing geopolitical tensions that could lead to global warfare over depleting oil and competing oil transaction currencies. What is not yet clear, and must be openly debated within societies and governments, is how to adjust the global economy to the formidable challenges presented by Peak Oil, and how to piece together a compromise between the US, EU, and Asia in regard to a more balanced global monetary system.

The success or failure to create multilateral accords toward these two colossal undertakings will define the human condition in the 21ˢᵗ century. This book examines the history of these events and offers numerous policy recommendations within a multilateral framework.

The liberty of speaking and writing guards our other liberties.

Dissent is the highest form of patriotism.

— Thomas Jefferson

Two

US Geostrategy and the Persian Gulf: 1945–2005

I hereby find that the defense of Saudi Arabia is vital to the defense of the United States.
— Franklin D. Roosevelt, US President 1933–1945, 1943[1]

We could solve all our economic and political problems by taking over the Arab oil fields [and] bringing in Texans and Oklahomans to operate them.
— Former US Saudi Ambassador, Chris Akins, commenting on an article by Miles Ignotus (pseudonym), "Seizing Arab Oil," *Harper's Magazine*, 1975[2]

The process of transformation, even if it brings revolutionary change, is likely to be a long one, absent some catastrophic and catalyzing event — like a new Pearl Harbor.

From an American perspective, the value of such bases [in Iraq] would endure even should Saddam Hussein pass from the scene. Over the long term, Iran may well prove as large a threat to US interests in the Gulf as Iraq has. And even should US-Iranian relations improve, retaining forward-based forces in the region would still be an essential element in US security strategy given the longstanding American interests in the region.
— Project for a New American Century (PNAC), "Rebuilding America's Defenses: Strategies, Forces and Resoaurces for a New Century," 2000[3]

First, for more than seven years the United States is occupying the lands of Islam in the holiest of its territories, Arabia, plundering its riches, overwhelming its rulers, humiliating its people, threatening its neighbors, and using its [military] bases in the peninsula as a spearhead to fight against neighboring Islamic peoples.

There is no better proof of all this than their eagerness to destroy Iraq, the strongest of the neighboring Arab states, and their attempt to dismember all of the states of the region, such as Iraq and Saudi Arabia and Egypt and Sudan into petty states, whose division and weakness would ensure the survival of Israel and the continuation of the calamitous Crusader [US] occupation of the lands of Arabia.

> — Osama bin Laden, "Declaration of the World Islamic
> Front for Jihad Against the Jews and the Crusaders," 1998[4]

Covert Hegemony to Neoconservative Domination

In February 1945, as allied victory in World War II was becoming assured, President Franklin D. Roosevelt held a meeting on a US Navy warship with Abdul-Aziz ibn Saud, known as Ibn Saud, the founder of the modern Saudi dynasty. Although the official record is somewhat silent about the issue of oil, it is generally agreed that after Roosevelt and King Saud met, the US tacitly agreed to protect the royal family against its external and internal enemies, and in return the US was assured privileged US access to the vast oil reserves of Saudi Arabia.[5] The Saudi dynasty has relied on US military agreements to arm and protect the Saudi monarchy as a quid pro quo, with Saudi Arabia traditionally ranking as one of the largest buyers of US arms. (Approximately 25 percent of total US armament exports from 1950 to 2000 were purchased by Saudi Arabia.)

Almost 60 years later another US president, George W. Bush, held meetings in the summer of 2001 at his private home in Crawford, Texas, with Saudi ambassador Prince Bandar. On September 13, 2001, just two days after the terrorist attacks in New York and Washington, President Bush dined with the Saudi ambassador at the White House.[6] This meeting occurred despite the fact that US intelligence agencies reported that Osama bin Laden, an exiled Saudi terrorist, had just attacked the US, murdering thousands. For many years he had received the majority of his funding from wealthy Saudis.

Even after the 9/11 tragedy, Saudi purchases of US armaments in 2002 were a very robust $5.2 billion.[7] These seemingly incongruous events are not surprising given an objective analysis of longstanding US foreign policies in the region. Over the past 60 years, a common trajectory of US foreign policy has been a continuous preoccupation with the fossil fuels of the Middle East, with particular focus on Saudi Arabia.

Following the oil embargos during the 1970s, American citizens were forced to become painfully aware of the importance of oil from the Persian Gulf region. The oil price shocks of 1973–1974 and again in 1979 resulted in the formulation of aggressive geostrategic planning that included a US military invasion to gain control over the oil reserves in the Persian Gulf. The origins of these policies became public in 1975, when Henry Kissinger stated the US was prepared to wage war over oil.

In 1980 President Jimmy Carter initiated the Carter Doctrine when he stated the US would use any force necessary, including military power, to repel foreign influence (i.e., Soviet) from the Persian Gulf oil supply.[8] In view of the Iran Revolution and Soviet invasion of

The oil price shocks of 1973–1974 and again in 1979 resulted in the formulation of aggressive geostrategic planning that included a US military invasion to gain control over the oil reserves in the Persian Gulf. The origins of these policies became public in 1975, when Henry Kissinger stated the US was prepared to wage war over oil.

Afghanistan in 1979, along with the "Cold War politics" during that time, the Carter Doctrine was an understandable policy statement. It was a clear announcement that the US military would intervene if the global oil spigot in the Middle East were threatened by our formal arch rival, the Soviet Union.

Subsequent to the demise of the Soviet Union in 1989, it would seem that planning for a US military invasion of the Persian Gulf would have diminished. However, in August 1990 Iraq invaded Kuwait, thereby affording Washington a new impetus and opportunity to position US military force in the region. In 1991 former president George H.W. Bush brought together a large UN coalition to forcibly drive Saddam Hussein's army out of Kuwait during Operation Desert Storm.

Following the 1991 Persian Gulf War, the US was "invited" by the Saudi monarchy to maintain US military forces near Riyadh. At the same time, the Department of Defense stored vast quantities of munitions and military material in Kuwait and Qatar in order to facilitate future combat operations without having to wait for the delivery of heavy equipment.[9] Moreover, during the 1990s Iraq's military force was systematically diminished through UN sanctions and continued aerial bombing strikes by US and UK aircraft. Operations using overt US military force in the Persian Gulf region were primarily limited to Iraq's air-defense installations, with the exception of the 1998 Operation Desert Fox bombing campaign of locations suspected of WMD production facilities.

Interestingly, just as the Iraq War was initiated in March 2003, an article by Robert Dreyfus in *Mother Jones Magazine* chronicled the resurrection of US geostrategy from the 1970s that advocated an invasion of the Persian Gulf. His award-winning article, "The Thirty-Year Itch," included an interview with James Akins, a former US diplomat, who confirmed the long-standing military plans to invade and control the oil in the Persian Gulf region.[10] Akins lucidly recalled his personal experiences when the original invasion plan surfaced almost 30 years ago. He stated: "It's the Kissinger plan. I thought it had been killed, but it's back."[11] The following excerpt from Dreyfus's article illustrated the historical context of the original Kissinger plan:

> In 1975, while Akins was ambassador in Saudi Arabia, an article headlined "Seizing Arab Oil" appeared in *Harper's* [*Magazine*]. The author, who used the pseudonym Miles Ignotus, was identified as 'a Washington-based professor and defense consultant with intimate links to high-level US policymakers.' The article outlined, as Akins puts it, 'how we could solve all our economic and political problems by taking over the Arab oil fields [and] bringing in Texans and Oklahomans to operate them.' Simultaneously, a rash of similar stories appeared in other magazines and newspapers. 'I

knew that it had to have been the result of a deep background briefing,' Akins says. 'You don't have eight people coming up with the same screwy idea at the same time, independently.'

'Then I made a fatal mistake,' Akins continues. 'I said on television that anyone who would propose that is either a madman, a criminal, or an agent of the Soviet Union.' Soon afterward, he says, he learned that the background briefing had been conducted by his boss, then Secretary of State Henry Kissinger. Akins was fired later that year.[12]

An overview of current global oil consumption illustrates the pervasiveness of the increasing oil demand in the global economy. Global oil use in 2004 was estimated at 82 million barrels a day (mb/d). In 20 years world oil consumption is projected to increase dramatically to 120 mb/d. By 2020 it is anticipated that the Asian economies, lead by China, will consume 25 percent of the world's energy; the US, 25 percent; Western Europe, 18 percent; Eastern Europe and the former Soviet Union, 13 percent; and Latin America, 5 percent.[13] In 2004 the US consumes approximately 20 mb/d, or nearly one out of every four barrels of global oil production. The US has an estimated 2 percent of the world's oil reserves but uses 25 percent of the world's oil. Twenty-four percent of US oil imports are from the Middle East. These trends are expected to rise sharply as other sources disappear.

The Middle East holds an estimated 65 percent of global oil reserves, with Saudi Arabia reported to hold the world's largest reserves (25 percent of the total). Recognizing that the Saudi monarchy has become increasingly alienated from Washington, has come under attack from probable Al Qaeda elements, along with the fact that most of the 9/11 hijackers were reported to be Saudi citizens, it is obvious that US policy-makers may be concerned about losing access to the eastern oil fields of Saudi Arabia should the monarchy fall. Iran and Syria have often been mentioned as potential targets under the "war on terror," but the neoconservatives have repeatedly suggested that Iraq is the first stage in a much larger project of *regional regime change*.

Cold War Geostrategy: Domestic Peak Oil in the Former Soviet Union

'In November 1985, oil was $30 a barrel,' recalled the noted oil economist Philip Verleger. By July of 1986, oil had fallen to $10 a barrel, and it did not climb back to $20 until April 1989. 'Everyone thinks Ronald Reagan brought down the Soviets,' said Verleger. 'That is wrong. It was the collapse of their oil rents.' It's no accident that the 1990s was the decade of falling oil prices and falling walls.

— Thomas Friedman, "A New Mission for America," 2004[14]

As illustrated throughout Daniel Yergin's classic book, *The Prize: The Epic Quest for Oil*, the pursuit of petroleum was a key strategic factor during both world wars and the Cold War.[15] Knowledgeable observers have suggested that the decline of domestic Russian oil production likely played a much larger role in ending the Cold War than what is typically acknowledged. History suggests that Saudi-induced low oil prices during the mid-1980s, in conjunction with a natural decline in Russian oil production, contributed to the economic decline in the downfall of the Soviet Union. Strategically, the Soviet invasion of Afghanistan accelerated their economic decline.

Recently declassified CIA documents suggested such topics were carefully analyzed with regard to the anticipated peak in Russian oil production. In March 1977 a CIA intelligence memorandum, "The Impending Soviet Oil Crisis," was issued by the Office of Economic Research and classified Secret.[16] It was made publicly available in January 2001 in response to a Freedom of Information Act (FOIA) request. This memorandum predicted an impending peak in Soviet oil production "not later than the early 1980s."[17] The authors noted this phenomenon would have important consequences regarding the Cold War standoff. Oil production charts within this document estimated the goal for Russian oil production in 1980 would be 12.9 mb/d, but the CIA predicted that peak oil would likely occur at 11.8 mb/d.

The CIA analysts were fairly close in their estimates; actual oil production in Russia showed a preliminary peak in 1983 with 12.5 mb/d, followed by the actual peak in 1987 at 12.6 mb/d. Russian oil production in 2004 is approximately 9 mb/d, approximately 25 percent less than its peak output.

The unnamed authors of the CIA document proffered: "During the next decade, the USSR may well find itself not only unable to supply oil to Eastern Europe and the West on the present scale, but also having to compete for OPEC oil for its own use." Additionally, this document forecast that peak oil within the Soviet Union would create adverse economic influences upon the Soviet Union's fiscal solvency. It stated, "When oil production stops growing, and perhaps even before, *profound repercussions will be felt on the domestic economy of the USSR and on its international economic relations.*"[18] [emphasis added] Indeed, ten years after this memo was written, Russia reached peak oil production. Two years later, the Berlin Wall came crashing down, and the Cold War was finally over.

In 1977 the CIA was undoubtedly interested in this subject as the US had reached domestic peak oil production in 1970–1971, an event that marked the end of an era, and a difficult period of economic decline for the US economy. Although difficult to imagine today, until that time America was the world's foremost oil producer, and its oil reserves were crucial in helping the Allies prevail in both the world wars of the 20th century. During much of the

Cold War, the former Soviet Union was the second-largest oil-producing nation (today Russia is the second-largest oil exporter in the world).

Evidently the CIA analysts who prepared this document clearly understood the importance of domestic oil production peaking in the US and predicted that the peaking of oil production in the USSR would have similar consequences for the Soviet Union.

Richard Heinberg, author and energy expert, postulated a compelling theory based on this CIA document — did a joint US/Saudi strategy facilitate economic decline of the USSR — which was at that time trapped in an expensive occupation and futile quagmire in Afghanistan? Heinberg suggested that former CIA Director William Casey may have advised the Reagan administration to persuade Saudi Arabia to dramatically increase oil production during the 1980s, knowing that Soviet oil production would reach its peak even sooner under such exacerbating economic pressure. Heinberg summarized:

> Throughout the last decade of its existence, the USSR pumped and sold its oil at the maximum possible rate in order to earn foreign exchange income with which to keep up in the arms race and prosecute its war in Afghanistan. Yet with markets awash with cheap Saudi oil, the Soviets were earning less even as they pumped more. Two years after their oil production peaked, the economy of the USSR crumbled and its government collapsed.[19]

Regardless of this hypothesis, it is a matter of historical record that Saudi Arabia increased its oil production significantly after 1985, which quickly reduced global oil prices by over 60 percent. This certainly had an adverse effect on the Soviet Union's main export income and, consequently, their ability to maintain foreign currency reserves when it was engaged in its own "Vietnam experience" against the Mujahideen of Afghanistan. Although still speculative at this point in history, it seems plausible that Washington might have utilized an innovative form of oil/economic warfare to cripple the Soviet Union's economy and thereby facilitate its ultimate collapse.

World Oil Consumption 2000 to 2020

> I cannot think of a time when we have had a region emerge as suddenly to become as strategically significant as the Caspian.
> —Former CEO of Halliburton, Dick Cheney, 1998[20]

> On our present course, America 20 years from now will import nearly two out of every three barrels of oil — a condition of increased dependency on foreign powers that do not always have America's interests at heart.
> — Vice President Cheney's Energy Task Force paper, 2001[21]

The Cheney report is very guarded about the amount of foreign oil that will be required. The only clue provided by the [public] report is a chart of net US oil consumption and production over time. According to this illustration, domestic oil field production will decline from about 8.5 million barrels per day (mb/d) in 2002 to 7.0 mb/d in 2020, while consumption will jump from 19.5 mb/d to 25.5 mb/d. That suggests imports or other sources of petroleum ... will have to rise from 11 mb/d to 18.5 mb/d. Most of the recommendations of the NEP [National Energy Policy] are aimed at procuring this 7.5 mb/d increment, equivalent to the total oil consumed by China and India.

— Michael Klare, international energy expert, "Bush-Cheney Energy Strategy: Procuring the Rest of the World's Oil," *Foreign Policy in Focus*, 2004[22]

In a speech to the International Petroleum Institute in London in late 1999, Dick Cheney, then CEO of the world's largest oil services company, Halliburton, presented a disconcerting forecast to his audience of oil industry insiders: "By some estimates there will be an average of two percent annual growth in global oil demand over the years ahead, along with, conservatively, a three percent natural decline in production from existing reserves."[23] Cheney ended his presentation on a profound note: "That means by 2010 we will need on the order of an additional fifty million barrels a day." That understated reference to an "additional fifty million barrels" per day is equivalent to more than five times the oil production of Saudi Arabia (current output of approx. 9 mb/d).

On January 20, 2001, President George W. Bush was sworn into office as the 43rd president. Nine days later he announced that Vice President Cheney would chair a cabinet-level group of advisors in the newly created National Energy Policy Development Group (NEPDG), commonly referred to as Cheney's Energy Task Force. This group began its meetings immediately, and on May 17, 2001, released their report, formally titled *National Energy Policy* (*NEP*).[24]

Perhaps it was no coincidence that Cheney, as Vice President, was chosen to head a Presidential Task Force on Energy as his first major assignment. As Engdahl noted, Cheney "knew the dimension of the energy problem facing *not only* the United States, but the rest of the world."[25] Although the full contents of meetings held by the NEPDG remain secret based on a ruling of the US Supreme Court, the original report illustrated the energy challenges that are facing the United States.

The Middle East is reported to contain approximately 65 percent of the world's "proven" oil reserves. Although such estimates are rightly viewed with considerable skepticism by many oil geologists, it is typically accepted as factual that Iraq alone has a reported 11 percent of the world's proven reserves, an estimated 112 billion barrels. The US Energy Department further stated that some analysts (the Baker Institute, Center for Global Energy Studies, and the Federation of American Scientists) believed that the vast western desert region of Iraq might hold up to an additional 100 billion barrels of oil, but this area has not been explored. The Department of Energy's website also lists a caveat, "Other analysts, such as the US Geological Survey, are not as optimistic, with median estimates for additional oil reserves closer to *45 billion barrels.*"[26] [emphasis added]

> The Middle East is reported to contain approximately 65 percent of the world's "proven" oil reserves. ... it is typically accepted as factual that Iraq alone has a reported 11 percent of the world's proven reserves, an estimated 112 billion barrels.

Michael Klare, an international expert on natural resource conflict and author of *Resource Wars*[27] and *Blood for Oil,*[28] provided the following analysis of the NEPDG report. The report made three key points about US energy challenges between 2000 and 2020:

> The United States must satisfy an ever-increasing share of its oil demand with imported supplies. (*Note: By 2020, daily US imports will total nearly 17 million barrels, or 65 percent of consumption, up from 10 m/bl, or 53 percent in 2000.*)
>
> The United States cannot depend exclusively on traditional sources of supply like Saudi Arabia, Venezuela and Canada. It will also have to obtain substantial imports from new sources, such as the Caspian states, Russia, and West Africa.
>
> *The United States cannot rely on market forces alone to gain access to these added supplies, but will also require a significant effort on the part of government officials to overcome foreign resistance to the outward reach of American energy companies.*[29] [emphasis added]

Instead of advocating various policies to reduce America's consumption of oil, either through conservation, improvements in efficiency, or the development of large-scale alterative energy sources, the 2001 Bush/Cheney energy policy implicitly assumed the US will continue to consume what is almost universally regarded as excessive oil consumption. According to Klare this was a "fateful decision." It means the US must find a way to increase oil imports from 11 mb/d to 18.5 mb/d by 2020. Klare noted, "*Securing that increment of imported oil — the equivalent of total current oil consumption by China and India combined — has driven an integrated US oil-military strategy ever since.*"[30] [emphasis added] The 2001 NEPDG energy plan obliquely inferred that the primary role of the US military in the beginning decades of the 21st century will be to "secure" physical control of the world's largest hydrocarbon reserves.

Klare and others have noted that the Bush administration has pursued a visible convergence of the US military with regard to energy issues. The influential Council on Foreign Relations (CFR) advocated that the Defense Department be included in Cheney's energy task force meetings. Secondly, a joint publication by the Council on Foreign Relations and the James A. Baker III Institute for Public Policy unequivocally, if obliquely, recommended "military interventions [to] secure" energy supplies.[31]

Geostrategic policies advocating an overt US military invasion of the Persian Gulf went below the surface during the 1980s and 1990s, but the group of strategists who later became known as "neoconservatives" maintained this viewpoint throughout this period. Most of these individuals served with the Reagan Defense Department, and some such as Cheney served in the former George H.W. Bush administration.

For many years successive US administrations have sought to control OPEC, which was largely accomplished by convincing the Saudis to invest heavily in the US financial instruments and armament procurements. However, with the possible exception of Russia, oil production in non-OPEC countries is now in permanent decline, giving the OPEC countries a dominant position in the global oil market into the foreseeable future.

Project for a New American Century (PNAC) Neoconservative Policies: 1992–2002

Our first objective is to prevent the re-emergence of a new rival, either on the territory of the former Soviet Union or elsewhere, that poses a threat on the order of that posed formerly by the Soviet Union.

There are three additional aspects to this objective: First, the US must show the leadership necessary to establish and protect a new order that holds the promise of *convincing potential competitors that they need not aspire to a greater role or pursue a more aggressive posture to protect their legitimate interests.* Second, in the non-defense areas, we must account sufficiently for the interests of the advanced industrial nations to discourage them from challenging our leadership or seeking to overturn the established political and economic order. Finally, *we must maintain the mechanisms for deterring potential competitors from even aspiring to a larger regional or global role.* [emphasis added]

— February 18, 1992, draft of the *Defense Planning Guidance for the Fiscal Years 1994–1999*, prepared by then

Undersecretary of Defense for Policy Paul Wolfowitz, for then
Secretary of Defense Cheney.[32]

The United States has for decades sought to play a more permanent role in Gulf regional security. While the unresolved conflict
with Iraq provides the immediate justification, the need for a substantial American force presence in the Gulf transcends the issue
of the regime of Saddam Hussein.

New methods of attack — electronic, 'non-lethal,' biological
— will be more widely available .... combat likely will take place
in new dimensions, in space, cyberspace, and perhaps the world of
microbes .... advanced forms of biological warfare that can target
specific genotypes may transform biological warfare from the
realm of terror to a politically useful tool.

— Project for a New American Century,
"Rebuilding America's Defenses: Strategies, Forces and
Resources for a New Century," 2000[33]

Despite the initial shock of the terrorist attacks in New York and Washington,
many aspects of current US geostrategy following 9/11 were apparently
planned in the late 1990s. A cursory analysis of various policy documents
published by PNAC relay sufficient details of the Bush administration's global
strategy. Interestingly, the American media and general population failed to
appreciate the implications of these radical policy papers published over a ten-
year period, beginning in 1992[34] and continuing into 1998[35] and 2000.[36]

In 1992, the final year of George H.W. Bush's presidency, Paul Wolfowitz
took the lead in drafting an internal set of military guidelines that is typically
referred to as the Defense Planning Guidance. Wolfowitz was then undersecretary of defense for policy (the Pentagon's third-highest-ranking civilian)
and originally authored this document for then Secretary of Defense Cheney.
This draft document advocated that, with the fall of the Soviet Union, a window
of opportunity was available for the US to exert an aggressive unilateral doctrine
with a stated goal of preventing any nation or any group of nations from
"aspiring to a larger regional or global role or pursue a more aggressive posture
to protect their legitimate interests."[37] The *Washington Post* summarized this
1992 draft with the following description:

The central strategy of the Pentagon's framework is to '*establish
and protect a new world order*' that accounts '*sufficiently for the
interests of the advanced industrial nations to discourage them from
challenging our leadership*,' while at the same time maintaining a
military dominance capable of '*deterring potential competitors from
even aspiring to a larger regional or global role.*'[38] [emphasis added]

This strategy for US global dominance requires a hybrid economic/military/ intelligence nexus in order to enforce American supremacy in the immediate post–Cold War period. Forebodingly, in this Defense document Wolfowitz defined "access to vital raw material, primarily Persian Gulf oil" as a key objective of US policy and advocated military intervention — *preemptive, if necessary* — to gain such access.[39] However, this document did not escape the public's attention once it was leaked to the press, instantly creating controversy in Washington DC and likely within the capitals of other nations. In 2003 PBS's *Frontline* interviewed *Washington Post* reporter Barton Gellman, who offered insight into the reactions of this story in 1992:

> You have to take yourself back to 1992. This is the first time that the Defense Department gathers itself to say, 'What is our new strategic mission in the world now that there is no more Soviet Union?'
>
> [And] they said, 'Our number one mission in the world, now that we are the sole superpower is to make sure we stay that way.' They wanted to pocket that gain. And what was so politically insensitive in this internal document, which wasn't meant for distribution, is it talked about not only Russia, but Germany, Japan, India, all as potential regional hegemons that could rise up to challenge the United States as at least a regional and, potentially, a global superpower. They said their number one mission is to quash that.
>
> *PBS reporter: What was the reaction?*
>
> Well, most of the countries I just named were on some kind of friendly terms, or central allies of the United States. They were none too pleased to be named as potential rivals. The public reaction was, 'Good God, we're supposed to have a peace dividend now. The Cold War is over. Let's get on with our lives. Of course, stay strong enough to protect ourselves. But what in the world are you doing, going out there and looking for trouble?'
>
> It was very controversial in Congress. There was an enormous amount of commentary by the opinion leaders saying, 'This is way over the top.' And, it was an election year. And they caved.[40]

Based on the largest worldwide protests in history during February 14–16, 2003, (estimated to have included 12 million people in 700 cities, representing 60 countries) the overall reaction of the global community protesting US ambitions for an Iraq War was assuredly unprecedented. Based on the political fall out in both the UN and NATO, the majority of governments sympathized with their citizens by expressing manifest intolerance of a US geostrategy based upon unilateral warfare and global domination.

Indeed, the world community seems increasingly intolerant and fearful of a hegemonic US superpower in the opening years of this new century. The failure of the Bush administration to gain UN authorization for the 2003 Iraq War, in conjunction with the largest anti-war protests in recorded history, showed that a great number of nations and their citizens still opposed the neoconservative agenda as "way over the top."

The supporters of PNAC openly seek to create a global empire, which in their terms is a blueprint for maintaining global US preeminence, precluding the rise of a great power rival, and shaping the international security order in line with American principles and interests. These policy-makers see little or no value in using America's "soft power." Contrarily, they advocate "hard power" policies, such as an aggressive militarization of US foreign policies, and provide an excellent contrast to the concept coined by Joseph Nye as America's traditional reliance on multilateral approaches when possible, or in his terms, "soft power."[41]

Instead of using America's soft power, the neoconservatives advocated grandiose unilateral policies designed to "discourage advanced industrial nations from challenging our leadership *or even aspiring to a larger regional or global role.*"[42] [emphasis added] What's more, this document stated that the doctrine of US global dominance must be pursued "as far into the future as possible."[43] Numerous governments have indicated their revulsion to such a contemptuous geostrategy, which is not in the least surprising.[44]

This small group of ideologues provided the basis for a new overt US foreign policy agenda. To appreciate the significance of 9/11 and how it has been used to pursue previously documented policies requires careful analysis. Individuals, such as Paul Wolfowitz, were considered fringe members of the Republican Party's far-right wing. After the 1992 elections, this group was out of power but began the process of preparing for the next opportunity when Republicans would win back the White House.

In 1997 like-minded members of this group had founded the Project for a New American Century (PNAC).[45] This organization included an impressive array of politicians and theorists: Donald Rumsfeld, Dick Cheney, Lynne Cheney, James Woolsey, Paul Wolfowitz, Richard Perle, James Bolton, Jeb Bush, Zalmay M. Khalilzad, William Bennett, and Dan Quayle. The views of PNAC members, despite their reputations and authority, were often regarded as perhaps too extreme by the mainstream conservatives who controlled the Republican Party.[46]

However, following the 2000 election of George W. Bush, these former political "outsiders" became powerful "insiders" within the White House, and were placed in positions where they could exert maximum influence on US policy: Dick Cheney as Vice President, Rumsfeld as Defense Secretary, Wolfowitz as Deputy Defense Secretary, I. Lewis "Scooter" Libby as Cheney's Chief of Staff, Elliot Abrams as the official in charge of Middle East policy at the National Security Council (NSC), Dov Zakheim as comptroller for the Defense Department, John Bolton as Undersecretary of State, Richard Perle as chair of the Defense Policy advisory board at the Pentagon, and Paula Dobriansky as the Undersecretary of State for Global Affairs in the Bush administration.[47] Additional members of the PNAC included Jeb Bush, younger brother of George W. Bush and Governor of Florida, and William "Bill" Kristol, editor of the *Weekly Standard* magazine.

The military–industrial–petroleum–intelligence nexus was also represented in PNAC by former Lockheed-Martin vice president Bruce Jackson, ex-CIA director James Woolsey, and senior fellow at the Hudson Institute, Norman Podhoretz, all of whom were signatories to the PNAC policy document, "Rebuilding America's Defenses: Strategies, Forces and Resources for a New Century."[48] In effect, PNAC members were able to construct incoming President George W. Bush's foreign policies. In his first eight months in power, some of these policies were openly pursued, such as insistence on a National Missile Defense (NMD) system and the cancellation of the Anti-Ballistic Missile (ABM) treaty.

However, these advisors were not able to pursue the more ambitious aspects of their global strategy. PNAC's famous strategy document from September 2000 lamented that the desired "transformation" of the US military would be a long and difficult process without a massive external threat to provide a catalyst for their larger goals. This document noted that perhaps only a "new Pearl Harbor" could facilitate their goals of military "transformation."[49]

> Tragically, the American media has still failed to offer much-needed analysis to inform the people of the imperial policies espoused by PNAC and the resulting international blowback stemming directly from the doctrine of US global domination.

Historians will undoubtedly record that it was the Bush administration's response to the historical opportunity presented in the aftermath of the 9/11 terrorist attacks that allowed the government to overtly pursue previously unpalatable foreign policies. Tragically, the American media has still failed to offer much-needed analysis to inform the people of the imperial policies espoused by PNAC and the resulting international blowback stemming directly from the doctrine of US global domination.

In contrast to the subservient media, information about this group and careful analysis of their policy documents can be found on numerous websites. Perhaps most significant is the widespread analysis by European policy-makers, many of whom have openly expressed significant concerns about the transformation of the US from a largely multilateralist nation to one that openly espouses an eagerness for global dominance and endless warfare. PNAC's policies are seen as an open US declaration to seek global domination — at any costs.

PNAC's strategy papers provided the theoretical basis for the controversial US defense document released in September 2002, "The National

Security Strategy of the United States of America" (NSS).[50] The Iraq War was the test case of the new "Bush doctrine" of "preventative warfare." One of the many US websites that analyze and critique neoconservative geostrategy is Bernard Weiner's informative "Crisis Papers."[51] Weiner, who has taught American politics and international relations at Western Washington University and San Diego State University, offered the following analysis of the underlying doctrine behind the NSS strategy, otherwise known as the Bush doctrine:

> The [National Security Strategy of the United States of America] document asserts as the guiding policy of the United States the right to use military force anywhere in the world, at any time it chooses, against any country it believes to be, or it believes may at some point become, a threat to American interests. No country has ever asserted such a sweeping claim to global domination as is now being made by the United States.
>
> Furthermore, it declares that '*The US national security strategy will be based on a distinctly American internationalism that reflects the union of our values and our national interests.*' This bold sort of internationalism may appear presumptuous to other countries, governments and religious groups when it proclaims that whatever is good for America is good for the world. As President Bush asserts in the introduction of the document, America's values '*are right and true for every person, in every society.*'[52] [emphasis added]

While many people from around the world naturally tend to harbor nostalgic notions of their own country, it is often problematic for a nation state to boldly proclaim that its *national interests* and *values* are true for every nation on Earth. The NSS did not address what constitutes national interests and, as such, represented another Orwellian phrase similar to the oft-repeated, but never actually defined, "American way of life." According to the Declaration of Independence, the unalienable universal rights of mankind are to "Life, Liberty and the pursuit of Happiness." Clearly preventative warfare is not one of the self-evident truths, but rather appears to be an aggressive strategy for enforcing our national interests upon other states.

The essential claim in the 2002 NSS document is the right of the US to take unilateral military action against another country *without* having to offer verifiable evidence that it is acting to prevent a clear and verifiable threat of attack. This assertion was used to justify the 2003 Iraq War and basically stated that the US has all-encompassing power to resort to violence whenever it decides to, while using very vague language that cannot withstand the scrutiny of critical analysis or international law: "We must be prepared to stop rogue states and their terrorist clients before they are able to threaten or use weapons of Mass Destruction."[53]

This philosophy represents a radical departure from the post–WW II period, as it does not apply to a nation's right to self-defense from imminent attack, but proclaims that any potential, ambiguous threats at some point in the future will be used to justify US military action. From a forthright geostrategic perspective, this policy appears to advocate the use of military force to overrule economic realities. As US policy-makers lose confidence in the economic strength and competitiveness of the American economic structure vis-à-vis its major international rivals, policy-makers may increasingly be fearful of dislocations within the domestic social structure. The ruling elites may view the application of US military power as the mechanism by which it can counteract some of the troubling economic reality.

Rarely mentioned in our censored press, but widely disseminated in the foreign media, is the disheartening realization that the majority of international legal opinion has interpreted the concept of "preventative war" as illegal under international law. The International Commission of Jurists denounced the invasion of Iraq, claiming the attack represented a "war of aggression."[54] In September 2004 UN Secretary General Kofi Annan unequivocally stated the UN's position on the war, "I've indicated that it was not in conformity with the UN Charter from our point of view, and from the Charter point of view it was illegal."[55] (Note: The US helped write the original UN charter and ratified it in 1948.)

The New Great Game: Geopolitical Tensions over Diminishing Hydrocarbon Reserves

The United States will find the world of liquefied natural gas potentially much more troubling than that of oil. To the extent that the so-called war on terror is a cover for increasingly desperate moves to control the world's dwindling oil supply, expansion into LNG, which is liquid natural gas, with its main production sources in politically anti-American states, threatens an even greater likelihood of endless war, covert disruption and forced regime change.

— Julian Darley, author of *High Noon for Natural Gas: The New Energy Crisis*, 2004[56]

Anxious to diversify its suppliers, Beijing has directed its state-controlled companies to buy into oilfields around the world .... 'It reflects the generally uneasy feeling in the government,' said Joe Zhang, head of China research at UBS in Hong Kong. 'Strategically, politically, militarily, somehow they don't feel comfortable.'

— "China Unable to Quench Thirst for Oil," *Financial Times*, 2004[57]

In 2003 China became the second-largest oil consumer of energy behind the US. This has far-reaching implications and provides further impetus to develop alternative energy sources in an effort to reduce geopolitical tensions. Gal Luft, Executive Director of the Institute for the Analysis of Global Security (IAGS) in Washington DC, and Anne Korin, Director of Policy and Strategic Planning at IAGS, noted that China may come into conflict over oil in the Middle East.

> [It] is worth bearing in mind that the US, which has been trying for three decades to break its addiction to Middle Eastern oil, has only become more dependent with each passing year. Whether the Chinese can do better remains at best an open question. For the time being, the trend lines are what they are: oil reserves elsewhere are being depleted faster than in the Middle East, and before too long that region will contain the last remaining reservoir of cheaply extractable crude. If each barrel the US needs is also sought after by China, a superpower conflict in the world's most unstable region can once again become an omnipresent danger. At that point, as Napoleon foresaw, the world will surely tremble.[58]

This warning provided yet another reason for the US government to undertake a sustained and concerted effort to reduce our excessive oil consumption. Although China's population is over four times that of the US (1.2 billion versus 300 million) and has accounted for the majority of economic growth in the opening years of the 21st century, its energy consumption is much less than that of the US. For example, in 2002 daily US oil consumption was a prodigious 7,191 mb/d, whereas China consumed a miserly 1,935 mb/d.[59] To place this imbalance in perspective at the individual level, the average American consumes 25 barrels of oil a year; in China, the average is 1.3 barrels.[60]

Notably, from the mid-1990s until early 2002 there were optimistic claims that the Caspian Sea region could have up to 200 billion barrels(b/bl) of untapped oil, making it the "oil find of the century."[61] Cheney's energy plan may have been written based on these optimistic estimates. The highly reputable *Jane's Intelligence Review* reported in March 2001 that the US was working with Russia to "tactically and logistically counter the Taliban" well before the September 11th attacks and the "war on terrorism" was declared.[62]

Furthermore, according to the French book, *The Forbidden Truth*, the Bush administration ignored the UN sanctions that had been imposed upon the Taliban and entered into secret negotiations with the supposedly "rogue regime" from February 2, 2001, to August 6, 2001.[63] According to this book, the Taliban were not cooperative, based on the statements of Mr. Naik, Pakistan's former ambassador. He reported that the US threatened a military option if the Taliban did not acquiesce to Washington's demands.[64] Fortuitous for Cheney's energy plan, as outlined in the May 2001 NEPDG report, a few months later Osama bin Laden delivered upon US soil the unprecedented 9/11terrorist attacks.

The pre-positioned US military, along with the CIA providing millions in cash for the Northern Alliance leaders, led the invasion of Afghanistan, and the Taliban were routed. The pro-Western Karzai government was ushered in. The $3.2 billion pipeline project was reinvigorated shortly thereafter, with an agreement signed between Turkmenistan, Afghanistan, and Pakistan in 2002.[65] According to Dale Allen Pfeiffer, an oil industry researcher for Michael Ruppert's website (www.fromthewilderness.com), after three exploratory wells were built and analyzed, it was reported that the Caspian region contained much smaller oil reserves than originally reported, although it does appear to have a lot of natural gas.[66] In fact, it was discovered that the Caspian oil is also of poor quality, with up to 20 percent sulfur content, expensive to refine, and creates huge volumes of environmentally damaging waste product.

In December 2001, just after US troops took over the capital of Afghanistan, British Petroleum (BP) announced disappointing Caspian drilling results. The consulting group PetroStrategies published a study estimating that the Caspian Basin contained only 8 to 39.4 b/bl of oil.[67] Shortly after this report was discussed in the petroleum news sources, BP and other Western oil companies began reducing investment plans in the region.[68]

Despite exaggerated claims of the "oil find of the century" and predictions of a new Saudi Arabia outside the Middle East, the US State Department announced in November 2002 that "Caspian oil represents 4% of world reserves. It will never dominate the world's markets."[69] Subsequently, several major companies dropped their plans for the pipeline, citing the massive project was no longer profitable.

Unfortunately, this unexpected realization about the Caspian Sea region has serious implications for the US, India, China, Asia, and Europe, as the amount of available hydrocarbons for industrialized and developing nations has been decreased. Although the contents of the Cheney's energy task force are still unpublished, Judicial Watch won a small victory in July 2002 with the release of a few documents under a Freedom of Information Act (FOIA). The following is a synopsis of the seven pages of disclosed documents from these secretive energy meetings held during early 2001:

- Detailed map of all Iraqi oil fields (an estimated 11 percent of world supply)
- Two-page specific list of all nations with development contracts for Iraqi oil and gas projects and the companies involved, "Foreign Suitors for Iraqi Oilfield Contracts," dated March 2001
- Detailed map of all Saudi Arabian oil fields (an estimated 25 percent of world supply)

- List of all major oil and gas development projects in Saudi Arabia
- Detailed map of all oil fields in the United Arab Emirates (an estimated 8 percent of world supply)
- List of all oil and gas development projects in the UAE[70]

It is widely reported as factual that Iraq holds 11 percent of the world's total oil reserves (112 billion barrels). However, due to armed conflict with Iran and then Kuwait, no geological surveys have been conducted in Iraq since the 1970s. The Russians, French, and Chinese were eager to lease Iraq's unexplored fields, which some organizations claimed may contain up to 200 billion barrels.[71] However, these appear to be markedly irresponsible claims, as technical reports suggest Iraq's recoverable oil may be significantly lower than expected, perhaps to only 15 to 25 percent of its 112 b/bl reserve estimates.[72]

Furthermore, the convergence of overt military actions to pursue energy policy requires the US president to obfuscate the underlying energy issues in an effort to create public support for such war. It would have not been easy to convince the masses that the Iraq War was based on the US' need to somehow acquire an additional 7.5 mb/d to meet projected energy consumption by 2020.

Obviously the UN would not sanction a war based on such a narrow self-interest. Hence, the Straussian/neoconservative ideology to create an external threat was actively pursued by our political leaders in order to deceive the domestic population, in an effort to pursue otherwise unpalatable foreign policies. Despite the success of the ruling elites to launch the Iraq War, two flaws in neoconservative geostrategy remain. First, the observation that neither the world community, nor the UN, is as easily propagandized as the domestic US audience. In other words, the tactics involving the creation of an ominous external threat to American security is ineffectual on the international stage.

Secondly, most of the countries targeted for increased oil supply to the US are typically plagued with either internal conflict based on differing ethnic groups or are anti-American based on perceptions or historical experience with unsavory US foreign interference. The Iraq War was claimed to be a logical extension of the "war on terror." However, the generalized failure of the international community to support the US occupation in the aftermath of the Iraq War exemplified the inherent weaknesses of neoconservative doctrine. Although only obliquely addressed by the mainstream media, international agreements and competition over oil exploration contracts in a post-sanction Iraq were key factors.

One of the documents that Cheney reviewed during the spring of 2001 was entitled "Foreign Suitors for Iraqi Oilfield Contracts."[73] These detailed reports are representative of those prepared by the highly regarded Swiss firm IHS Energy (formerly Petroconsultants). A careful analysis of these two pages suggests that, around 1997 many nations, including China, Russia, and France, approached the Saddam Hussein regime to secure oil exploration contracts. Apparently an international consensus was beginning to emerge that Iraq's WMD program had been effectively dismantled and the 1991 UN sanctions against Iraq would soon be lifted. After the sanctions were lifted, those nations awarded oil lease contracts by the Iraqi government stood to gain — but with Saddam Hussein likely excluding the US and UK oil companies due to his animosity over ongoing bombing campaigns in southern and northern Iraq.

These documents reveal that energy giants, such as Russia's Lukoil and France's TotalFinaElf, had signed "production-sharing contracts"(PSCs) going back to 1997. In total, over 30 nations were listed as foreign suitors for Iraq's oil.[74] The two conspicuous nations missing from this list were the United States and United Kingdom (two small UK companies were listed, but not British Petroleum/BP). Incidentally, the Clinton administration unilaterally pulled the UN weapons inspectors out of Iraq and launched a bombing campaign in December 1998, Operation Desert Fox. This effectively ended the UN inspection process within Iraq, but foreign oil companies continued to pursue contractual agreements with Saddam Hussein until 2002, believing the UN sanctions would ultimately be lifted. In the meantime the US and UK continually blocked motions to lift the sanctions despite the ongoing humanitarian crisis in Iraq.

Figure 2.1 below helps illustrate why neither Washington nor London was unable to gain approval for the Iraq War at the UN Security Council. According to the International Energy Agency's "World Energy Outlook 2001," these contracts for Iraqi oil were worth up to $1.1 trillion.[75]

According to an article in the *Observer*, both European and Russian officials voiced concerns about an "oil grab" by Washington in the event of a US

Company	Country	Iraq Reserves (billion barrels)	Area or Oil Field
Elf Aquitaine, Total SA* (Now part of TotalFinaElf)	France	9-20, 3.5-7	Majnoun, Nahr Umr, etc.
Lukoil, Zarubezneft, Mashinoimport	Russia	7.5-15	Rafidain, West Qurnah, etc.
China National Petroleum	China	Under 2	North Rumaila
ENI/Agip	Italy	Under 2	Nasiriya
Japex	Japan	n/a	Gharraf
Ranger, CanOxy, etc.	Canada	n/a	Block 6, Ratawi

2.1: *Iraqi oil contracts. Source: IEA "World Energy Outlook 2001"* invasion of Iraq.[76] It is reasonable to assume that the governments of the US, UK, France, Germany, Russia, or China were likely motivated more by geostrategic interests than the deplorable human rights conditions in Iraq.

> The Russian official said his government believed the US had brokered a deal with the coalition of Iraqi opposition forces it backs whereby support against Saddam Hussein is conditional on their declaring — on taking power — all oil contracts conceded under his rule to be null and void.
>
> "The concern of my government," said the official, "is that the concessions agreed between Baghdad and numerous enterprises will be reneged upon, and that US companies will enter to take the greatest share of those existing contracts. Yes, you could say it that way — an oil grab by Washington."
>
> — A government insider in Paris told the *Observer* that France also feared suffering economically from US oil ambitions at the end of a war."[77]

These concerns about a US *oil grab*, as expressed by various foreign governments, were not unfounded accusations, considering the explicit comments of former CIA director R. James Woolsey. In an interview with the *Washington Post* before the war, he warned, "France and Russia have oil companies and interests in Iraq. They should be told that if they are of assistance in moving Iraq toward decent government, we'll do the best we can to ensure that the new government and American companies work closely with them." But he added, "If they throw in their lot with Saddam Hussein, *it will be difficult to the point of impossible to persuade the new Iraqi government to work with them.*"[78] [emphasis added] Woolsey's unveiled message was quite clear about future oil prospects in Iraq: Join the "coalition of the willing" — or your oil contracts will be voided.

A review of Iraq's oil production history shows a peak in December 1979 at 3.7 mb/d. In 1980, shortly after the Iran-Iraq War started, Iraq's oil production decreased. Likewise, one month before Saddam Hussein's August 1990 invasion of Kuwait, Iraq's daily oil production was near the previous peak, with July 1990 oil production reaching 3.5 mb/d. However, during the decade of the 1990s, Iraq's oil infrastructure deteriorated under the UN sanctions. According to the Energy Information Administration, Iraq's oil production reached perhaps 2.0 mb/d, with "gross" production (including re-injection, water cut, and unaccounted-for oil) of around 2.2 mb/d. For the first ten months of 2004, Iraqi crude oil output was averaging 2.0 mb/d.[79]

Before the 2003 invasion it was widely speculated that a reconstituted Iraqi oil production infrastructure would garner billions in new investment that could potentially double oil production, reaching up to 6 mb/d. It was also presumed that such oil production exports would pay for the majority of Iraq's reconstruction costs.

However, in 2001 and in 2003 it was reported that, during the UN embargo period throughout the 1990s, Iraqi oil engineers were injecting 400,000 barrels of oil back into the giant Kirkuk field in an effort to maintain reservoir pressure. Over time this poor engineering technique will degrade the internal structure of the reservoir, thereby jeopardizing future production output in order to maintain current production levels. As an oil field matures, the internal oil pressure begins to drop. In order to maintain internal pressure, large amounts of water or oil can be injected back into the reservoir, but eventually the field will "water out," often resulting in a drastic collapse in output.

Similar concerns have arisen regarding the world's largest oil find, Ghawar in Saudi Arabia. This mature field produces over half of all Saudi oil, approximately 4.5 mb/d. However, in order to achieve this output, Saudi engineers are injecting 7 million barrels of seawater per day into Ghawar, a sign that the world's largest oil field is nearing a collapse of output.[80]

Regarding Iraq, apparently the lack of spare parts and inability to conduct engineering repairs in the reservoirs throughout the 13 years of comprehensive UN sanctions (1991 to 2003) resulted in severe, and potentially permanent, damage to Iraq's two major oil fields, and likely other fields as well. If these reports are even only partially accurate, Iraq's oil production capability may never reach oil production levels of 5-6 mb/d that was proclaimed prior to the 2003 invasion.

> In June 2001 the UN reported that, without immediate and extensive repairs of Iraq's two main oil reservoirs, the fields may become permanently damaged, thereby significantly decreasing the amount of recoverable oil.

Given these disconcerting issues, some oil geologists have downgraded Iraq's oil reserve figures to approximately half of what is typically reported as its reserves: 112.5 billion barrels. In June 2001 the UN reported that, without immediate and extensive repairs of Iraq's two main oil reservoirs, the fields may become permanently damaged, thereby significantly decreasing the amount of recoverable oil.

The January 2004 newsletter for the Association for the Study of Peak Oil & Gas (ASPO) addressed the issue of damaged oil reservoirs as reported by the UN and inferred that a realistic downgrade of Iraq's oil reserves was warranted. Additionally, the ASPO omitted the "political oil" reserve revisions typical of the late 1980s and concluded that Iraq's recoverable oil reserves are more likely in the 50-billion-barrel range.[81]

> The report says that it may now be possible to recover only 15% to 25% of the oil in place. Meanwhile the occupying forces are concentrating on trying to repair the surface facilities being hesitant

to address the subsurface for fear, as the *New York Times* no less admits, the objective of the invasion should become self-evident. It looks as if a serious downward revision of Iraq's future production potential is called for. The published reserve estimate of 112.5 Gb looks increasingly unreliable. Perhaps it makes more sense to revert to something around 50 Gb, closer to what was reported prior to the anomalous jump to 100 Gb in 1988, when the OPEC countries were vying with each other for quota based on reported reserves.[82]

This UN report likely presented a paradox for the Bush administration — had the 1991 UN sanctions been lifted, the French, Russian, and Chinese oil-leasing contracts could have been legally implemented. These nations would then have been in the enviable position of pouring massive reinvestment into Iraq's oil sector in an effort to make the necessary upgrades and engineering repairs.

On the other hand, lifting of the UN sanctions would have presumably denied the major US and UK oil companies from oil exploration contracts inside Iraq, while also allowing higher volumes of Iraqi oil production sales denominated in the euro. Given the disconcerting reports of deterioration within Iraq's major oil reservoirs, a larger question should have been contemplated in 2001, What course of action in Iraq would be beneficial to the global community? It was not in anyone's interests, including the people of Iraq or the international community, to allow Iraq's oil reserves to be adversely, and perhaps permanently, damaged due to the insistence of continued US/UK-sponsored sanctions.

The evidence of Iraq's effective disarmament was growing by 1997–1998, but in an effort to keep "foreign suitors" from beginning oil exploration in Iraq — at the exclusion of the major US and UK oil conglomerates — the plan under the Bill Clinton, George W. Bush, and Tony Blair administrations appears to have been an active attempt to block and postpone any attempts to lift the UN sanctions until Saddam Hussein was replaced with a pliant regime. The real costs of preserving Iraq's oil profits for the US/UK corporate–military–industrial–petroleum–banking conglomerate can be now measured in lost human lives: American, British, and Iraqi — estimated in excess of 100,000 violent deaths.

There were alternatives to an invasion of Iraq, but sacrifice in the pursuit of nonviolent approaches to our energy and economic challenges was not what the Bush administration was able, or willing, to ask of the American people. Nonetheless, previously "pro-war" commentators such as *New York Times* columnist Thomas Friedman are now advocating that the US earnestly seek alternative energy strategies:

If Bush made energy independence his moon shot, he would dry up revenue for terrorism; force Iran, Russia, Venezuela, and Saudi Arabia to take the path of reform ... strengthen the dollar; and improve his own standing in Europe, by doing something huge to reduce global warming. He would also create a magnet to inspire young people to contribute to the war on terrorism and America's future by becoming scientists, engineers and mathematicians.

'This is not just a win-win,' said the Johns Hopkins foreign policy expert Michael Mandelbaum. 'This is a win-win-win-win-win.'

Or, Bush can ignore this challenge and spend the next four years in an utterly futile effort to persuade Russia to be restrained, Saudi Arabia to be moderate, Iran to be cautious and Europe to be nice.

— Thomas L. Friedman, "A New Mission for America," *International Herald Tribune*, December, 2004[83]

West Africa: Expanding the War on Terror, or War on Global Oil Control?

I think Africa is a continent that is going to be of very, very significant interest in the 21st century ... we're going to have to engage more in that theater ... [warning that West Africa's ungoverned regions] could become terrorist breeding grounds.

— General James Jones, head of the US European Command, statement before a Senate Panel in May 2003, as quoted in the *Washington Times*, September 2003[84]

The US is always looking for alternative sources of oil. We need to find sources that we can depend on, and certainly the Gulf of Guinea is one of those areas, but oil is not the driving force in this region. Clearly, shoring up security in these regions helps us in our global war on terrorism, which is a major linchpin of our current foreign policy.

— State Department official, *Washington Times*, September 2003[85]

The [West African] people are fed up and angry at the exploitation of their resources.

— Mr. Ayittey of American University, *Washington Times*, September 2003[86]

Why does America end up supporting dictators and autocrats around the world?

Unfortunately, American oil and gas or mining companies are very likely to support a dictatorship because it makes the natural resource extraction and sale that much easier and more profitable. US oil companies are in Nigeria, its mineral companies are in Sierra Leone. Under lobbying pressure, the American government ends up supporting its largest natural resource companies and quickly becomes an ally of the dictator's regime and an enemy of his people.

— John Talbot, *Where America Went Wrong and How to Regain Her Democratic Ideas*, 2004[87]

According to a September 2003 article in the *Washington Times*, the US is on a global "hunt for new oil," with West Africa emerging as a key strategic area of interest.[88] Negotiations are underway for multiple US military outposts in this region. Currently the US receives about 14 to 15 percent of its oil imports from Africa, with Nigeria and Angola serving as the two prime producers there. Cheney's 2001 National Energy Plan estimated the US could receive up to 25 percent of its total energy from Africa. For comparison, currently the US receives approximately 30 percent of its imports from Canada and Mexico, with 26 percent imported from the Persian Gulf.

While the oil reserves in West Africa are believed to be around 77 billion barrels, this pales in significance to the estimated total reserves in the Middle East of a reported 686 billion barrels. Nonetheless, at least six nations in West Africa will likely become more important during this decade as global oil production winds down in the US, UK, and elsewhere. According to Michael Rodgers, senior director for PFC Energy in Washington,

> Several other West African countries — like Chad, Congo-Brazzaville, Equatorial Guinea, and Sao Tome and Principe — are emerging as new and potentially strong oil producers. West African oil production, currently at 3.5 million barrels per day, could top 6 million barrels per day in the next decade.[89]

Despite the oil wealth in Nigeria and Angola, the *Washington Times* article noted that human rights abuses and poverty levels rank very high in the two most oil-rich nations of Africa. Likewise, these conditions of economic disparity have created both ethnic and political conflicts that plague this region. Furthermore, much of the societal strife in these nations appears to be directed at Western oil companies that are seen as exploiting the natural resources of the region without reinvesting in the native country. The indigenous antagonism toward US oil companies has created an expansion of the so-called war on terror into West Africa. Timothy Burn of the *Washington Times* outlined the growing risks associated with African oil exports:

> Political and ethnic strife are rampant throughout West Africa. The presence of huge amounts of oil has fueled the unrest, as billions

of dollars in petroleum revenue pour into government coffers. Little finds its way to impoverished local populations.

Militant protesters in West Africa often aim their wrath at Western oil companies, accusing them of exploiting Africa's oil wealth while their nations struggle under poverty.[90]

The anger and frustration espoused by the impoverished populations in West Africa sound eerily reminiscent of claims stated by Osama bin Laden regarding the exploitation of oil wealth and corrupt Middle Eastern governments. Since the mid-1990s, the Saudi government has been perceived by bin Laden and his followers to be a corrupt regime that has transferred vast wealth into Western oil companies, presumably US oil companies. Regarding Nigeria and Angola, if the indigenous populations become increasingly militant with feelings of exploitation, the US strategy of relying on West African sources of oil may not be a viable long-term national security strategy.

To mitigate such conflicts, transparent policies should be pursued with respect to oil export profits. For example, Prime Minister Blair has called for more openness in the financial dealings between oil companies and oil-rich nations. One organization advocating transparency is Publish What You Pay. Their goal is to "help citizens of resource-rich countries hold their governments accountable for how revenue from oil is distributed, and thereby is designed to improve the living standards of local populations, rather than lining the pockets of corrupt government leaders."[91] It would appear that increasing the transparency behind these financial agreements could lessen social discord. This effort is spearheaded by billionaire financier George Soros, but not surprisingly, the Bush administration is opposed to such transparency.

Oil and War in the 20th Century: The Emerging Role of the US Military in the 21st Century

The need for oil certainly was a prime motive [in Hitler's decision to invade Russia] ...

— Albert Speer's testimony at Nuremburg War Trials,
German Minister for Armaments and War Production,
1941–1945[92]

The thrust is clear: Once it has seized the oil wells of west Asia, the US will determine not only which firms would bag the deals, not only the currency in which oil trade would be denominated, not only the price of oil on the international market, but even the destination of the oil.

— "Behind the Invasion of Iraq,"
Aspects of India's Economy, 2002[93]

Iraq is hardly the only country where American troops are risking their lives on a daily basis to protect the flow of petroleum. In Colombia, Saudi Arabia, and the Republic of Georgia, US personnel are also spending their days and nights protecting pipelines and refineries, or supervising the local forces assigned to this mission. American sailors are now on oil-protection patrol in the Persian Gulf, the Arabian Sea, the South China Sea, and along other sea routes that deliver oil to the United States and its allies. *In fact, the American military is increasingly being converted into a global oil-protection service.* [emphasis added]

— Michael Klare, "Transforming the American Military into a Global Oil-Protection Service," October 7, 2004[94]

During the two great wars of the 20th century, oil often proved to be the defining natural resource that was required to project military power on the sea, air, and land. Indeed, oil factored in the victory or defeats in major military campaigns throughout the 20th century. During both of the world wars, the US had an abundance of oil. The transatlantic transport and supply of this oil was critical to our success in helping our allies prevail during both world wars. Conversely, while Germany had a large supply of domestically sourced coal, she had little domestic oil. The geological history of Germany ultimately impaired its goal of an empire.

It is estimated that during WW I a staggering 6 out of 7 million barrels of oil used by the English and French to defeat the Axis powers were provided by the United States. Lord Cuzon, chairman of the Inter-Allied Petroleum Conference famously remarked after WW I, "The Allied cause had floated to victory upon a wave of oil."[95] In WW II, the German U-boat fleet tried to stop the flow of US oil being shipped to England but was ultimately unsuccessful after the allies invented underwater sonar technology.

A young German soldier who fought in WW I became convinced in the intervening two decades between the world wars that one of the reasons for Germany's defeat in WW I was due to its lack of crude oil. This man was Adolph Hitler, later the chancellor of Germany, who, according to his generals, was fascinated with the history of oil. By the time Hitler had begun his imperialist campaign in Europe, German scientists had developed a process that broke down coal molecules to produce synthetic oil for fuel and lubrication (Fischer-Tropsch process). Despite this breakthrough, the German army still sought sources of crude oil to power the Nazi military machines. Naturally, Hitler told the German people his invasion of Russia was absolutely necessary to "save the Western world" from the barbaric and Godless communists.

After the war the true strategic reasons for the Russian invasion were revealed. Albert Speer, the German Minister for Armaments and War

Hitler told the German people his invasion of Russia was absolutely necessary to "save the Western world" from the barbaric and Godless communists. After the war Albert Speer, the German Minister for Armaments and War Production, stated that "the need for oil certainly was a prime motive" in the decision to invade Russia.

Production, stated during his interrogation in May 1945 that "the need for oil certainly was a prime motive" in the decision to invade Russia.[96] Indeed, Hitler's invasion of Russia in 1941 was in large part initiated so the Nazi war machine could reach the oil-rich Caucus region of southern Russia. Hitler reportedly told Field Marshall von Mannstein, "Unless we get the Baku oil, the war is lost."[97] By the winter of 1942, the Russians had stopped the German offensive. In turn, the inability of the German Wehrmacht to gain control over the oil-rich Baku region played an important factor in thwarting Hitler's dreams of an empire.

As illustrated by Daniel Yergin's epic analysis of oil-related conflict during the 20th century, political leaders resorted to both deception and fear as methods to disguise their imperial conquests of gaining control over oil deposits in various places around the world. The 21st century is showing a similar pattern, using the "external threat" of terrorism to scare the masses into compliance for geostrategic maneuvers.

A cursory review of recent US military activity shows a pattern of military basing activity that translates to deployments in areas with either energy reserves or oil pipelines. Since 9/11 US military deployments have included areas ranging from South America to the Caspian Sea region, stretching down to the Middle East and over to West Africa. Undeniably, these worldwide military deployments are in areas that lack evidence of Al Qaeda, but do fall within US "strategic interests" as they designate the locations of oil and gas deposits, the associated pipelines, or proposed routes, such as the Baku-Tbilisi-Ceyhan pipeline. This drive to establish new US military bases has not escaped the attention of world leaders.

Consequently, it is naïve to believe recent US military deployments were designed to fight terrorism, rather than to ensure US dominance over oil supplies and Western oil interests, should indigenous populations protest against foreign oil companies. Naturally, any indigenous protests against perceived exploitation of their countries' natural resources by Western oil and gas interests will likely be considered as "terrorism." Also, if Iraq is any indicator of the future, oil exporting nations that switch their oil export currency to the euro might also find they are the next US target in the "war on terror."

An Australian newspaper noted that to US policy-makers "defence redefined means securing cheap energy." This aspect of geostrategy appeared in an article by Lieutenant Colonel Liotta, professor of national security affairs at the Naval War College. According to this report, Liotta's article advocated the use of military force "for more than simply protecting a nation and its people from traditional threat-based challenges." Liotta argued that defense meant protecting the US lifestyle, the circumstances of "daily life."[98] This obliquely advocated a military strategy of *waging war* to maintain our excessive consumption of oil, *regardless of whether or not our nation faces any threat.*

Moreover, former British MP Meacher characterized US strategic maneuvers as revolving around a "bogus" war on terror. After reviewing the goals outlined in PNAC doctrine, Meacher concluded that, "all this analysis must surely be that the 'global war on terrorism' has the hallmarks of a political myth propagated to pave the way for a wholly different agenda — the US goal of world hegemony, built around securing by force command over the oil supplies required to drive the whole project."[99]

In May 2001, four months before 9/11, General Franks reviewed war plans that were to be used in the upcoming campaign in Afghanistan. At that time, Michael Klare observed that US military planning had become increasingly defined as providing "*resource security as their primary mission.*"[100] [emphasis added] Although this was hardly addressed in the US media, in April 2002 Franks testified that one his key missions as commander of the Persian Gulf/South Asia region was to provide "access to [the] region's energy resources."[101]

While it is true the US Navy plays an important role in keeping the sea routes safe for the transportation of oil, it is interesting to note that in the months prior to 9/11, US policy planners were increasingly devising military frameworks around potential energy issues. According to Klare's book, *Blood and Oil*, a top-secret document dated February 3, 2001 directed the "NSC (National Security Council) staff to cooperate with the NEPDG in *assessing the military applications of the energy plan*"[102] [emphasis added]. According to Jane Meyer of the *New Yorker*, who has reportedly seen a copy of the document, it envisioned the melding of two White House priorities: "review of operational policies toward rogue states [such as Iraq] and actions regarding the "capture of new and existing oil and gas fields."[103] Klare succinctly appraised the 2001 Quadrennial Defense Review (QDR) and related US joint energy-military policy documents:

> In fact, it is getting harder to distinguish US military operations designed to fight terrorism from those designed to protect energy assets. And the administration's tendency to conflate the two is obvious in more than just the Gulf and Caspian areas. In Latin America, the US Southern Command has been ordered to strengthen the Columbian army's ability to defend oil pipelines against guerrilla attack — again on the basis of expanding the war against terrorism. In the Caucasus, the European Command is

doing its part in the war on terror by training Georgian forces to protect the soon-to-be-completed Baku–Tbilisi–Ceyhan pipeline; terrorism and the vulnerability of the oil supplies are also providing the justification for Eurcom's efforts to enhance America's power-projection capacity in Africa.[104]

Recent strategy documents prepared by US government officials, remarks of high-ranking members of the US armed forces, and new military bases depict an open declaration by both the civilian leadership and military commanders that the US military's role in the new century is not limited to protecting the Constitution from enemies both foreign and domestic, but is an overt attempt to gain access to, or more accurately *domination* over, the world's largest oil reserves — all under the guise of the "war on terror." Europe, Russia, and China are naturally resisting this strategy.

Despite the unprecedented resistance at the geopolitical level against the war, the Bush administration launched Operation Iraqi Freedom in March 2003. Today, US soldiers, US contractors, and a handful of international coalition members are suffering under daily attacks and violent hostage-taking strategy by Iraqi insurgents. Meanwhile US political leaders use ambiguous phrases to justify their imperial goals with lofty statements, such as *securing access to energy, providing economic security, and spreading democracy.* Despite these proclamations, most industrialized and developing nations simply engage in legal trade agreements with the nations who export their natural resources such as oil, and typically leaders do not resort to Orwellian phraseology to justify faraway wars against "terror" or obfuscate their hidden agenda under the impressive-sounding slogan of "spreading democracy."

It is important to realize that, according to Cheney's energy plan, the US oil consumption will grow by an additional 7.5 mb/d by 2020. Current global production is around 82 mb/d, which is stretching the supply of all oil producers. As OPEC's President Yusgiantoro warned in August 2004, "There is no additional supply."[105] Furthermore, in December 2004 Igor Bashmakow, the executive director of the Russian Center for Energy Efficiency, stated that if Russia does not increase its abysmally low energy efficiency it "may lead to a situation where Russia *will be forced to stop all exports of energy sources such as oil and gas as early as 2010.*[106] [emphasis added] If these sentiments by energy experts are accurate, the question becomes, who will provide the projected 18–20 percent increase in demand by the year 2020?

Technical data on oil discovery and production, in conjunction with the analyses of numerous veteran oil geologists, clearly indicate that 7.5 mb/d of additional oil supply may only be possible under one ominous scenario — by strategically using the US military to thwart oil exports from the Middle East into China, India, and perhaps the EU. This is an aggressive and destabilizing strategy that has predictably produced geopolitical tensions.

Current US geostrategy, as articulated by the PNAC documents and subsequent NSS policy, is a bold attempt to justify unilateral military action anywhere on the globe, including the potential militarization of space. This remarkable merging of foreign policy with overt military doctrine provides further evidence that US policy-makers are acutely aware of the upcoming phenomenon known as global Peak Oil. Indeed, this realization would explain current geopolitical tensions and the growing expansion of US military deployments in the Middle East, Central Asia, West Africa, and Latin America.

America does not go abroad searching for monsters to destroy.

— President John Quincy Adams, 1821

Three

Global Peak Oil:
The Millennium's Greatest Challenge

All truth passes through three stages: First it is ridiculed. Second, it is violently opposed. Third, it is accepted as being self-evident.

> — Schopenhauer, Philosopher

The world is not running out of oil — at least not yet. What our society does face, and soon, is the end of the abundant and cheap oil.

> — Colin J. Campbell, founder of the Association for the Study of Peak Oil and Gas (ASPO), 1998[1]

Every generation has its taboo, and ours is this: that the resource upon which our lives have been built is running out. We don't talk about it because we cannot imagine it. This is a civilization in denial.

> — George Monibot, the *Guardian* (UK), December 2003[2]

By the time this is being read, currently available oil production capacity all around the world will be producing flat out. How sustainable this proves to be remains to be seen.

> — Chris Skrebowski, editor, *Petroleum Review*, August 2004[3]

You shall know the truth and the truth shall make you free.

> — Inscription on the marble entranceway of the CIA headquarters, Langley, Virginia[4]

Global Peak Oil: The Greatest Story Never Told

For the past 100 years the industrialized world has become dependent upon the very cheap and abundant energy provided by hydrocarbons; it is this energy supply that has created the global economy. At the nation-state level, economic development requires sources of energy, and currently, hydrocarbons comprise 90 percent of the world's transportation fuel and 40 percent of the world's primary energy.

The United States remains the world's largest energy consumer; it represents 5 percent of the world's population, but consumes more than 25 percent of the world's oil production. The US was estimated to consume 7.5 billion barrels of oil in 2004, despite the fact that its oil production was then at its lowest level since the early 1950s and was declining by more than 2 percent per year.[5] It is projected that by 2010 the United States will have less than 15 billion barrels of domestic oil reserves and will have to import 65 percent of its projected oil demand by 2020 (estimated at 26 mb/d).[6,7]

The concept of Peak Oil was first illustrated in bell-shaped curves that US geophysicist M. King Hubbert developed when working for Shell Oil in Houston. He studied the past production characteristics of individual oil fields all across the US and developed a methodology to predict the natural peak and decline of oil fields. During a petroleum conference in 1956 he explained his research and predicted that US oil production in the lower 48 states would peak between 1966 and 1972.[8] Although he was a respected geophysicist at the time, his prediction was strongly criticized by others in the oil industry. Similar to the story of the tragic figure of Cassandra in Greek mythology, no one believed Hubbert's predictions about a future in which US oil production would soon peak and then enter a permanent state of slow decline.

However, Hubbert's methodology for predicting future oil recovery based on an analysis of past oil production data was proven correct when the US reached peak oil production in 1970. Kenneth Dreffeyes, his colleague, recalled this event when he read a rather cryptic sentence in the 1971 *San Francisco Chronicle*: "The Texas Railroad Commission announced a 100 percent allowable for next month."[9] Dreffeyes knew that during the 1960s the Texas Railroad Commission had been given the task of determining when peak oil production would occur in the lower 48 states. After reading that sentence, Dreffeyes realized that Hubbert's controversial prediction of 16 years before was correct.

Peak oil *discovery* in the lower 48 states occurred in 1930 in the east Texas oil field, with domestic US oil *production* peaking 40 years later. Conventional oil production peaked in 1970 at 9.5 mb/d and had slowly declined to around 4.4 mb/d by 2004.[10] These same bell-shaped curves for oil production have now been repeated in 50 oil producing nations.

The most crucial observation in this graph is the fact that *global oil discovery peaked in 1964*. Simply put, we cannot burn what we have not found, and

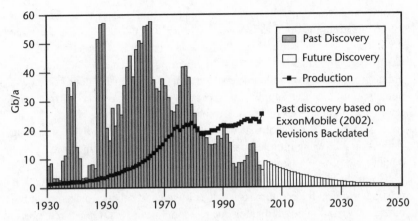

3.1: *Global oil discovery since 1930, with projections to 2050*
Source: Institute for Environmental and Legal Studies[11]

over the past 40 years we have found increasingly smaller amounts of oil. Due to advances in exploration technology, most regions whose geological characteristics indicate hydrocarbon deposits have already been explored. As noted in an excellent article by the Institute for Environmental and Legal Studies (of Mauritius Island), "planet Earth has been searched for oil pretty thoroughly. Few areas are left for exploration. Indeed exploration has now shifted to very inhospitable places like the Arctic or the Deep Sea, off continental shelves."[12]

Oil industry consultant and economist Michael Lynch is often regarded as the "leading critic of the peak-oil theorists."[13] He and other commentators often argued that the decline in oil discoveries since the 1960s is an artifact of economics and that "it's not geology that['s] causing that drop" in global oil discovery.[14] Lynch argued that increased oil exploration and drilling will result in sufficient new discoveries.[15] Some oil geologists refer to advocates of this nonfinite viewpoint of oil as "flat-earth economists."

Indeed, an objective review of the empirical facts refutes Lynch's claims. Referring again to the article "Fossil Fuels and Human Civilization," the facts are self-evident: "While oil discoveries fell in the seventies and eighties, the number of wildcats (exploratory drills) increased dramatically in the seventies but then fell sharply by 1985 wielding few large discoveries. It is no longer safe to assume that any increases in exploration will yield large finds."[16]

Regardless of the ongoing battle between the "peak-oil theorists" versus the "flat-earth economists," many industry observers have noted that investments by several major corporations in oil exploration have tapered off during the last few years. These business decisions are simply based on reduced expectations of finding major oil fields and reduced expectations of a positive

Return on Investment (ROI) for the small finds. The fact is oil companies cannot find enough new discoveries that will be able to replace the large declining fields. In November 2004 the UK-based Oil Depletion Analysis Centre (ODAC) analyzed 68 global "mega projects" that are scheduled to go online from 2004 to 2010 and reported that, if oil demand does not ease, a potentially permanent supply-side shortage could occur after 2007. Upon reviewing this analysis, ODAC Board member Chris Skrebowski stated, "This could very well be a signal that world oil production is rapidly approaching its peak, as a growing number of analysts now forecast, especially in view of the diminishing prospects for major new oil discoveries."[17]

Given the rising price and global demand for oil, especially by China, it is no longer logical for economists, such as Lynch and others, to claim that the oil industry's lack of investment is due to economic factors. Objectively speaking, decreasing finds are to be expected with any finite natural resource created under a process of fossilization millions of years ago.

Figure 3.2 is a model of global Peak Oil based on the technical analysis by the Association for the Study of Peak Oil and Gas(ASPO). Each oil field in the world follows a basic bell-shaped curve, with the composite view of the world's thousands of oil fields as one gigantic, uneven bell-shaped curve. In their mid-2004 update the ASPO model predicted the "Peak" would arrive two years earlier, in 2008 instead of 2010.

Although there are currently mitigating issues in global oil production with regard to Iraq, it should be noted that during 2004, evidence mounted that we may be reaching a plateau in Peak Oil production — reinforced by some petroleum experts who have stated oil production is now "flat out."[19] Establishing when global Peak Oil occurs will be determined in the subsequent year or two after the actual peak in oil production.

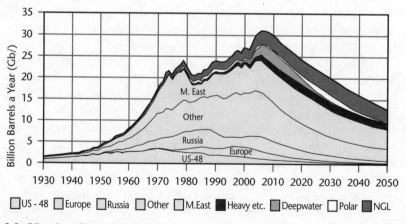

3.2: *Oil and gas liquids, 2004 scenario*   Source: *ASPO website*[18]

The Paradigm Shift: Energy Return on Energy Invested (EROEI)

One of the crucial concepts required to understand the importance of Peak Oil relates to a phenomenon in physics commonly described as Energy Return on Energy Invested, or EROEI. Unlike the traditional financial metric, Return on Investment (ROI), EROEI refers to the amount of *energy spent* compared to the amount of *energy extracted*. EROEI is the ratio between energy expended to extract a barrel of oil, versus the energy provided by that barrel of oil.

Fifty years ago when some of the super-giant oil fields were still being discovered, one of these could produce an EROEI of 200, that is, energy 200 hundred times *greater* than the energy actually expended to extract the oil. In contrast, oil wells in deep water currently achieve an EROEI of less than 5. Oil removed from the tar sands, as found in Canada, have a very low EROEI of 1.5, along with a slow extraction process.

Once global Peak Oil is reached and exceeded, a critical point is attained on the downward side of Hubbert's curve, when it requires *more energy* to extract a given unit of oil than what it will produce if extracted. Of the remaining oil in the ground or at the bottom of the ocean, a positive EROEI is required if that oil is to be used as transportation fuel. To reiterate, when the *energy* required to extract very low-grade or geographically undesirable oil is *equal to or greater than* the energy that would be provided by that new barrel of oil, it will no longer be logical to expend the energy to extract the oil. In such a scenario, the EROEI for that oil field becomes an energy sink, and the oil will simply remain in the ground.

It is for these reasons that the world will never technically run out of oil; rather, it will ultimately become simply too energy-intensive to extract low-quality or geographically inaccessible oil. Unlike ROI calculations, the amount of *money* invested in a mature oil field is completely irrelevant if the energy required to extract the oil is greater than the energy that would be derived from recovering the oil.

Despite the historic, social, economic, and geopolitical implications of global Peak Oil, many governments still appear reluctant to publish this information — even though the facts regarding global oil discovery and production are perfectly apparent to the rational observer. Instead, the global society has acquired an unfounded belief that more oil will be discovered as needed in order to further economic growth, but this is a false construct.

Reported Oil Reserves versus Technical Analysis

> The pessimists use technical data, whereas the optimists use the political data.
>
> — Jean H. Laherrère, renowned oil geologist,
> ASPO Conference, May 2003[20]

Dr. Salameh tackles the thorny question of how accurate are Middle East reserve estimates. His conclusion that these may be overstated by up to 300 bn [billion] barrels, or roughly five North Seas, will certainly give pause for thought. If his assessments are right, the world faces very major challenges in developing and securing the oil supplies it will require.

— Chris Skrebowski, *Petroleum Review*,
Editorial, August 2004[21]

> All objective oil geologists agree that global Peak Oil will occur — the real debate centers around exactly *when* it will happen.

All objective oil geologists agree that global Peak Oil will occur — the real debate centers around exactly *when* it will happen. One of the great difficulties of predicting Peak Oil is the ambiguous definition of "oil reserves;" another issue is the politically motivated reporting of oil reserve data. Typically, the mass media, government spokespersons, and economists utilize the suspicious political oil reserve figures as if they were facts. At the opposite extreme is the network of oil geologists, scientists, and interested citizens who attend annual conferences sponsored by the Association for the Study of Peak Oil and Gas. Of course various intelligence agencies, such as the CIA, also fall into the latter technical camp whose primary mission is to provide rigorous, unbiased, analytical intelligence.

IHS Energy (formerly Petroconsultants) is regarded as the premier source of technical data on the world's hydrocarbon reserves. The main asset of this Geneva-based company is their proprietary databases containing all significant information on the world's petroleum concessions, companies, exploration, and development wells outside the US and Canada. IHS Energy has proprietary data on virtually all discoveries, production history by country, fields, and company, as well as details pertaining to geophysical surveys. The detailed reports produced by this firm are not inexpensive, as their elite clientele pay approximately $35,000 for these reports. The oil and gas industry recognizes that no other organization has such a comprehensive database on the upstream petroleum industry. According to Kenneth Dreffeyes, a 40-year veteran oil geologist, the CIA was rumored to be one of the largest clients for Petroconsultants.[22]

The most obvious examples of politically motivated reporting occurred from 1986 to 1990 when OPEC countries revised their oil reserve numbers in quota wars. In essence, OPEC members added about 300 billion barrels of oil to their reported reserves. Without doubt, the sensitive nature of publishing technical oil reserve data is often relegated to opaque ministries within various governments and is typically performed without any type of third-party verification. According to Jean Laherrère, veteran oil geologist and member of ASPO, "*oil is so important that publishing reserve (even production) data has become a political act.*"[23] [emphasis added] For example, Russia's reserves are considered a state secret, and thus disclosure of its official reserve data is subject to a penalty of seven years in jail.[24] Nonetheless, the value of Russia's reserves are well known, and trained geologists use past production data to build empirical models of Hubbert's curve to calculate likely oil reserve data in all oil-producing nations.

The temptation for OPEC countries to manipulate their reserve data was based on proposals during the 1980s in which oil production quotas were to be proportional to one's "proven reserves." Consequently, in 1988 Venezuela began listing its heavy oil as part of its proven reserves, thereby more than doubling its reported reserves from 25 billion barrels to 56 billion barrels. Unlike light, sweet crude, heavy oil is not currently suitable for use as transportation fuel, such as gasoline or diesel fuel, but is used instead for various industrial purposes. Unlike mankind, all oil was not "created equally."

The emergence of "political oil" reserve data during the 1980s is easily appreciated in the following chart of reported "proven reserves" by the main OPEC oil producers. OPEC data is likely significantly overstated based on analysis of technical data — before the advent of "political oil." In Figure 3.3, please note the transitions to the shaded areas regarding reserve figures. This suspicious "political" data illustrates why transparency and technical analysis is critical to develop models regarding Peak Oil.

	1980	1981	1982	1983	1984	1985	1986	1987	1988	1989	1990
UAE	28	29	31	31	30	30	30	31	92	92	92
Iran	58	57	57	55	51	48	48	49	93	93	93
Iraq	31	30	30	41	43	44	44	47	100	100	100
Kuwait	65	66	64	64	64	90	90	92	92	92	92
Saudi Arabia	163	165	165	162	166	169	169	167	167	170	257
Venezuela	18	18	20	21	25	26	26	25	56	58	59

	1991	1992	1993	1994	1995	1996	1997	1998
UAE	92	92	92	92	92	92	92	92
Iran	93	93	93	90	88	93	93	90
Iraq	100	100	100	100	100	112	112	112
Kuwait	94	94	94	94	94	94	94	94
Saudi Arabia	257	258	259	259	259	259	259	259
Venezuela	59	63	63	64	65	65	72	73

3.3: *OPEC's "Political" Oil Reserve data*

Source: Oil and Gas Journal, *"Statistical Review of World Energy 2003."*[25]

If OPEC's reported reserves are to be believed, then 1988 was a year in which four OPEC members suddenly "discovered" they had a combined total of 189 billion barrels of extra "proven oil reserves." One reason for these absurdly exaggerated figures was Kuwait's decision in 1985 to increase its "proven reserves" by almost a third, from 64 billion to 90 billion barrels of oil. Even Saudi Arabia engaged in creative accounting in 1990 when it declared its proven reserves went from 170 billion barrels to 257 billion barrels — despite the fact that *no* giant oil fields had been discovered to justify these huge upward revisions.

From 1985 to 1990, the aggregate "proven" oil reserve data for those six countries went from 379 billion barrels to proven reserves of 693 billion barrels. However, according to retired oil geologist Colin Campbell, the actual oil discoveries during this time period were *around 10 billion barrels.*[26] Despite these reported reserves appearing to be blatant political figures, the US government and most of the media continue to report these fantastic reserve numbers as if they were somehow factual.

Could the world's reported oil reserve data for the six largest OPEC producers — together containing an estimated 65 percent of global figures — be overstated by almost 40 percent, or 300 billion barrels? Many veteran oil geologists have stated this may indeed be the case due to political/economic reasons and an ambiguous definition of proven reserves.

Most recently, Canada engaged in somewhat confusing reporting of its oil deposits by broadening its definition of reserves to include all of its oil sand. In 2003 the oil sands found in Alberta were listed as proven oil reserves, causing Canada's oil reserves to increase in one year from 4.9 billion barrels to an incredible 180 billion barrels.[27] As a result, according to the United States Geological Survey (USGS), Canada is now listed as having more "proven oil reserves" than Iraq, second only to Saudi Arabia.

While it is true that Canada does have billions of barrels of oil trapped in sand, separating the sand from this heavy oil requires huge amounts of *energy*, mainly tremendous volumes of high-pressure water that must be heated, usually by natural gas. This process also produces an enormous amount of wastewater that is environmentally dangerous and reportedly carcinogenic. Unfortunately, considering the fresh-water requirements, environmental damage, and a low Energy Return on Energy Invested (EROEI), oil extraction from Canada's immense deposits of tar sands will never be a panacea for either Canadian or US energy needs.[28]

ANWR: False Panacea

A brief discussion of oil exploration prospects in the Alaska National Wildlife Refuge (ANWR) is warranted at this point. Despite the ongoing political debate between the Republicans and Democrats over possible oil exploration in ANWR, this area is of little importance with regard to US energy needs. In fact, it is not helpful to frame this debate as oil/energy lobbyists versus environmentalists, which is based on the false panacea attributed to this issue.

It is perhaps more useful to analyze other Alaskan oil fields to place the ANWR debate into the proper context. The Badami oil field between Prudhoe Bay and ANWR is about to be shut down according to British Petroleum (BP).[29] The cumulative production results of this field was 4 million barrels, but at the time of development it was reported to have 120 million barrels. (Actual production was only 1/30 of the original projections.) Likewise, it was forecasted that its peak production would reach 35,000 b/d. However, the actual peak oil production was only a fraction of the original projections, reaching only 3200 b/d.[30]

The USGS (Open file 98-34) estimated in 1999 that technically recoverable oil for ANWR would range from 5.7 to 16 billion barrels, with a mean of 10.3 billion barrels. The US Department of Energy (SR/O1G/2000-02) forecasted that ANWR would achieve peak output between 1.0 and 1.3 mb/d 20 years from start.[31] Notably, current US oil consumption is approximately 20 *million barrels per day*, thus illustrating that an additional 1 mb/d 20 years from now will provide *less than 1/25 of daily projected demand* (projected US demand in 2020 is 26mb/d). In other words, from an objective perspective ANWR's production would be far too little and too late, or as oil geologist Jean Laherrère stated, "a very quick and negligible blip in the production curve."[32]

In conclusion, if oil exploration and drilling were to take place in ANWR — even under a "best case" production scenario — Americans must be realistic that it will not provide a panacea for US oil consumption. The political rhetoric surrounding ANWR is inappropriate considering that its potential contribution to projected US energy demand and national security is quite negligible — unless of course certain politicians are attempting to gain millions in campaign cash from petroleum companies seeking favorable oil leases in ANWR.

Glimpse of Alternative Energy Technologies

After oil, the most important hydrocarbon for energy use is natural gas, or methane gas using the industry's terminology. The situation regarding natural gas is no better than that of oil. Energy experts, such as Matthew Simmons, have stated that enduring natural gas shortages in the US are imminent. He predicted this may result in power interruptions similar to what happened on August 14, 2003, when 57 million people in northern US and into Canada experienced a power blackout.

Due to provisions within the NAFTA treaty, Canada is currently exporting 50 percent of its natural gas to the US, but this practice may not be sustainable as its own domestic supply will soon peak. According to Julian Darley, a British environmental researcher and author of *High Noon for Natural Gas*, both the US and Canada are experiencing near-critical declines in natural gas production.[33]

A few of the well-known alternative energy technology options are discussed below. Some of the interesting newest technologies such as thermal depolymerization do not have published EROEI data, but readers are encouraged to review any prospective alternative technologies with net energy in mind.[34] The main point to reinforce regarding discussions centered on alternative energies is that any meaningful analysis must be based on the crucial factor of EROEI, *a metric reflecting physics, not money.* Jeff Wright, author of this book's foreword, evaluated various alternative energy sources as found in Richard Heinberg's book on Peak Oil, *The Party's Over: Oil, War and the Fate of the Industrialized Societies.*[35]

In the following excerpt, Wright stressed the importance of EROEI when analyzing any type of alternative energy technology, especially claims of an energy panacea. He discounted the possibility of using shale oil for a variety of reasons, despite the fact that there are potentially tens of billions of recoverable barrels in the US. The reason is simple, "The EROEI factor of shale oil is way too low (0.7) to be useful. It takes too much energy to produce the equivalent energy from shale oil."[36]

Wright also noted two important environmental artifacts encountered when extracting shale oil. First, it is an extremely dirty process, considering that it takes "more than 100 gallons of water to produce a gallon of shale oil." Secondly, the amount of wastewater produced means that when replacing "all of our [conventional] oil with shale we [will] need to *find a large basin to hold a new Lake Erie of wastewater.*"[37] [emphasis added]

Additionally, Wright addressed the question of nuclear power that according to Heinberg is an energy source that requires a complex analysis of EROEI. The results are somewhat disappointing when the *fully loaded* costs of nuclear power are factored in:

> The costs for nuclear-generated electricity (1.8¢ – 2.2¢/kWh) are operating costs only, including fuel, maintenance, and personnel ... such figures omit costs for research and development, plant amortization and decommissioning, and spent-fuel storage. Fully costed, nuclear power is by far our most expensive conventional energy source. Indeed, total costs are so high that, following the passage of energy deregulation bills in several states, nuclear plants were deemed unable to complete, and so utility companies like California's PG & E had to be bailed out by consumers for nuclear-related 'stranded costs.'[38]

Heinberg persuasively argued that nuclear power, as currently implemented, is a dead-end solution when viewed from an EROEI perspective. He concluded:

Industrial societies have, in energy terms, been able to afford to invent and use nuclear technologies primarily because of the availability of cheap fossil fuels with which to subsidize the effort.[39]

Another alternative energy resource that warrants brief inclusion in this text is the so-called hydrogen economy. Bill Butler has provided a succinct analysis of the issues surrounding the hydrogen economy on his website, "The Great Rollover Juggernaut."[40] Butler generally dismissed the popular myth that hydrogen will somehow become our energy panacea after Peak Oil. On his website he exposed why hydrogen fuel cells may not provide the answer to the global transportation challenges following Peak Oil.

> This is everyone's 'favorite solution' to the gasoline problem. Nice, clean, efficient hydrogen for fuel cells to power automobiles. It is quite true that if you have an adequate supply of hydrogen, you could use it instead of the present internal combustion engine. There is a bit of a problem that everyone ignores. Where do you get the hydrogen and how much will it cost?
>
> Today hydrogen is produced by reacting methane gas and steam yielding carbon monoxide and hydrogen .... In terms of useful energy, this is less efficient than just burning the methane. As noted above, natural gas is going to be in short supply after a couple of decades. Scratch natural gas as a source for hydrogen. Perhaps nuclear or 'renewable' based electric power can produce hydrogen via electrolysis (or some other electric process), or some biomass-based reaction can produce hydrogen sometime in the distant future, but this is at best decades away — and very expensive.[41]

Butler's online critique of hydrogen referred to several reports on this subject, including a technical report entitled "Energy and the Hydrogen Economy." The report concluded with a warning: "The 'Pure-Hydrogen-Only-Solution' may never become reality."[42] He also lamented that the US was about to spend billions on hydrogen "pork barrel projects" that may not provide real benefits. A July 2003 white paper by TMD Management warned that hydrogen is not the panacea as sometimes described by proponents:

> In most instances, the total energy cost of producing, compressing, liquefying, transporting and delivering it to the user will be far higher than the energy recovered from it. In addition, it is inconvenient and often dangerous to use. It makes no contribution whatever to energy independence — i.e., to weaning the US off imported energy supplies — and almost no real contribution to eliminating or minimizing environmental issues such as global

warming — that all has to be dealt with at the hydrogen or energy manufacturing plant and is independent of the choice of fuel.[43]

Richard Heinberg's second book on energy, *Powerdown*, carefully examined the unwarranted hype about hydrogen-based energy sources and listed several experts who warned against the uninformed who may be "High on Hydrogen."[44] A paper published in *Science* by Alex Farrell, assistant professor of energy and resources at UC Berkeley, and David Keith, associate professor of engineering and public policy at Carnegie Mellon, reached similar conclusions about the unrealistic expectations of hydrogen-based transportation systems.[45] During an interview, Farrell surmised, "Hydrogen cars are a poor short-term strategy, and it's not even clear that they are a good idea in the long-term."[46]

The only renewable energy that could theoretically be implemented on a worldwide basis to replace the depletion of oil and natural gas is the enormous solar energy captured every day by the world's tropical oceans. During the 1970s, promising research on Ocean Thermal Energy Conversion (OTEC) was conducted by the US government along with Japan.[47] OTEC is a renewable system that produces electricity — and potable water — based on the temperature variance between the warm surface water in the tropics and the consistently cold water found at a depth of 1000 meters.[48] Unfortunately, in 1982 the Reagan administration cut much of the funding for OTEC research and development.

However, Hawaii has continued developing OTEC technology with positive results. The process itself of developing and implementing alternative sources of energy requires large amounts of energy, and so it is critical that the global community immediately invest in a fleet of 50- to 100-Megawatt OTEC "plantships" and other renewable technologies while we still have a *surplus* of energy based on fossil fuels. While potential solutions such as OTEC continue to be researched, the success of any alternative energy inevitably depends much on their EROEI. While the OTEC process is inefficient when compared to burning hydrocarbon molecules, in the long-term it is clearly superior, considering that it is renewed every day by sunlight and, if properly implemented, is much more environmentally benign than any fossil fuel-based system.[49]

Regarding some of the more popular alternative energy sources, Heinberg warned that we should not allow a false belief in a miraculous conversion to a hydrogen economy, or another energy panacea, thereby creating a mentality of "waiting for the magic elixir."[50] After analyzing all the currently available alternative energies, he concluded in his second book that there is no foreseeable magic elixir, and therefore *self-limitation* is the only realistic and sustainable alternative for the human species. Heinberg titled his book after his term for the bold, personal, and societal strategy of reducing overall energy consumption in a hopefully managed environment, *Powerdown.*

It is unpredictable how the current global financial system will react to Peak Oil. From an economic perspective, after Peak Oil the global oil supply will begin its long and irreversible decline, regardless of economic theorems regarding supply and demand. Peak Oil will ultimately produce the decline of a pervasive source of electrical energy that will no longer be aligned with current economic theorems of unlimited growth. The result will be a *demand-side* rebalancing.

Perhaps an entirely new paradigm will eventually evolve that includes metrics such as EROEI, incorporating new theorems that refer to "ecological economics." This system would take into consideration the *ecosystem*, including biophysical laws and related *ecological limitations*. In my opinion, whoever successfully constructs a viable mechanism for ecological economics will likely deserve the Nobel Peace Prize.

Peak Oil and the War on Terror

> Oil fuels military power, national treasuries, and international politics. It is no longer a commodity to be bought and sold within the confines of traditional energy supply and demand balances. Rather, it has been transformed into a determinant of well-being, of national security, and of international power.
>
> — Robert E. Ebel, Director of the energy program, Center for Strategic and International Studies, *Mother Jones Magazine* [51]

> Bush and Blair have been making plans for the day when oil production peaks, by seeking to secure the reserves of other nations.
>
> — George Monibot, "Bottom of the Barrel," *Guardian*(UK)[52]

> 'The US has usurped the right to attack any part of the globe on the pretext of fighting the terrorist threat .... [We have concluded that al-Qaeda] is not a group but a notion .... The fight against that all-mighty ubiquitous myth deliberately linked to Islam is of great advantage for the Americans as it targets the oil-rich Muslim regions,' Shebarshin emphasized.
>
> — Leonid Shebarshin, ex-chief of the Soviet Foreign Intelligence Service, and head of the Russian National Economic Security Service consulting company, as interviewed for the *Vremya Novostei* newspaper, mosnews.com.[53]

Although the documents used during Vice President Cheney's 2001 energy meetings have been blocked from public review, one individual who was present during some of those meetings has been active in publicly discussing Peak Oil. Matthew Simmons, an investment banker in Texas and CEO of Simmons and Co. International, was a key advisor to the Bush administration and participated on Cheney's 2001 Energy Task Force. In May 2003 at an ASPO conference in Paris, France, Simmons stated:

> I think basically that now, the peaking of oil will never be accurately predicted until after the fact. But the event will occur, and my analysis is leaning me more by the month, the worry that peaking is at hand; not years away. If it turns out I'm wrong, then I'm wrong. But if I'm right, the unforeseen consequences are devastating. But unfortunately the world has no Plan B if I'm right. The facts are too serious to ignore. Sadly the pessimist-optimist debate started too late.[54]

Simmons hopes he is wrong, but as illustrated in the 1980's OPEC quota wars, there is considerable evidence to suggest that Saudi's oil reserves have been exaggerated for the past 15 years, perhaps by as much as 40 percent. His analysis of over 200 technical reports on Saudi's oil production provided evidence that cast doubt on Saudi Arabia's ability to effectively serve as the swing producer in the global oil market. Simmons stated that Saudi Arabia may essentially be "out of spare capacity."[55]

The peak of domestic oil production in the UK may have provided one of the reasons British Prime Minister Blair endorsed the Iraq War. The UK has no significant oil reserves other than the North Sea, which reached peak production in 1999. Unfortunately, the precipitous decline rate in North Sea oil production from 2000 to 2004 is undoubtedly quite disconcerting to the British government, as the depletion rate is reported to be rather steep at around 6.1 percent per year.[56]

Like the US, the UK will soon import the majority of its oil. Perhaps Blair agreed to the invasion given that British Petroleum (BP) has been the only non-US oil company that has been stated in the mix for oil exploration privileges in the post-Saddam Iraq.[57] Of course, unlike EU nations such as France and Germany, the UK has not yet ascended to the euro currency.

The neoconservatives have repeatedly suggested that Iraq is the first stage in a much larger project of regional regime change, with Iran, Syria, and even Saudi Arabia as candidates for regime change and so-called democratization. Given that the Saudi monarchy is increasingly alienated from the US, has come under attack from supposed Al Qaeda elements, and that most of the 9/11 hijackers were reported to be Saudi citizens, it is likely that US policy-makers have military contingency plans for an invasion of the eastern oil fields of Saudi Arabia.

Realistically, US troops were stationed after the 1991 Gulf War not to ensure the flow of oil, but to ensure that the House of Saud was not overthrown.

Despite irresponsible rhetoric about using the US military to seize control of Saudi Arabia's oil fields, any such invasion to grab the oil fields would be an irrational strategy unless the government and military were fully willing to engage in a genocidal war of massive attrition — throughout the entire region. Obviously this would also result in an unprecedented recruitment opportunity for the Al Qaeda terrorist organization.

> Realistically, US troops were stationed after the 1991 Gulf War not to ensure the flow of oil, but to ensure that the House of Saud was not overthrown.

In April 2003, just after the Iraq War began, the Bush administration quietly removed the remaining US military personnel from Saudi Arabia.[58] It does not require a logical stretch to understand that maintaining US hegemony in accordance with stated neoconservative doctrine requires military bases in the Persian Gulf — even if "Saddam Hussein [should] pass from the scene."[59] As the intelligence firm Stratfor suggested, "other locations, from the Horn of Africa to Syria to *Saudi Arabia could fall under US sights*, and Riyadh will carefully gauge its reaction to the diplomatic dustup *to remain just outside the US area of operations*."[60] [emphasis added]

In 2004 Saudi Arabia rejected oil-lease contracts with US companies for its natural gas fields and awarded these natural gas contracts to Russia, China, Italy, and Spain. Stratfor's analysis asserted these exploration contracts were "clearly politically motivated."[61] In a somewhat oblique fashion, Stratfor also suggested Washington might "begin to set its sights" on Saudi's oil fields.[62]

There is every reason to assume that the Bush administration understood the essential outlines of the situation. The president, vice president, and national security advisor are former oil industry executives. Matthew Simmons, one of the Energy Task Force petroleum analysts, repeatedly warned his clients of coming energy-supply crises in both oil and natural gas.[63] Declassified CIA documents concerning the peak of Russian oil production revealed that the CIA had been carefully monitoring global petroleum supplies as far back as 1977.[64] Furthermore, the CIA is reported to be the largest client of the highly regarded firm IHS Energy (formerly Petroconsultants). Their 1995 report, "The World's Oil Supply (1930 – 2050)", predicted that the peak of global oil production would occur in the decade following 2000.[65]

When we examine what is known about today's existing oil production, global oil reserves, and where they are in light of the analysis of Peak Oil, it becomes much clearer why both Bush and Cheney would be willing to risk so much in terms of America's standing among allies and other nations relating to their geostrategy of occupying the oil fields of Iraq. It is reasonable to assume that Cheney probably knew during the late 1990s exactly what the global oil reserve situation was when he was former CEO of Halliburton Corporation, the world's largest oil services company. I am not alleging a conspiracy but merely presenting facts indicating that Bush and Cheney had information and motives that neither was willing to publicly state.

Undoubtedly, the alternative to the Iraq War would have required asking the American people to make sacrifices, while Washington engaged in multilateral negotiations with respect to oil currency and energy depletion issues. Regrettably, one of the most tragic missed opportunities that pragmatic US leadership could have provided in the aftermath of 9/11 was the need for US energy reform. We could have received an inspiring call to duty, a John F. Kennedy type of speech challenging our nation to "go to the moon" by the end of this decade regarding energy policy and energy independence.[66] Instead the message we heard was: *Unite. Go shopping, and don't be afraid to fly.* Failing to rally the citizenry for the truly patriotic purpose of strengthening the nation was perhaps the greatest missed opportunity since the end of the Cold War.

Nevertheless, it is still plausible that under enlightened leadership, policymakers who effectively advocate meaningful energy reform — beginning with Americans' excessive consumption levels — could move the US forward in pursuing the crucial patriotic goal of enhancing our security by becoming one of the world's leaders in advocating, developing, and implementing alternative energy technologies. The effective adoption of such a domestic energy strategy could potentially provide the US with a unique opportunity to reinvigorate its manufacturing industry. Indeed, this could restore its leadership role.

The United States desperately needs a real national energy policy, instead of an endless war on terrorism. Today's blowback is partly due to the US' ongoing support of corrupt Middle East regimes and dictatorships. Creating a more equitable global monetary system, while maintaining a strong transatlantic relationship with Europe, is in the long-term national security interest of the US. Hopefully, monetary and energy reform could mitigate future armed or economic warfare over oil, thus ultimately fostering a more stable, safe, and prosperous 21st century.

Clearly, for the past 25 years, successive US administrations in both major political parties have failed to make the necessary preparations regarding energy transformation required today. Jimmy Carter, who lost his bid for reelection in 1980, was the only president who attempted to seriously address this issue. Peak Oil will affect the entire world, and as such, the US is not alone in facing this dilemma, but Americans use one out of every four barrels of world oil production and arguably waste the most energy.[67] Time is not on our side, as Mother Nature will not wait for politicians or scientists to "go figure out something."

In truth, some commentators have suggested our collective failure to devise a sustainable energy infrastructure in conjunction with the global depletion of hydrocarbons could adversely erode our civil liberties and democratic processes.

Retired US Special Forces soldier Stan Goff offered a sobering, yet alarming, analysis in his online essay, "The Infinite War and Its Roots":

> When I was working in Special Forces, we were part of a foreign policy doctrine called Internal Defense and Development (IDAD). That was old school. As I prepared to leave the Army, there was much emphasis, doctrinally and technologically, on something called Operations Other Than War (OOTW). The process of uneven development has begun to culminate in the concentrated urbanization of much of the world's population.
>
> One is the ever-closer relationship and blurring of lines between military and police. The other is the technological development of sub-lethal weapons systems and highly sophisticated population control measures for both police and military — globalized military policing. This is one key component in the mad doctrine of 'full spectrum dominance' championed by the feverish Secretary of Defense Donald Rumsfeld.
>
> This dialectical relation between energy, currency, and the military is at least one key concrete condition for us to understand if we are to see into the mind of capital (big business and its political establishment) in this period of imperialism in crisis.
>
> It is this inevitable attack on the living standards of average Americans that will either wake us to the folly of this manufactured patriotism and push us into resistance to this regime, or in the worst case, into atavistic racialism and fascism. Which it will be depends in some part on how effective some of us are at telling people in advance what they can expect ... and why.[68]

Post-Peak Oil World: Three Scenarios

> During times of universal deceit, telling the truth becomes a revolutionary act.
>
> — George Orwell, author of *Nineteen Eighty-Four* [69]

Undeniably, the passing of Peak Oil and the slow, but irreversible, depletion of hydrocarbon resources will entail monumental effects on geopolitics, domestic politics, economics, and societal structure itself. Given the focus of this book, geopolitical considerations will be the primary category addressed. Acknowledgement of Peak Oil likely implies the development of three potential scenarios by the end of this decade and into the next.

The first possibility is the status quo, a principally unipolar global community with the US remaining the sole superpower. Clearly, attempting to maintain the US in this role is the basis of neoconservative geostrategy, which openly stated in 1992 the US imperative of "convincing potential competitors that *they need not aspire to a greater role or pursue a more aggressive posture to protect their legitimate interests* .... We must maintain the mechanisms for deterring potential competitors from even aspiring to a larger regional or global role."[70] [emphasis added]

This strategy of dominance requires the US military to not only physically patrol the major sea lanes used by the world's 3500 oil tankers, but also increasingly attempt to *physically control* the regions with the world's largest remaining hydrocarbons — thereby invoking indigenous opposition. This doctrine could only be attempted by outright imperial military force, massive oppression of the indigenous populations in the oil-rich regions, along with suppression of political dissent at home.

From a macroeconomic perspective, global trends suggest the likely emergence of a multi-polar world, which itself can be destabilizing if poles act unilaterally, as opposed to multilaterally. In the second scenario, real attempts to arrive at a multilateral compromise would prove to be the paramount goal. This is my preferred outcome, as the challenges presented by Peak Oil *cannot be resolved by military force* — but in fact would only be exacerbated by the levels of capital, energy, and men that would ultimately be wasted on military operations when these resources should be allocated towards Energy Reconfiguration. Moreover, the monetary and energy issues inherent in Peak Oil could only be resolved with broad international cooperation between the major industrial nations, most likely within a UN framework.

The foremost multilateral treaty developed thus far in response to the dilemma presented by global Peak Oil is the Uppsala Accord, also called the Rimini Accord.[71] Researchers at the Uppsala University in Sweden, in conjunction with oil geologists Colin J. Campbell and Kjell Aleklett, based this protocol on a global rationing system that reflected individual and aggregate depletion rates.

Despite the inherent difficulties of implementing the Uppsala Accord on a worldwide basis, it is irrefutable that any multilateral accord will be preferable to warfare between industrialized nation states or alliances of states, many of whom are nuclear powers. The only rationale strategy would include the G–8 nations plus China and India, in conjunction with the UN, to devise an exceedingly difficult treaty regarding the allocation of hydrocarbon reserves. Failure to reach a multilateral accord could result in the systemic breakdown of international relationships and the destabilization of the global community.

This segues into the worst-case scenario, the surfacing of a fragmented, *unilateral and multi-polar* world that seeks to gain control over its hydrocarbon reserves in an effort to deny other industrialized nations their requisite access to energy. Richard Heinberg called this the Last One Standing scenario, warning that geopolitical tensions are likely to result in depressing global resource warfare. He somberly stated that this scenario could lead to *"the general destruction of human civilization and most of the ecological life-supporting systems of the planet."*[72] [emphasis added] Clearly, a fragmented multi-polar world engaged in unilateral attempts to dominate the world's energy reserves would create an unstable and highly dangerous geopolitical environment.

Irrefutably, the potential outbreak of global warfare over depleting hydrocarbons would be the most tragic outcome for humanity. Even if a nation state or group of nation states could militarily prevail over the other industrialized nations, the so-called winner would likely end up energy poor within a generation due to the tremendous resources in men, energy, and finances that would be required to suppress both their competing states and the indigenous populations whose geological history happened to retain the last viable hydrocarbon reserves on the globe. The chaotic post war situation in Iraq clearly illustrates the inherent fallacy of imperial strategies premised on US geostrategic domination of hydrocarbon reserves in the Middle East, Central Asia, and West Africa.

If we are to have a multi-polar world, let us hope it is a balanced one, in which incorrigible greed would give way to enlightened cooperative action, with leaders committed to arrive at multilateral compromises and concessions. Although not guaranteed of success, the only rational policy regarding global Peak Oil is an unprecedented attempt at international cooperation and coordination. A collective approach is the only strategy that could conceivably result in the development and implementation of both *demand-side strategies* and *alternative energy technologies* in the post-Peak Oil world. Developing and adhering to a multilateral, compromising approach to Peak Oil is the foremost challenge to mankind at the dawning of the 21st century.

> Cheap oil is dead. You are never going to see oil priced at $25 a barrel again …. We are approaching the plateau of production; these are the first signs that we are there. As I said, cheap oil is history.
>
> — Ali Bakhtiari, head of strategic planning, Iranian National Oil Company (NIOC), August 2004[73]

> The conclusion is clear: if we do not immediately plan to make the switch to renewable energy — faster, and backed by far greater investment than currently envisaged — then civilisation faces the sharpest and perhaps most violent dislocation in recent history.
>
> — Michael Meacher, former member of British Parliament, UK Environment Minister, 1997 to 2003[74]

We have only a dwindling amount of time to build lifeboats — that is, the needed alternative infrastructure. It has been clear for at least 30 years what characteristics this should have — organic, small-scale, local, convivial, cooperative, slower paced, human-oriented rather than machine-oriented, agrarian, diverse, democratic, culturally rich, and ecologically sustainable.

A transition to a lower level of social-technological complexity need not be violent, need not be chaotic, and need not entail the loss of the values and cultural achievements of which we are most proud as a society. And the end result could be far more humane, enjoyable, and satisfying than life currently is for citizens of this grandest of empires.

— Richard Heinberg, "Beyond the Peak," December 2004[75]

Four

Manifest Subterfuge: Disguising the Macroeconomic and Geostrategic Rationales for War

The [UN] sanctions exist ... for the purpose of keeping in check Saddam Hussein's ambitions toward developing weapons of mass destruction .... And frankly they have worked. He has not developed any significant capability with respect to weapons of mass destruction. He is unable to project conventional power against his neighbors.

> — Secretary of State Powell, February 24, 2001[1]

Simply stated, there is no doubt that Saddam Hussein now has weapons of mass destruction.

> — Vice President Cheney, August 26, 2002[2]

Our conservative estimate is that Iraq today has a stockpile of between 100 and 500 tons of chemical weapons agent. That is enough agent to fill 16,000 battlefield rockets. Even the low end of 100 tons of agent would enable Saddam Hussein to cause mass casualties across more than 100 square miles of territory, an area nearly five times the size of Manhattan.

> — Secretary of State Powell, February 5, 2003[3]

Intelligence leaves no doubt that Iraq continues to possess and conceal lethal weapons.

> — President George W. Bush, March 17, 2003[4]

We are asked ... to accept ... that Saddam decided unilaterally to destroy those weapons .... I say that such a claim is palpably absurd.

— Prime Minister Blair, March 18, 2003[5]

Goering: Why, of course, the people don't want war .... That is understood. But, after all, it is the leaders of the country who determine the policy and it is always a simple matter to drag the people along, whether it is a democracy or a fascist dictatorship or a Parliament or a Communist dictatorship.

Gilbert: There is one difference. In a democracy, the people have some say in the matter through their elected representatives, and in the United States only Congress can declare wars.

Goering: Oh, that is all well and good, but, voice or no voice, the people can always be brought to the bidding of the leaders. That is easy. All you have to do is tell them they are being attacked and denounce the pacifists for lack of patriotism and exposing the country to danger. It works the same way in any country.

— Gustave Gilbert, a German-speaking intelligence officer and psychologist, interviewed and recorded the observations of Hermann Goering, Nazi Reichsmarshal and Luftwaffe chief, during the Nuremberg War Criminal trials, April 18, 1946[6]

Buildup to Gulf War II: Saddam Hussein and Weapons of Mass Destruction

The propaganda tactics for promoting war, as bluntly revealed by an unrepentant Hermann Goering, are just as effective today as they were during the 20th century. When the press becomes subservient to the desires of political leaders, even modern democracies, such as the US and UK, are not immune to the historical effectiveness of propaganda to bring a frightful population "to the bidding of the leaders."

Regarding Iraq, the effective use of propaganda techniques by the Bush administration was especially critical, given their unique task of justifying the US' first-ever "preventative war." However, well before this campaign, it is clear that invading Iraq was a priority from the beginning. Former secretary of the treasury Paul O'Neill recalled that, during the very first national security meeting of the Bush administration, toppling Saddam Hussein was its focus. *The Price of Loyalty* revealed that this was at the top of the national security agenda just ten days after George W. Bush was sworn in as the 43rd president, a full eight months before the September 11th terrorists attacks.[7]

Despite over 400 unfettered UN inspections before the 2003 invasion, and hundreds more after the war, there has been no reported evidence that Iraq had reconstituted any aspects of its previous WMD program. In fact, researchers had carefully deconstructed most of the WMD claims made by the Bush and Blair administrations before the Iraq War, but the media did not provide proper analysis of these counterclaims.[8] On March 6, 2003, less than two weeks before the outbreak of the Iraq War, Hans Blix, the chief UN weapons inspector, testified to the UN Security Council that, "No proscribed activities, or the result of such activities, from the period of 1998-2002 have, so far, been detected through inspections."[9] The following day International Atomic Energy Agency (IAEA) Director General Mohamed ElBaradei informed the UN Security Council of his finding, "After three months of intrusive inspections, we have to date found *no evidence or plausible indication of the revival of a nuclear weapons programme in Iraq.*"[10] [emphasis added]

> Despite over 400 unfettered UN inspections before the 2003 invasion, and hundreds more after the war, there has been no reported evidence that Iraq had reconstituted any aspects of its previous WMD program.

Nonetheless, the "imminent threat" to national security purported by the Bush and Blair administrations was used to justify initiating the war a few days later. Of critical note is that had the UN weapons inspectors been able to complete their prewar inspection in the spring of 2003, Blix would have declared Iraq to be disarmed and free of WMD. According to Blix, "Had we had a few months more [of inspections before the war], we would have been able to tell both the CIA and others that there were no weapons of mass destruction [at] all the sites that they had given us."[11] This would have ended the 1991 UN sanctions against Iraq and allowed Saddam Hussein's contractual agreements with TotalELF, Lukoil, and Sin-oil (French, Russian, and Chinese) oil firms to begin exploration in Iraq — with an alternative euro-driven oil transaction currency. Obviously this was not an acceptable outcome to the US and UK governments and the powerful oil interests (BP, Exxon-Mobil, TexacoChevron, and Shell Oil) who influence such political decisions. Five months before the war, Peter Beaumont and Faisal Islam's article in the the *Guardian* noted these contentions:

> Disclosure of talks between the oil executives and the INC [Iraqi National Congress], which enjoys the support of Bush administration officials — is bound to exacerbate friction on the UN Security Council between permanent members and veto-holders Russia, France, and China, who fear they will be squeezed out of a post-Saddam [Hussein] oil industry in Iraq.
>
> Although Russia, France, and China have existing deals with Iraq, [Iraqi National Congress founder Admad] Chalabi has made clear that he would reward the US for removing Saddam with lucrative oil contracts, telling the *Washington Post* recently, "American companies will have a big shot at Iraqi oil."[12]

Documents and maps released from Vice President Cheney's spring 2001 National Energy Policy Development Group (NEPDG) supported this assertion. On September 19, 2002, Secretary of Defense Rumsfeld stated, "No terrorist state poses a *greater or more immediate threat to the security of our people and the stability of the world* than the regime of Saddam Hussein in Iraq."[13] [emphasis added] Although Rumsfeld's bold claim regarding the "immediate threat" to the US came a year later, it is quite clear he wanted to attack Iraq just hours after the 9/11 strikes, when *CBS News* reported that he had requested, "best info fast. Judge whether good enough hit S.H. at same time. Not only U.B.L."[14] (S.H. and UBL refer to Saddam Hussein and Usama bin Laden, often spelled as Osama bin Laden.)

Furthermore, despite President Bush's repeated claims, the CIA and the 9/11 Commission did not find any links between Saddam Hussein and Al Qaeda, although the CIA made intense efforts before and after the invasion. It is now obvious that Iraq did not pose an imminent threat to the United States, nor to its neighbors in the Middle East.

The so-called war on terrorism was promoted to obfuscate the real objectives from the global community, while domestic dissent was thwarted by incessant claims of an ominous external threat, further traumatizing the citizenry. After the September 11th tragedy, these policies of a world order dominated by US military power were being implemented under the indefinable threat of "terrorism." Some researchers and a former member of the British parliament have suggested that 9/11 was a necessary precondition to create generalized societal fear, and as such the executive branch exploited the tragedy to pursue previously unpalatable foreign policies in various areas of US strategic interest.[15, 16, 17] The governing principles of the neoconservatives are easier to appreciate after analyzing the work of Leo Strauss, who is often described as the original advocate of modern neoconservative ideology.

Leo Strauss 1899–1973: Philosophical Father of the Neoconservatives

> Because mankind is intrinsically wicked, he has to be governed .... Such governance can only be established, however, when men are united – and they can only be united against other people.
>
> Those who are fit to rule are those who realize there is no morality and that there is only one natural right — the right of the superior to rule over the inferior .... The people are told what they need to know and no more.
>
> — Leo Strauss, thoughts on government and the wise elites' need for secrecy, *Natural Right* and *History and Persecution and the Art of Writing*[18]

> Everybody sees what you appear to be, few feel what you are, and those few will not dare to oppose themselves to the many, who have the majesty of the state to defend them .... Let a prince therefore aim at conquering and maintaining the state, and the means will always be judged honourable and praised by everyone, for the vulgar is always taken by appearances ....
>
> — Niccolo Machiavelli, *The Prince*, 1513[19]

> In order to achieve the most noble accomplishments, the leader may have to 'enter into evil.' This is the chilling insight that has made Machiavelli so feared, admired, and challenging. It is why we are drawn to him still.
>
> — Michael A. Ledeen, leading neoconservative at the American Enterprise Institute (AEI), advisor to President Bush's political strategist Karl Rove, as quoted in his book, *Machiavelli on Modern Leadership: Why Machiavelli's Iron Rules Are As Timely and Important Today As Five Centuries Ago*, 1999[20]

It is widely acknowledged that the Bush administration was not honest about the reasons it gave to the public for the invasion of Iraq. Paul Wolfowitz, former deputy secretary of defense, acknowledged that the "intelligence" used to justify the war was always "murky" and that the main rationale for the Iraq War, "disarming Saddam" of a supposed reconstituted WMD program, was in essence a "bureaucratic decision."[21] Wolfowitz's neoconservative colleague Richard Perle admitted that the war was in violation of international law but nonetheless stated it was the "right thing" to do.[22]

This philosophy of governance openly advocates an end-justifies-the-means mentality, allowing deception, violence, and the abrogation of international law. Many Americans have difficulty believing the Bush administration purposely engaged in a campaign of diversion and deception to convince the public that an invasion of Iraq was urgent and necessary. However, while the idea is disconcerting, it is hardly surprising, given the self-proclaimed philosophical underpinning of neoconservative ideology.

In 1938 German political philosopher Leo Strauss arrived in the US, an ethnic Jew and refugee from Nazi Germany. As a professor at the University of Chicago, he specialized in philosophical analysis of the classic Greek tradition and basic philosophical questions, including the structure of society and whether it can be governed on rational principles. Wolfowitz, a leading advocate of neoconservatism, was introduced to Straussian ideology while earning his PhD under him at the University of Chicago.[23]

Shadia Drury, professor of political theory at the University of Regina in Saskatchewan, wrote an extensive analysis of Straussian ideology in two books, *The Political Ideas of Leo Strauss*[24] and *Leo Strauss and the American Right*.[25] She deftly argued that the use of deception and manipulation in current US policy flows directly from the doctrines espoused by Strauss, including the philosophy that deception is the normal process in politics. Therefore secrecy is a paramount goal of government, especially regarding foreign policy issues.

According to Drury, Strauss believed that society comprised three classes of people, of which only the "wise elite" were capable of governing. He proposed that the elites were required to engage in "perpetual deception" over those that were to be ruled.

> There are indeed three types of men: the wise, the gentlemen, and the vulgar. The wise are the lovers of the harsh, unadulterated truth. They are capable of looking into the abyss without fear and trembling. They recognise neither God nor moral imperatives. They are devoted above all else to their own pursuit of the "higher" pleasures.
>
> The second type, the gentlemen, are lovers of honour and glory. They are the most ingratiating toward the conventions of their society — that is, the illusions of the cave. They are true believers in God, honour, and moral imperatives. They are ready and willing to embark on acts of great courage and self-sacrifice at a moment's notice.
>
> The third type, the vulgar many, are lovers of wealth and pleasure. They are selfish, slothful, and indolent. They can be inspired

to rise above their brutish existence only by fear of impending death or catastrophe.[26]

In Strauss's framework, "those who are fit to rule are those who realize there is no morality and that there is only one natural right — the right of the superior to rule over the inferior .... The people are told what they need to know and no more."[27] While the elite are capable of absorbing the absence of any moral truth, Strauss thought, the masses could not be exposed to the truth or they would fall into nihilism or anarchy. His ideology of governing via secrecy, deception, and the imperative of a broad external threat to "inspire the vulgar many" provides a tragic parallel to the neoconservative strategy regarding Iraq.

Strauss was openly contemptuous of secular democracy — he stated that religion is absolutely essential for imposing moral law on the masses (or vulgar many). At the same time, he stressed, religion is to be reserved for the masses, as the ruling elite need not be bound by it. He argued it would be illogical for the rulers to be bound by religion, since the truths proclaimed by religion are in his words "a pious fraud."[28] Hence, secular society is the least desirable situation because it leads to individualism, liberalism, and relativism.

Ironically, while these traits are those the founders of the United States viewed as most desirable, in the Straussian ideology these ideals only promote dissent, which weakens society's ability to cope with external threats. Strauss was ambivalent as to which religion was needed to facilitate social control of the masses, only that a religion was required.

Strauss also believed that the inherently aggressive nature of human beings could only be restrained by a powerful nationalistic state: "Because mankind is intrinsically wicked, he has to be governed .... Such governance can only be established, however, *when men are united — and they can only be united against other people.*"[29] [emphasis added] Drury observed that the requirement of "perpetual war" in the Straussian political framework and an "external threat" must exist, even if it is manufactured. She concluded with this foreboding analysis of how Straussian philosophy permeated the underlying neoconservative political strategy:

> In short, they all thought that man's humanity depended on his willingness to rush naked into battle and headlong to his death. Only perpetual war can overturn the modern project, with its emphasis on self-preservation and 'creature comforts.'
>
> This terrifying vision fits perfectly well with the desire for honour and glory that the neo-conservative gentlemen covet. It also fits very well with the religious sensibilities of gentlemen. The combination of religion and nationalism is the elixir that Strauss advocates

as the way to turn natural, relaxed, hedonistic men into devout nationalists willing to fight and die for their God and country.

I never imagined when I wrote my first book on Strauss that the unscrupulous elite that he elevates would ever come so close to political power, nor that the ominous tyranny of the wise would ever come so close to being realized in the political life of a great nation like the United States. But fear is the greatest ally of tyranny.[30]

Straussian ideology regarding foreign policy, plainly Machiavellian in orientation, was expanded and formally articulated by neoconservative groups, such as the Project for a New American Century (PNAC) and the American Enterprise Institute (AEI). Karl Rove, President Bush's political advisor, boasted that he read Machiavelli's *The Prince* for insights into his political strategy.[31] Straussian governing philosophy requires strict secrecy, and this was certainly the case with the preplanned invasion of Iraq.

In January 2003, the *Washington Post* reported that six days after the 9/11 attack, President Bush approved a 2½-page document marked Top Secret outlining the plan for a war in Afghanistan. Interestingly, according to "senior administration officials," this document also contained a footnote that "*directed the Pentagon to begin military options for an invasion of Iraq.*"[32] [emphasis added]

In his second book on the Bush administration, *Plan of Attack*, *Washington Post* reporter Bob Woodward revealed that President Bush privately asked Donald Rumsfeld to create a secret war plan for Iraq on November 16, 2001.[33] According to Woodward, on that same day General Franks received a formal request from Rumsfeld to draft a "commander's estimate," basically the notification to prepare a specific plan to invade Iraq. Franks, occupied with the one-month-old war in Afghanistan, was reportedly shocked and incredulous at this request. After settling down, he remarked, "Man, I just can't imagine this is something we're going to be doing anytime soon."[34]

Woodward's book and a subsequent interview with *CBS News* reinforced that Bush decided to invade Iraq well before he received congressional permission on the Iraq War Resolution. In the summer of 2002 Bush approved, without congressional authorization or notification, the secret reallocation of $700 million designated for Afghanistan to be secretly spent on "preparatory tasks" in the Persian Gulf region (i.e., 30 projects that included upgrading airfields, bases, fuel pipelines, and munitions storage depots to accommodate a massive US troop deployment).[35] Setting aside the Constitutional and legal issues raised by this abuse of power, these decisions exposed intentional obfuscation in the fundamental decision-making process in the executive branch. During this time the Bush administration continued to deny that a decision had been made regarding an invasion of Iraq, but the facts speak for themselves.

As Straussian theory requires, an "external threat" was created during the autumn of 2002. This campaign was designed to create the requisite societal fear so the "wise" rulers could pursue a strategy kept secret from the "vulgar masses." Religion has often been invoked as a divine force guiding our political leaders in a battle of "good versus evil," while the mantra "United We Stand" created the necessary hyper-nationalism to drown out critical analysis of the facts surrounding the coming war. Under the threat of mushroom clouds, our prime nemesis, Osama bin Laden, was skillfully transformed by the Bush administration into our old-yet-new public enemy number one, Saddam Hussein.

Straussian Governance: Conspiracy Inside the Pentagon

> One of the reasons I left was my sense that they were using the intelligence from the CIA and other agencies only when it fit their agenda. They didn't like the intelligence they were getting, and so they brought in people to write the stuff. They were so crazed and so far out and so difficult to reason with — to the point of being bizarre. Dogmatic, as if they were on a mission from God. If it doesn't fit their theory, they don't want to accept it.
>
> — Former CIA official interviewed by Seymour Hersh,
> for *New Yorker*, May 2003[36]

> I'd love to be the historian who writes the story of how this small group of eight or nine people made the case [for war] and won.
>
> — W. Patrick Lang, former chief of Middle East intelligence,
> Defense Intelligence Agency (DIA)[37]

The first groundbreaking story about the Office of Special Plans (OSP), and the neoconservative operatives within it, was provided by investigative reporter Seymour Hersh of the *New Yorker*.[38] Additional information that confirmed OSP activities was revealed in interviews with Lt. Colonel Kwiatkowski, a former Pentagon employee and author of this book's epilogue. These individuals exposed how a small clique of neoconservative ideologues, along with an Iraqi exile group previously discredited by the CIA, conspired to provide most of the fraudulent "intelligence data" that the executive branch publicized during the lead-up to the war. According to Hersh, proponents of Straussian ideology were placed in key positions within the ad hoc "intelligence units" that prepared information specifically for the president and vice president in their efforts to prepare the public for war.[39]

Evidently during 2001–2002 the Defense Intelligence Agency (DIA) and CIA were not providing Secretary of Defense Rumsfeld with intelligence information that would justify invading Iraq. Our intelligence agencies surmised that Iraq's previous WMD program was dormant, and in 1998 they determined that Saddam Hussein had no ties to Al Qaeda.[40] Undeterred, in the summer of 2002 Rumsfeld set up two unofficial and autonomous intelligence units within the Pentagon. The smaller "cell" was a two-man operation with an impressive sounding name, Counter-Terrorism Evaluation Group, or CTEG.[41] Rumsfeld assigned Douglas Feith, the third-highest-ranking civilian in the Department of Defense, to set it up. Feith staffed this cell with two staunch neoconservatives, David Wurmser and F. Michael Maloof, for the somewhat ambiguous purposes of reviewing "the vast amount of existing intelligence on terrorist networks, think through how various terrorist organizations relate to each other, and how they relate to different groups that support them."[42]

Former intelligence professionals claimed that this secretive unit, operating from a secure room on the third floor of the Pentagon, ultimately succeeded in circumventing the CIA and DIA by briefing the White House directly on dubious reports of a "relationship" between Saddam Hussein and Al Qaeda. According to investigative journalists Robert Dreyfuss and Jason Vest, the CTEG was successfully used "*to disparage, undermine, and contradict the CIA's reporting*, which was far more cautious and nuanced than Rumsfeld, Wolfowitz, and Feith wanted."[43] [emphasis added]

The neoconservative operatives in this obscure intelligence cell collaborated with the other Rumsfeld-inspired intelligence unit within the Pentagon, known as the Orwellian-sounding Office of Special Plans (OSP). According to former Pentagon employees who observed OSP activities, its sole purpose was to promote the Iraq War by creating a worst-case scenario regarding Iraq's supposed "vast" and "reconstituted" WMD program. The head of this unit was William "Bill" Luti, who earned his PhD under Leo Strauss. Not surprisingly, Luti is an acknowledged disciple of Straussian theory.[44]

Based on what was witnessed and was revealed during 2003–2004, the purpose of these two "intelligence units" was to bypass the CIA and DIA, and provide "faith-based intelligence" to Cheney and Bush. In a twist of bizarre humor, members of the OSP accurately referred to themselves as the "cabal."[45] Figure 4.1 adapted from *Mother Jones* magazine illustrates how these two units bypassed the CIA and DIA, while the Iraqi National Congress (INC) simultaneously fed deceptive information to former secretary of state Powell on Iraq's supposed WMD program.

Since the Roman Empire, people have long suffered when leaders espoused a governing philosophy that political order is stable only if the people are united by fear of an external threat. Straussian governance philosophy *requires* people to be united under fear and hatred. The goals of the OSP and CTEG, apparently, were to demonstrate a broad external threat — even if such a threat had to be invented. Luti and members of the OSP vigorously pursued this challenge during the autumn of 2002 and succeeded brilliantly. To date, no professional intelligence analysts in the CIA, DIA, MI5, or MI6 have provided

The Lie Factory

The White House
President George W. Bush
Vice President Dick Cheney
Lewis "Scooter" Libby

Office of Net Assessement	**The Pentagon**	**Defense Policy Board**
(Recruited from Pentagon's Iraq Intelligence team) Andrew Marshall Harold Rhode	Donald Rumsfeld Paul Wolfwitz Douglas J. Feith	Richard Perle Newt Gingrich James Woolsey

Counter-Terrorism Evaluation Group (CTEG)	**Near East and South Asia Affairs (NESA)**	**US State Department**
(Secretive 2-member intelligence "cell") David Wurmser F. Michael Maloof	William "Bill" Luti (Deputy Undersecretary of Defense of NESA in charge of Office of Special Plans/OSP)	Colin Powell (Used primarily for February 5, 2003 presentation to the UN on WMD issues)

Central Intelligence Agency (CIA)	**Office of Special Plans (OSP)**	**Iraqi National Congress (INC)**
(Intelligence analysis ignored or subverted by Pentagon)	Abram N. Shuisky Colonel William Bruner Michael Rubin	Ahmad Chalabi - Founder "Curveball" - supposedly a secret "Iraqi defector"

Defence Intelligence Agency (DIA)
(Intelligence analysis ignored or subverted by Pentagon)

National Security Agency (NSA)
(unknown activity regarding war)

4.1: *Flow of information*
Source: Mother Jones, *February 2004*[46]

credible evidence linking Saddam Hussein to Osama bin Laden, Al Qaeda, or to the 9/11 attacks.[47, 48]

The main rationales for the Iraq War were woven into a propaganda campaign developed by an unprecedented US government conspiracy, perpetrated by two relatively small intelligence cells, as well as a few discredited Iraqi exiles in the INC. Further, this campaign was facilitated by far-right news sources such as the *Weekly Standard*, *National Review*, the *Wall Street Journal's* editorials, and *Fox News*. Much of the disinformation propagated before the war was discernibly deceptive, but now the evidence of a Pentagon-based conspiracy is simply irrefutable.

The British people were also subjected to an impressive propaganda campaign, but with a slightly narrower focus that suggested Iraq had simply not disarmed and minus the claims of a "relationship" between Saddam Hussein and Osama bin Laden. Immediately after the Iraq War began, the British press revealed a clandestine intelligence unit, Operation Rockingham, remarkably similar to the Pentagon's OSP. According to former weapons inspector Scott Ritter, Operation Rockingham "cherry-picked" information about WMD for Prime Minister Blair and "only put forward a small percentage of the facts when most were ambiguous or noted no WMD .... It became part of an effort to maintain a public mindset that Iraq was not in compliance with the inspections. *They had to sustain the allegation that Iraq still had WMD [when] UNSCOM was showing the opposite.*"[49] [emphasis added]

Like the OSP, this unit acted as the interface with MI5, MI6, GCHQ, and Defence Intelligence. As such they effectively passed on dubious information to the Joint Intelligence Committee (JIC) in an effort to create a worst-case scenario — using, for example, the infamous claim of Iraq's capability to launch a WMD attack "within 45 minutes."

While Downing Street has not addressed the issue of the secretive Operation Rockingham, one British Intelligence official told the *Sunday Herald*, "I'd like to know if troops were sacrificed because we kept hyping up weapons of mass destruction."[50] Like the Pentagon's OSP unit, Operation Rockingham successfully frightened the people into compliance and "to the bidding" of their leader, Prime Minister Blair.

Straussian Necessity of an External Threat: Mushroom Clouds to Inspire the Vulgar Many

> Many of us are convinced that Saddam will acquire nuclear weapons fairly soon. Just how soon we cannot gauge.
> — Vice President Cheney, August 26, 2002[51]

> The problem here is that there will always be some uncertainty about how quickly he can acquire nuclear weapons, but we don't want the smoking gun to be a mushroom cloud.
> — National Security Advisor Rice, September 8, 2002[52]

> Facing clear evidence of peril, we cannot wait for the final proof ... the smoking gun ... that could come in the form of a mushroom cloud.
> — President George W. Bush, October 7, 2002[53]

> An Iraqi nuclear weapon might bring 'the sight of the first mushroom cloud on one of the major population centers on this planet.'
> — General Franks, November 12, 2002[54]

We know he's been absolutely devoted to trying to acquire nuclear weapons, and we believe he has, in fact, reconstituted nuclear weapons.

— Vice President Cheney, March 16, 2003[55]

I don't believe anyone that I know in the administration ever said that Iraq had nuclear weapons.

— Secretary of Defense Rumsfeld, May 14, 2003[56]

Yeah, I did misspeak .... We never had any evidence that he had acquired a nuclear weapon.

— Vice President Cheney, September 14, 2003[57]

This final quote from Cheney is rather surprising considering his comments of August 2002 and March 2003. These intervening months just before the war were remarkable. Senior members of the executive branch and a top US military commander appear to have made a coordinated attempt to create massive societal fear. Repeated references to *nuclear weapons, smoking gun,* and *mushroom clouds* were clearly aimed at instilling Strauss's "fear of impending death or catastrophe" in the American public's imaginations.[58] However, if one can overcome that fear and critically examine the available facts, it appears highly doubtful that Saddam Hussein could have reconstituted an undetected nuclear weapons program under the UN sanctions. Likewise, Saddam Hussein — an emphatically secular leader — was unlikely to provide any weapons to Islamic terrorists.

Despite inherent logical contradictions of an unprovoked WMD attack by the Iraqi government, in August 2002 Cheney introduced the notion that Saddam Hussein would acquire nuclear weapons "fairly soon." Not coincidentally, on the one-year anniversary of the September 11th attacks, Rice famously remarked that failure to "disarm" Saddam might produce a "smoking gun" in the form of a "mushroom cloud." Introducing the terrifying image of a mushroom cloud to the American citizens when their emotions were heightened was a highly effective method for instilling generalized fear.

The *coup de grâce* to "inspire" the American people that an imminent "external threat" existed from a nuclear-armed Saddam Hussein was provided by General Franks and Rumsfeld. On November 12, 2002, Franks warned that inaction might produce the "first mushroom cloud on one of the major population centers on this planet."[59] Two days later Rumsfeld stated, "Within a week, or a month, Saddam could give his WMD to al Qaeda."[60]

Tragically, the subservient US media conglomerates uncritically repeated and amplified the government's fear-inspiring propaganda campaign. Members of Congress who questioned the drive to war were quickly denounced. These events vividly illustrate how the power wielded by a few government officials can easily bring a frightful population "to the bidding of the leaders." Just as Hermann Goering stated, political leaders seeking war will always attack the pacifists for "lack of patriotism and exposing the country to danger. It works the same way in any country."[61]

The following information was never discussed by the US government or our subservient media conglomerates, as it would have exposed the fallacy of the prime rationale for the Iraq War. First, we all hope the US government will never have to conduct a forensic analysis of radioactive isotopes that would remain after a rogue nuclear explosion. However, the National Nuclear Security Administration (NNSA) and associated US military laboratories can analyze these unique radiation signatures to determine the origin of major sources of plutonium or uranium required in any nuclear weapon.

For example, if a nuclear warhead were stolen and detonated, the US could determine whether the fissile material came from Britain, China, France, India, Israel, Pakistan, Russia, or the United States. Furthermore, if Al Qaeda were to seek a nuclear weapon, it would most likely go to where this is most plentiful and least secure — the former states of the Soviet Union. Reports to Congress by US intelligence agencies and non-proliferation organizations have repeatedly stated that the real risk for a rogue group acquiring an unsecured nuclear weapon was, and still is, a former Soviet Union-based weapon, not from the Middle East. The second most likely nuclear proliferation threat is Pakistan, which according to foreign media sources was engaged in a "sophisticated black market" of selling nuclear WMD components to numerous nations.[62]

These are well-understood risks, despite the corporate media's lack of reporting these facts in the run-up to the Iraq War. Incidentally, a report presented to Congress in September 2002 regarding a "Terrorist Nuclear Attack" illustrated that US forensic capability itself "could help to deter other nations from giving nuclear material to a terrorist group."[63] The report clearly illustrated that government personnel deemed any potential detonation of a rogue nuclear device within the US as likely being of Russian origin — not from Iraq, Iran, or North Korea. Furthermore, if such an event were to occur, first it would be assumed by the US government that the bomb material was stolen from Russia, and secondly, it would be unlikely that Russia would have conducted any such attack.

Although this is a highly disconcerting subject, it is important to realize that professionals within the US government are operating under the assumption that a rogue nuclear explosion would likely be a terrorist attack and not an attack from a hostile nation. Although a brutal and despicable individual, Saddam Hussein is like other dictators who enjoy their power and position. He was not interested in provoking the US to attack Iraq, and as a secular dictator, nor was he interested in associating with fundamentalist terrorist groups like Al Qaeda. Saddam ruled over the most secular state in the Middle East and loathed religious zealots like Osama bin Laden.

Despite Bush's and Cheney's Orwellian references to Saddam Hussein's "relationship" with bin Laden, the CIA stated that Saddam Hussein never reciprocated contacts from bin Laden during the 1990s — in fact, he actually rebuffed Al Qaeda's overtures. The Congressional 9/11 investigation's final report reiterated this, finding "no credible links" between Saddam and Al Qaeda. The President said the Commission was "wrong," while the Vice President has never offered *any evidence* to support his continued claims to the contrary.[64] The modus operandi of Bush and Cheney appears to be based on Goebbels's advice on propaganda, "Repeat a lie often enough, and it becomes the truth."

Despite Bush's and Cheney's Orwellian references to Saddam Hussein's "relationship" with bin Laden, the CIA stated that Saddam Hussein never reciprocated contacts from bin Laden in the early 1990s — in fact, he actually rebuffed Al Qaeda's overtures.

Regardless, it is a matter of historical record that Saddam Hussein was warned through diplomatic channels during the 1991 Operation Desert Storm that launching a WMD attack against the UN coalition forces would result in an overwhelming US military response, one that would have ended his regime — if not his life. Obviously he was shrewd enough to avoid engaging in such self-defeating tactics and refrained from using WMD against UN forces.

Thus, a cursory analysis of Saddam Hussein's history and desire to hold onto power, and some basic common sense, exposes that the prime rationale for the 2003 war was always based on flawed logic, paranoia, or simply the desire to unite the "vulgar many" under fear. Numerous countries dislike US foreign policies, but even the most brutal dictators would likely be deterred from providing WMD to Al Qaeda in order to preserve their own survival. The American people must not let fear tactics overrule the facts or their ability to think critically.

US Government in the New Century: Political Fundamentalism and Tragic Hubris

I'm the commander — see, I don't need to explain — I do not need to explain why I say things. That's the interesting thing about being president. Maybe somebody needs to explain to me why they say something, but I don't feel like I owe anybody an explanation.

— President George W. Bush, as quoted in Bob Woodward's book, *Bush at War*[65]

God told me to strike at al Qaeda and I struck them, and then he instructed me to strike at Saddam, which I did, and now I am determined to solve the problem in the Middle East. If you help me I will act, and if not, the elections will come and I will have to focus on them.

— President George W. Bush, as reported by former Palestinian Prime Minister Mahmoud Abbas, 2003[66]

All's fair in war ... and in love. Practicing deceit to fulfill your heart's desire might be not only legitimate, but delicious!

— Michael Ledeen, as quoted in his book, *Machiavelli on Modern Leadership: Why Machiavelli's Iron Rules Are As Timely and Important Today As Five Centuries Ago*,1999).[67]

It is a disconcerting fact that fewer than two dozen men, all the way up to the president and vice president, were able to instill massive levels of irrational fear into the American citizenry by creating visions of nuclear or biochemical disaster. Thus far in our new era of political fundamentalism Congress appears to have neither the interest nor the ability to hold accountable any members of the secretive groups that operated out of the Pentagon. The same disinformation originating from the OSP and CTEG was used to sway the congressional votes on the Iraq War resolution — that was intentionally forced onto Congress just a few weeks before the 2002 mid-term elections.

One of the early whistle-blowers who witnessed the prewar activities of the OSP firsthand was US Air Force Lieutenant Colonel Kwiatkowski. She worked in the Near East South Asia (NESA), a policy arm of the Pentagon, from May 2002 until February of 2003. Before resigning, she began writing forceful articles about her experiences in the Pentagon. The following interview with Kwiatkowski illustrated how a small but radical group of ideologically "pure" neoconservatives successfully bypassed the CIA and DIA.

> All primary staff work was conducted by political appointees [that is, by those with no experience in working with intelligence, but Rumsfeld's hand-picked aides who would give him what he wanted] .... What I saw was aberrant, pervasive and contrary to good order and discipline. If one is seeking the answers to why peculiar bits of 'intelligence' found sanctity in a presidential speech, or why the post-Hussein occupation has been distinguished by confusion and false steps, one need look no further than the process inside the Office of the Secretary of Defense ....
>
> The answers [to questions about why the invasion] had been heavily crafted by the Pentagon, and to me, they were remarkably inadequate ....
>
> I suggested to my boss that if this was as good as it got, some folks on the Pentagon's E-ring may be sitting beside Hussein in the war crimes tribunals. Hussein is not yet sitting before a war

crimes tribunal. Nor have the key decision-makers in the Pentagon been forced to account for the odd set of circumstances that placed us as a long-term occupying force in the world's nastiest rat's nest, without a nation-building plan, without significant international support and without an exit plan. Neither may ever be required to answer their accusers, thanks to this administration's military as well as publicity machine, and the disgraceful political compromises already made by most of the Congress.[68]

The US' five subservient media conglomerates dutifully and uncritically repeated the propaganda of the Bush/Cheney administration essentially verbatim. The chief weapons inspector during 2002–2003, Hans Blix,[69] and former UN weapons inspector Scott Ritter,[70] have both written books reflecting the actual facts about Iraq's supposed WMD program. Additionally, Dilip Hiro's book *Secrets and Lies* carefully listed the prewar claims versus the actual results of the failed search for WMD within Iraq.[71]

According to former CIA employees, OSP members are dangerous ideologues who have seriously damaged the credibility and sense of mission within the CIA.[72] Aside from the Iraq debacle, CIA officers are reportedly distraught with the White House at the apparently politically motivated "outing" of Valerie Plame, an undercover CIA asset involved in investigating the proliferation of WMD technology. This unprecedented retaliatory act was detailed by her husband, former ambassador Joseph Wilson, in *The Politics of Truth.* [73] He clarified that, despite claims by the administration, Saddam Hussein had not sought to buy uranium yellowcake from Niger, but this disclosure from a veteran diplomat was met with nefarious retaliation by political operatives. According to John Dean, a lawyer in the Nixon administration who became famous during the Watergate scandal, Plame's "outing" may have violated the Espionage Act of 1917 and the Intelligence Identities and Protection Act of 1982, both of which are serious felonies.[74]

During a June 2003 interview, Ray McGovern, a retired 27-year CIA veteran, stated that there is an "incredible amount of unease and disarray" between the neoconservatives and US intelligence professionals.[75] According to him, "the primary function of the Central Intelligence Agency is to seek the truth regarding what is going on abroad and be able to report that truth without fear or favor."[76] However, under the Bush administration the ability of CIA employees to present data without fear of retaliatory actions has been, in McGovern's view, "corroded, or eroded, very much."[77]

During a 2003 interview with *Salon*, Thomas Powers, a widely respected authority on the US spy business, stated that the CIA was facing a "demoralized rank and file, a lack of resources," and was "effectively hamstrung" by the Bush administration. Powers acknowledged that these political manipulations

Allegations about Iraqi WMD	Findings
Precursor Chemicals: 3,307 tons	Found: None
Tabun, nerve agent	Found: None
Mustard agent	Found: None
Sarin, nerve agent	Found: None [A single unmarked and presumably discarded 1980s vintage "dud" artillery shell used as an improvised explosive device (IED) by Iraqi insurgents during May 2004. Details added by author]
VX nerve agent, 1.6 tons	Found: None
Anthrax spores raw material: 25,550 liters	Found: None
Ricin	Found: None
Botulinnum toxin	Found: One vial of Sarin B, 10 years old, in an Iraqi scientist's domestic refrigerator
Alfotoxins	Found: None
Mobile bio-weapons laboratories	Found: None [Two suspected mobile trailers found to be harmless, possibly purchased from the UK in 1987 as atmospheric hydrogen balloon labs for artillery aiming purposes. Details added by author]
Bombs, rockets, and shells for poison gas, up to 30,000 shells	Found: None
L-29 unmanned aerial vehicles for delivering biological and chemical weapons	Found: None
Nuclear weapons material	Found: None [corroded parts from a single 12-year-old centrifuge buried under a rose bush in the backyard of a former Iraqi scientist. Details added by author]
Al Hussein surface-to-surface missiles with 410 mile/650 kilometer range, up to 20	Found: None

4.2: *Iraqi WMDs and means of delivery -- alleged vs. found*
Sources: The Guardian *(UK), September 25, October 3, and October 7, 2003*

had compromised the CIA's ability to protect US national security. Regarding the OSP, Powers stated:

> [Donald Rumsfeld and the OSP] wanted the war so badly that they were doing everything they could to create pressure for it. With the Office of Special Plans, they were essentially saying to

the CIA, 'OK, you're not giving us what we want, so we're going to create a new CIA.'[78]

With their mission accomplished, Rumsfeld disbanded the OSP in September 2003, and the CTEG was disbanded in February 2004. Despite the so-called congressional investigation into "intelligence failures," there is reportedly "strong resistance" by the Republicans to investigate the activities of the Rumsfeld/Feith conspiracy.[79] It is highly doubtful the US Congress or UK Parliament will expose the truth in the near future. The publicly available facts, and statements by former intelligence professionals, clearly illustrate that the purposeful maneuverings of the OSP and CTEG were not "intelligence failures" at all, but rather a remarkable *success* in "uniting the vulgar many" with fear. Regardless of whether these individuals are ever held accountable, it is clear that the main justifications for the war were based on a mixture of deceptive premises and, in some cases, outrightly fraudulent information.

Following the Iraq War the Bush administration began to "purge" the CIA of analysts who provided analysis that contradicted the dogmatic notions of the neoconservatives. Jim Pavitt, a 31-year CIA veteran who retired in August 2003 as a departmental chief, said that he could not recall a time when such "viciousness and vindictiveness" had occurred in a battle between the White House and the agency.[80] In 2004 Vince Cannistraro, former CIA head of counter-terrorism and member of the National Security Council under Ronald Reagan, made the following understatement, "These have been an extraordinary four years for the CIA and the political pressure to come up with the right results has been enormous, particularly from Vice-President Cheney."[81]

The internal battle between the White House and the CIA erupted into public view during the summer of 2004. The first sacrificial lamb was the unexpected resignation in June of CIA Director George Tenet for supposedly "personal reasons." The newly appointed Director Porter J. Goss began to remove anyone not deemed sufficiently "ideologically pure." A memorandum written by Goss was leaked in which he warned CIA employees not to "identify with, support or champion opposition to the administration or its policies."[82] This memo coincided with resignations of many senior CIA staff; including John McLaughlin, the deputy director and head of clandestine operations, and Jami Miscik, the deputy director for intelligence and head of the analytical section. Michael Scheuer, the former head of the UBL unit and author of *Imperial Hubris,* also resigned at this time.

Considering the ongoing wrath of "viciousness and vindictiveness" emanating from the White House, it was not entirely surprising that immediately after the November 2004 election a "purge" of the CIA was implemented. Basically, numerous "realists" within the CIA have been removed in order to fill these slots with political appointees — or "true believers." This purging of

reality-based analysts with faith-based political fundamentalists will likely produce a dangerous myopia within the CIA.

In January 2005 the *Washington Post* revealed that the Bush administration
had decided to create a "new CIA" — without involving Congress. Apparently,
in 2002 Rumsfeld set up the Strategic Support Branch, his own clandestine
espionage unit operating out of the Pentagon. This unit had reportedly been
operating in secret for two years inside Afghanistan, Iraq, and other places that
were not disclosed.[83] According to Stephen A. Cambone, the undersecretary
for intelligence and neoconservative protégé, he defined the "war on terror"
as ongoing and indefinite, and thereby saw no need to notify Congress of its
deployment orders. In other words, Rumsfeld's newest espionage unit will
remain largely unaccountable to the Joint Chiefs, Congress, and the taxpayers.
This dangerous secrecy follows a pattern that has been evident throughout
the Bush administration.

Referring again to first-hand observations of Kwiatkowski, the deceptive
machinations underlying the Iraq War were carefully hidden from the public,
as she stated in this interview with *LA Weekly*:

> *Marc*: So if, as you argue, they knew there weren't any of these
> WMD, then what exactly drove the neoconservatives to war?
>
> *Karen*: The neoconservatives pride themselves on having a
> global vision, a long-term strategic perspective. And there were
> three reasons why they felt the US needed to topple Saddam, put
> in a friendly government and occupy Iraq .... One of those reasons
> is that sanctions and containment were working and everybody
> pretty much knew it .... The second reason has to do with our mil-
> itary-basing posture in the region. We had been very dissatisfied
> with our relations with Saudi Arabia, particularly the restrictions
> on our basing .... The last reason is the conversion, the switch Saddam
> Hussein made in the Food for Oil program, from the dollar to the
> euro. He did this, by the way, long before 9/11, in November
> 2000.[84]

In order to facilitate the goals as articulated by Kwiatkowski, on May 9,
2003, the Bush administration presented UN Security Council Resolution 1483
that proposed the cessation of sanctions against Iraq and granted US/UK
sole control of Iraq's oil production revenue.[85] Interestingly, the Bush administration blocked Blix and the UN inspectors from returning to Iraq in the
postwar period and successfully had the UN sanctions lifted regardless of
Iraq's WMD status. Why? The Bush administration simply had decided that
it was unacceptable for any of the "foreign suitors of Iraqi oil" to gain control of an estimated 40 billion barrels of Iraqi oil — or for that oil be sold in
euros by the French and perhaps later by the Russians.

Had the UN inspectors declared Iraq free of WMDs, the oil lease contracts and exploration rights held by the French, Russians, and Chinese could have been legally initiated. Lifting the UN sanctions would have also allowed foreign investment to begin rebuilding and exporting Iraq's vast reserves, while simultaneously impeding the ability of major US/UK oil companies to gain lease contracts for Iraqi oil, given Saddam Hussein's loathing of the US/UK post–1991 sanction policies toward Iraq. Although hardly covered in the US media, it was briefly reported that the Bush administration's lawyers were studying international law in an effort to nullify these contracts while Iraq was governed by the US-appointed Coalition Provisional Authority (CPA). While this type of subterfuge at the highest levels of government was nothing new, there was a surprisingly intense reaction from the international community, manifested in the failure of the US to acquire the UN's authorization for invading Iraq.

March 19, 2003: An Oil Currency War to Enforce Dollar Hegemony within OPEC

Oil is Allah's gift to the Arab People.

— Optimistic Arab saying

There will be no democracy for the Arab People until the oil runs out.

— Cynical Arab saying

You can't distinguish between al Qaeda and Saddam when you talk about the war on terror.

— President George W. Bush, September 2002[86]

In the real world … the one factor underpinning American prosperity is keeping the dollar the World Reserve Currency. This can only be done if the oil producing states keep oil priced in dollars, and all their currency reserves in dollar assets. If anything put the final nail in Saddam Hussein's coffin, it was his move to start selling oil for euros.

— Richard Benson, "Oil, the Dollar, and US Prosperity," www.prudentbear.com, August 2003[87]

There were only two credible reasons for invading Iraq: control over oil and preservation of the dollar as the world's reserve currency.

— John Chapman, "The Real Reasons Bush Went to War," the *Guardian* (UK), July 2004[88]

In December 2002, I wrote an Internet essay hypothesizing that one of the real reasons for the upcoming war to topple Saddam Hussein was the Bush administration's desire to install a puppet government in Iraq — and to immediately revert Iraq's oil exports to a dollar standard.[89] This reconversion was not the sole issue per se, but preventing any further momentum toward a petroeuro is likely an unspoken component of neoconservative strategy for US global domination. Notably, when the euro was launched in 1999, Iran expressed interest in switching to a petroeuro, but the euro's subsequent decline in 2000 temporarily reduced momentum. Undeterred, Saddam Hussein was the first OPEC member to make the switch. While deceiving the American people into the Iraq War, this administration sent a message to other OPEC producers — *You are either with us or against us.*

Given neoconservative doctrine with regard to thwarting any nation, or group of nations, from "even aspiring" to challenge the US' role in global affairs, it is quite realistic to presume that Saddam Hussein sealed his fate when he decided to switch to the petroeuro in late 2000. At that point, another manufactured Gulf War become inevitable under the Bush administration. To be sure, Paul O'Neill's and Richard Clarke's books exposed that one of Bush's primary foreign policy objectives within his first month in office was to topple Saddam Hussein.

Aside from the reserve currency and the Saudi/Iraq/Iran oil issues, everything was peripheral and of marginal consequence to this administration. The dollar-euro threat is powerful enough that the US risked domestic and international economic backlash in the short-term to stave off the long-term dollar crash that would result from a collective OPEC switch from dollars to euros. The Bush administration planned to reverse the various trends mentioned above by seizing the world's richest oil-producing regions. Robert Dreyfuss outlined the development of these strategic goals in his 2003 Project Censored award-winning essay "The Thirty-Year Itch."

> *The administration believes you have to control resources in order to have access to them,*' says Chas Freeman, who served as US ambassador to Saudi Arabia under the first President Bush. 'They are taken with the idea that the end of the Cold War left the United States able to impose its will globally — and that those who have the ability to shape events with power have the duty to do so. *It's ideology.*[90] [emphasis added]

This information about Iraq's oil currency switch appeared in the US corporate media for a single 24-hour news cycle on October 30, 2000.[91] This newsworthy item never again showed up in the US media in the 2½ years leading up to the Iraq War. Likewise, the Bush administration has never spoken about it. Regardless, this quasi state secret can be found in a Radio Free Europe article discussing Saddam Hussein's switching his oil sales to the euros effective November 6, 2000:

> Baghdad's switch from the dollar to the euro for oil trading is intended to rebuke Washington's hard line on sanctions and encourage Europeans to challenge it. But the political message will cost Iraq millions in lost revenue. RFE/RL correspondent Charles Recknagel looks at what Baghdad will gain and lose, and the impact of the decision to go with the European currency.[92]

At the time of the switch many analysts were surprised that Saddam Hussein was willing to give up approximately $400 million (£270 million) in annual oil revenue for what appeared to be a political statement. However, the steady depreciation of the dollar against the euro since late 2001 meant that Iraq had profited handsomely from the switch in their transaction and reserve currencies. Indeed, the *Observer* surprisingly divulged these facts one month before the war in an article aptly titled "Iraq Nets Handsome Profit by Dumping Dollar for Euro."[93] Although the switch appeared to be censored within the US corporate broadcast media, this UK article revealed that the euro had gained 25 percent against the dollar following Iraq's decision:

> A bizarre political statement by Saddam Hussein has earned Iraq a windfall of hundreds of millions of euros. In October 2000 Iraq insisted upon dumping the US dollar — 'the currency of the enemy' — for the more multilateral euro.[94]

This UK news item by Islam Faisal was the only mainstream prewar story that specifically addressed the *financial windfall* of Iraq's oil currency switch to the euro. Due to the euro's steady appreciation relative to the dollar from 2001 to early 2003, Iraq's UN reserve fund swelled from around $10 billion to €26 billion.[95]

One week later a follow-up article appeared, just three weeks before the Iraq War began, entitled "When Will We Buy Oil in Euros?" According to Fadhil Chalabi of the Center for Global Energy Studies, Saddam Hussein's switch to the euro was "a political move [designed] to show that the euro could be a substitute for the dollar in denominating the oil price."[96] This article ended with a rhetorical question that historians will likely study in the coming years, "So is the euro the missing link between the 'axis of evil' and the 'axis of weasel'? It is greatly appreciated in the former and was invented in the latter."[97]

This strikingly honest news story revealed what appears to be an *ongoing* secret withheld from US citizens by the corporate media — but well known by Internet readers: the critical, but obfuscated, fact, *"that two-thirds of [Iraqi oil] is being snapped up by US companies, can only be paid for in euros."*[98] [emphasis added] Under the Oil for Food program, the US typically purchased around 65 percent of Iraq's total oil exports, which from 2001 to early 2003 was approximately 2.5 billion out of a total production of 3.3 billion barrels.

Despite months of debate in the mass media about fictitious threats from Iraq's "vast stockpile" of WMD and deceptive references suggesting Iraqi involvement in 9/11, the US media completely omitted the simple fact that, from 2001 up until the 2003 invasion, US petroleum conglomerates were paying for Iraq's oil in euros — *not dollars*.

Despite months of debate in the mass media about fictitious threats from Iraq's "vast stockpile" of WMD and deceptive references suggesting Iraqi involvement in 9/11, the US corporate media completely omitted from the information flow the simple fact that, from 2001 up until the 2003 invasion, US petroleum conglomerates were paying for Iraq's oil in euros — *not dollars*.

What would be the effect if most OPEC members made a sudden (collective) switch to euros, as opposed to a gradual transition? While highly unlikely, this would create monumental turmoil in the global financial markets. According to a former US government analyst:

> The effect of an OPEC switch to the euro would be that oil-consuming nations would have to flush dollars out of their (central bank) reserve funds and replace these with euros. The dollar would crash anywhere from 20–40% in value and the consequences would be those one could expect from any currency collapse and massive inflation (think Argentina currency crisis, for example). You'd have foreign funds stream out of the US stock markets and dollar denominated assets, there'd surely be a run on the banks much like the 1930s, the current account deficit would become unserviceable, the budget deficit would go into default, and so on. This could result in your basic 3rd world economic crisis.[99]

Although the above scenario is highly unlikely, and most assuredly undesirable to the global economy, under certain economic conditions or significant geopolitical tensions, it is plausible. The US economy is intimately tied to the dollar's role as reserve currency. This does not mean that the US couldn't function otherwise, but means that the transition would have to be gradual to avoid precipitous economic dislocations — and the ultimate result would probably be the US and the EU switching roles in the global economy. Referring again to Spiro's analysis of petrodollar recycling:

> So long as OPEC oil was priced in US dollars, and so long as OPEC invested the dollars in US government instruments, the US government enjoyed a double loan. The first part of the loan was for oil. The government could print dollars to pay for oil, and the American economy did not have to produce goods and services in exchange for the oil until OPEC used the dollars for goods and services. Obviously, the strategy could not work if dollars were not a means of exchange for oil.

The second part of the loan was from all other economies that had to pay dollars for oil but could not print currency. Those economies had to trade their goods and services for dollars in order to pay OPEC. Again, so long as OPEC held the dollars rather than spending them, the US received a loan. It was therefore important to keep OPEC oil priced in dollars at the same time that the government officials continued to recruit Arab funds.[100]

Avoiding the Iraq War would have required a more honorable US administration that could have convened a meeting of the G–8 industrialized nations in an effort to negotiate a graduated oil-pricing option that included the dollar and the euro. Of course, such an accord now seems inevitable by 2010.

Unfortunately the Bush administration chose a military option instead of a multilateral conference on monetary reform and appears completely unable to advocate any energy policy except one that encourages more consumption. After toppling Saddam Hussein, the US clearly intends to keep a large and permanent military force in Iraq. Indeed, there never was an exit strategy because the military is needed to protect the newly installed regime and to send a message to other OPEC producers that they might receive regime change if they convert their oil payments to euros. The geopolitical tensions between the US and other industrialized nations have been further exacerbated in the aftermath of the Iraq War, as Saddam Hussein's contracts with French, Russian, and Chinese firms appear to have been nullified.

It may surprise many Americans that the 2003 Iraq War was the *third* US-sponsored regime change in Iraq since WW II.[101] Therefore, we should not naïvely believe that the Bush administration intends to establish democratic rule in Iraq, assuming it is possible. As Americans, we engaged in wishful thinking that somehow the US military was capable of invading Iraq and "installing" democracy. In contrast, we are an empire trying to reaffirm our position as the world's only superpower, thus altruism is not our goal. It is simply to install a pliant puppet-regime that will align itself with US corporate interests, mainly to revert to petrodollar recycling and award Iraq's oil contracts only to US and UK companies, thereby nullifying the contracts revealed by Cheney's Energy Task Force as "foreign suitors of Iraqi oil."

The US economy has acquired significant structural imbalances, including a massive $665 billion trade account deficit in 2004 (almost 6 percent of GDP), a $7.6 trillion deficit (65 percent of GDP), and the recent return to annual budget deficits in the hundreds of billions. These imbalances are exacerbated by the Bush administration's ideologically driven tax and budget policies that have produced a $413 billion budget deficit in 2004, and projected an unprecedented ten consecutive years of deficits totaling a massive $5.9 trillion by 2014.[102] These factors would collapse the currency of any nation under the "old rules." The dollar is still predominant despite these structural imbalances, but for reasons rarely discussed in public.

The "safe harbor" status of the US dollar since 1945 rests on it being the World Reserve Currency. In conjunction with the oil industry's historical roots in Texas in the early 20th century, it has traditionally assumed the role of the main currency for international oil transactions. The dollar's monopoly began to breakdown in the early 1970s due in part to the debts of the Vietnam War, with its associated drain of the US' gold reserves, and the emergence of reinvigorated European and Japanese economies. Secret, unilateral US agreements with Saudi Arabia in 1974 thwarted movement toward a basket of multiple currencies for international oil trades. This has produced a *fundamentally* unbalanced global economy.

For the past 30 years the US Federal Reserve has printed hundreds of billions of oil-backed petrodollars, which US consumers provide to other nations by purchasing imported goods. Then those nations use these dollars to purchase oil/energy from OPEC producers. These billions of surplus petrodollars are recycled from OPEC and invested back into the US via Treasury bills or other dollar-denominated assets, such as US stocks, bonds, and real estate. The structural imbalances in the US economy are sustainable as long as

- nations continue to demand and purchase oil for their energy/ survival needs,

- the world's monopoly currency for global oil transactions remain the US dollar, and

- the three internationally traded "crude oil markers" remain denominated in US dollars.

These underlying factors of dollar supremacy, along with the "safe harbor" reputation of US investments, propelled the US to economic and military hegemony in the post–WW II period. However, the introduction of the euro is a significant new factor, and it appears to be the primary threat to US economic domination.

US policy-makers are undoubtedly aware of the EU's impressive expansion plans that will by default shift more economic power to Europe. In late 2002 it was agreed that the EU would expand in May 2004 with ten additional member states, thereby creating a 25-nation economic block, the EU-25. This successful integration resulted in an aggregate GDP of $9.6 trillion and 450 million people, directly competing with the US economy ($10.5 trillion GDP, 280 million people). Significantly, even before enlarging, the EU purchased more of OPEC's oil exports than did the US.

Facing these geopolitical potentialities with the attending macroeconomic threat of a powerful euro, in conjunction with the global energy challenges,

I hypothesized in December 2002 that the Bush administration sought to topple Saddam Hussein in 2003. Such a strategy would be pursued as a pre-emptive attempt to prevent the initiation of Iraqi oil lease contracts with various foreign nations, and the reconversion of Iraq's oil export transaction currency to the dollar. Regarding Iraq, the facts speak for themselves.

Just as hypothesized, after toppling the Saddam Hussein regime, the Bush administration quickly reconverted Iraq's oil transaction currency to the dollar. On April 28, 2003, *msnbc.com* published the first and *only* article in the mainstream US media since the autumn of 2000 that specifically addressed Iraq's oil export switch to the euro, the Iraq War, and underlying petrodollar issues. The following excerpts are from Howard Fineman's article "In Round 2, It's the Dollar Versus the Euro" (implying that the Iraq War was Round 1):

> A new world is being created. Ironically, the most troublesome clash of civilizations in it may not be the one the academics expected: not Islamic fundamentalists vs. the West in the first instance, but the United States against Europe.
>
> To oversimplify, but only slightly, it's the dollar vs. the euro ....
>
> The Europeans and the United Nations want the inspections regime to resume because as long as it is in place, the UN Oil for Food program remains in effect. *Not only does France benefit directly — its banks hold the deposits and its companies have been involved in the oil sales — the entire EU does as well, if for no other reason than many of the recent sales were counted not in dollars but in euros.*
>
> Sometime in the next few weeks, push will come to shove. There are storage tanks full of Iraqi crude waiting in Turkish ports .... There may come a time when the smart thing to do is turn the whole Iraq situation over to the UN. This is not that time. Meanwhile, if the rest of the world tries to block any and all Iraq oil sales, it's possible that American companies will find a way to become the customer of first and last resort ....
>
> And we'll pay in dollars.[103][emphasis added]

Although Fineman addressed this subject somewhat obliquely, his final sentence is quite candid. Indeed, my original thesis from the Internet essay regarding the macroeconomic strategy of the Bush administration was confirmed a few months after the Iraq War had begun.

On June 5, 2003, an article in *Financial Times* briefly mentioned that the first "postwar" Iraqi oil sales returning to the international markets were once again denominated in US dollars — not euros, thus confirming my original hypothesis that the US would immediate seek to reconvert Iraqi oil exports to the dollar.

The tender, for which bids are due by June 10, switches the trans-action back to dollars — the international currency of oil sales — despite the greenback's recent fall in value. Saddam Hussein in 2000 insisted Iraq's oil be sold for euros, a political move, but one that improved Iraq's recent earnings thanks to the rise in the value of the euro against the dollar.[104]

Not surprisingly, the US corporate media has not run a single news story on the reconversion of Iraq's oil exports from petroeuros to petrodollars. The swiftness with which the Bush administration achieved this tactical goal was impressive. This hidden fact helped illuminate one of the crucial, yet over-looked, macroeconomic rationales for the 2003 Iraq War.

Another goal of the neoconservatives was to use the "war on terror" as the publicly expressed premise in an attempt to dissolve OPEC's decision-making process, thus ultimately frustrating the cartel's inevitable switch to pricing oil in euros. How would the Bush administration break up the cartel's price con-trols in a post-Saddam Iraq? First is the redenomination of Iraq's oil exports to the dollar standard. Additionally, investigative journalist Greg Palast dis-covered that some advisors to the Bush administration recommended initiating massive Iraqi oil production far in excess of OPEC quotas, thereby disrupting the cartel's pricing leverage.[105] Regardless of the outcome of this aspect of prewar discussions, it is irrefutable that the US has established 14 new military bases in Iraq in an effort to gain strategic control of Iraq's oil.

In the buildup to the war, Nayyer Ali offered a succinct analysis of why Iraq's underutilized oil reserves would not be a "profit-maker" for the US government, but they would achieve the more important goal of providing the economic leverage to potentially dissolve OPEC's price controls, thus ful-filling the US' long-sought goal of disbanding the OPEC cartel:

> Despite this vast pool of oil, Iraq has never produced at a level proportionate to the reserve base. Since the Gulf War, Iraq's pro-duction has been limited by sanctions and allowed sales under the Oil for Food program and what else can be smuggled out .... If Iraq were reintegrated into the world economy, it could allow massive investment in its oil sector and boost output to 2.5 billion barrels per year, or about 7 million barrels a day.
>
> What would be the consequences of this? There are two obvi-ous things.
>
> First would be the collapse of OPEC, whose strategy of limit-ing production to maximize price will have finally reached its limit .... This would lead to the second major consequence, which is a collapse in the price of oil to the 10-dollar range per barrel.

The Iraq War is not a moneymaker. But it could be an OPEC breaker. That however is a long-term outcome that will require Iraq to be successfully reconstituted into a functioning state in which massive oil sector investment can take place.[106]

The American people were oblivious to the potential economic risks regarding the Iraq War. The Bush administration believed that by toppling Saddam Hussein they would remove the juggernaut, thus allowing the US to control Iraq's huge oil reserves and finally break up and dissolve the pricing power of the ten remaining OPEC producers. However, the US occupation of Iraq may be exacerbating tensions within OPEC, providing further impetus toward a petroeuro.

Only time will tell, but from a purely monetary and economic perspective, it would be natural for some OPEC members and non-OPEC oil exporters, such as Russia, to protect their investments and debt obligations by pricing oil in the euro, given its higher valuation. Governments in many oil-producing states will naturally attempt to maintain social stability in their countries by allocating oil profits for domestic infrastructure improvements, which will become increasingly difficult if the dollar remains lower relative to the euro.

Operation Ajax to Operation Iraqi Freedom: 50 Years of History Lessons Not Heeded

In 1953 the United States played a significant role in orchestrating the overthrow of Iran's popular prime minister, Mohammad Mossadegh. The Eisenhower administration believed its actions were justified for strategic reasons. But the coup was clearly a setback for Iran's political development. And it is easy to see now why many Iranians continue to resent this intervention by America in their internal affairs .... Neither Iran nor we can forget the past. It has scarred us both. But the question both countries now face is whether to allow the past to freeze the future or to find a way to plant the seeds of a new relationship that will enable us to harvest shared advantages in years to come, not more tragedies.

— Secretary of State Albright, speech given at the American-Iranian Council, Washington, DC, March 17, 2000[107]

Operation Ajax was the CIA's first "dirty tricks" campaign to destabilize a Middle Eastern government — the US overthrew a secular democracy in Iran and installed a totalitarian regime, essentially in order to protect Western corporate oil profits.

Important history lessons following the 1953 coup of Iran are revealed in Stephen Kinzer's excellent book, *All the Shah's Men: An American Coup and the Roots of Middle East Terror.*[108] Kinzer, a veteran foreign correspondent for the *New York Times*, interviewed numerous Iranians about the overthrow of Prime Minister Mossadegh. The sordid history of foreign interference helps explain why Iran is governed today by theocratic mullahs instead of secular leadership as practiced under its brief period of democratic governance.

During the 1940s the Anglo-Iranian Oil Company reaped over 80 percent of the profits from Iran's oil exports. For example, in 1947 the British oil company reported an after-tax profit of $40 million but gave Iran only $7 million and failed to live up to its earlier agreements to spend some of the profits to improve the deplorable conditions at the main oil fields in Abadan.[109] The widespread abuses and arrogance of the British-controlled company had increased the level of social discontent within Iranian society.

These sentiments were shared by an Iranian politician in his early 60s, Mohammed Mossadegh, a staunch nationalist and anti-communist. He insisted that Iran be allowed to audit the accounting books from the Anglo-Iranian Oil Company (later to become BP). This was a matter of due diligence to Mossadegh, who believed that Iran was not getting sufficient financial returns from exporting its vital oil resources. Observing this brewing crisis, the US government stepped into the fray.

In 1949 George McGhee of the US State Department reviewed the financial reports of the Anglo-Iranian Oil Company and noted that it sold its oil for between 10 and 30 times the production cost, concluding that the company was "exceptionally profitable." McGhee sought to prevent a looming disaster by warning the British that this company had become "genuinely hated in Iran" and suggested it was time to begin sharing the oil wealth in a more equitable profit-sharing arrangement.[110] In a striking example of arrogance, the British told McGhee they would train more Iranians for supervisory positions, but they refused to offer any financial disclosures to the Iranian government, nor would they offer to split the oil profits. The British remarkably claimed, "One penny more and the company goes broke."[111]

British intransigence ignited Mossadegh's candidacy. On April 28, 1951, the Iranian parliament, or *Majlis*, elected him as prime minister by a vote of 79 to 12.[112] His one condition for accepting this position was the fateful decision that made him a national hero to the people of Iran, but despised by British oil interests.

Following the British refusal to a more equitable distribution of oil profits, in 1951 Mossadegh fulfilled his promise to nationalize Iran's oil resources. He then offered Anglo-Iranian Oil Company a 50/50 split on the oil proceeds, but the British rebuked it. British Prime Minister Arden organized a blockade of Iran, froze its financial assets, and claimed that the nationalization of Iran's oil was illegal. However, the World Court upheld Mossadegh's action. In 1951, *Time* named Mossadegh Man of the Year, describing him as "the Iranian George Washington" but also as an exasperating, "defiant man [who] dissolved one of the remaining pillars of a great empire."[113]

Undeterred by this turn of events or Mossadegh's popularity with the Iranian people, Churchill asked Truman to help overthrow Mossadegh and regain British control over Iran's oil export revenue. Truman declined and attempted to foster diplomatic mediation. However, the Dulles brothers had already conceived a plot when Eisenhower became president in January 1953. (Allen Dulles was the CIA Director, and according to Kinzer, John Dulles was a lawyer who represented various US/UK oil companies.)

In February 1953 Allen Dulles sent Eisenhower a preposterous intelligence estimate suggesting that a "Communist takeover is becoming more and more of a possibility" within Iran.[114] Eisenhower then agreed to a covert operation code-named Ajax, after which the CIA successfully overthrew Mossadegh in August 1953. The CIA then installed Mohammed Shah, a member of the Iranian monarchy who later became despised as a US puppet. The Shah used the brutal SAVAK secret police force to maintain his grip on power. Due to widespread political imprisonments, torture, and killings, his rule ultimately radicalized Iranian society. This blowback resulted in the ousting of the Shah to the US and the Iranian Revolution of 1979. Based on Kinzer's research, it is clear that many Iranians were very pro-US before the covert actions by the CIA:

> 'Why did you Americans do that terrible thing?' a relative of Mossadegh demands of Kinzer. 'We always loved America. To us, America was the great country, the perfect country, the country that helped us while other countries were exploiting us. But after that moment, no one in Iran ever trusted the United States again. I can tell you for sure that if you had not done that thing, you would never have had that problem of hostages being taken in your embassy in Tehran. All your trouble started in 1953. Why, why did you do it?'[115]

The answer to her question can be summarized in one word — greed, stemming from powerful oil interests that enacted unwarranted influence on British and American foreign policies. Not much has changed in the past 50 years; the Western participants in the Middle East are essentially the same, but the US is now the principal provocateur. The main differences today are that the propaganda used to justify regime change is now based on a "terrorist threat" as opposed to a "communist threat," and that the main actors are more desperate due to the imminent arrival of Peak Oil, which has resulted in *overt* military operations as opposed to the previous tactics of quiet, *covert* operations.

Regrettably, many Iranians have not forgiven the US government for what it did to their country 50 years ago. The ramifications of this 1953 plot and subsequent tyrannical rule by the Shah greatly agitated Iranian society, ultimately fostering the spread of a radical Islamic fundamentalism, which continues to fracture US-Iranian relations. Even on the 50th anniversary of the coup (August 2003), the conservative Islamic mullahs in Iran did not acknowledge Mossadegh's secular legacy. However, according to reporter Dan de Kuce of the *Guardian*, for many Iranians that coup was a tragedy from which their country has never recovered. On this anniversary he noted, "Perhaps because Mossadegh represents a future denied, his memory has approached myth."[116]

Undoubtedly, Bush's declaration of Iran as part of an "axis of evil" has even further damaged the US-Iran relationship, while paradoxically appearing to facilitate Iran's trade relationships with the EU, Russia, and China. Obviously, therefore, any future US military or covert action against Iran would likely be entirely unilateral, as even the British government has rejected overt "regime change" in Iran.

The Iraq Conundrum: Tactical Victory but Strategic Failure

In military campaigns I have heard of awkward speed but have never seen any skill in lengthy campaigns. No country has ever profited from protracted warfare. Those who do not thoroughly comprehend the dangers inherent in employing the army are incapable of truly knowing the potential advantages of military actions.

— Sun-tzu, *The Art of War*, 400–320 BC[117]

A guerrilla war is not a war of technology versus peasantry. Rather, it is a contest of endurance and national will. The side with the greatest moral commitment (ideological, religious, or patriotic) will hold the ground at the end of the conflict. Battlefield victory can be almost irrelevant, since victory is often determined by morale, obstinacy and survival.

— General Nawroz, US Army (retired), Foreign Military Studies Office Analysis: Soviet Invasion of Afghanistan[118]

You are going to be the proud owner of 25 million people .... You will own all their hopes, aspirations, and problems. You'll own it all .... So you need to understand that this is not going to be a cakewalk in the woods .... You need to understand not just a military timeline but other things that are going to be facing you.

— Colin Powell advising President George W. Bush about the need for a broad international coalition before the Iraq War, as quoted in Bob Woodward's book, *Plan of Attack*, 2004[119]

> We are going to fight them and impose our will on them and we
> will capture or ... kill them until we have imposed law and order
> on this country. We dominate the scene and we will continue to
> impose our will on this country.
>
> — Paul Bremer, pro-consul of the Coalition Provisional
> Authority (CPA), speaking in Baghdad, July 2003.[120]

Clearly, the US military was tactically successful in its goal of quickly toppling
the Saddam Hussein government while preventing major damage to Iraq's oil
infrastructure. However, diplomatically and strategically the Bush administration was destined to fail before the invasion began. It is obvious the
governments of the EU, Russia, and to a lesser degree China do not, and will
not, endorse the neoconservative agenda of US global domination, which by
default requires that neither the EU nor its euro be allowed to gain a
foothold in the oil currency market. Equally, it does not allow France, Russia,
or China to implement their oil exploration and production sharing contracts
within Iraq, thereby challenging US hegemony in the Persian Gulf.

The neoconservatives determined the only US strategy that could prevent
such events was a military invasion of Iraq that toppled Saddam Hussein's
government, thereby allowing the installation of a puppet regime that would
align itself with the interests of the US corporate–military–industrial–petroleum
conglomerate.

What the Bush administration and neoconservative strategists failed to
realize was that their open declaration of US strategic plans for global domination would naturally create an equal but opposite reaction from other
industrialized powers. This was symbolized by an unusual geostrategic alignment between the EU and Russia. China's role has been somewhat enigmatic,
but they did not approve of the invasion either. Whether or not this alignment solidifies in the near-term will likely become evident if a new "Iranian
crisis" should occur during Bush's second term in office.

First, it is important to clarify the objectives underlying the various prewar maneuvers, which appeared to be haphazard, but have since created the desired effect. None of these nations who opposed the Iraq War wish to destroy America. The Europeans certainly, but also the Russians and even the Chinese do not dislike the US nearly enough. France and Germany simply want Washington to reduce its intrusive mingling in European affairs, while allowing the euro to follow its natural trajectory in the global financial markets.

None of these nations who opposed the Iraq War wish to destroy America. France and Germany simply want Washington to reduce its intrusive mingling in European affairs, while allowing the euro to follow its natural trajectory in the global financial markets.

Most nations, particularly Russia, wish to reverse the current US military encroachment in the Middle East and Central Asia regions. As for China, it wants to reduce US influence in the Far East, and like Russia, sees US military bases as an encroachment into their backyard. The Chinese government likely desires that US alliances with South Korea and Japan become more neutral from a military perspective. Also, China certainly does not appreciate the current US encirclement policy being pursued via military basing in states to its east and naval maneuvers.

In general, these nations, along with most of the world, simply desire a multilateralist America more inclined to operate in tandem with the global community. From a cynical perspective, they would prefer a US more willing to share the spoils and less driven to bully its way through international relations. The Iraq invasion has resulted in unprecedented levels of US isolation and a reduction of political leverage.

This was achieved by denying the neoconservatives UN authorization to use military force against Iraq, while simultaneously functioning to weaken the US' tactical position. Even though the initial military operations were a resounding success, the diplomatic obstacles that were placed in the way provided for an unstable and now rather unclear aftermath. This was all accomplished without apparent direct antagonism, but rather with shrewd diplomacy. Assuming these nations wish to avoid American domination, they will continue to separate themselves from the dollar. This broad separation during 2003–2004 at least raises the possibility of a coordinated maneuver to reduce dollar hegemony.

One key question involves how much inherent weakness in the American economy is perceived by these world leaders. The finance ministers of the European Central Bank (ECB), International Monetary Fund (IMF), and Bank of International Settlement (BIS) have all gone on record with rather scathing criticism of the Bush administration's tax and economic policies.[121, 122] Likewise, Russia, China, and a few other Far Eastern nations have expressed their skepticism through their own recent fiscal policy decisions.[123, 124] This raises the question; did these nations hold a general expectation that the US economy was, or is, heading for a major downfall regardless, thereby eliminating much of the presumed motivation to avoid antagonizing the US?

One of the principle exacerbating issues with Iraq's conundrum is its unemployment rate, estimated to be a stunning 67 percent.[125] Paradoxically, the supposed flood of reconstruction jobs are almost exclusively reserved to non-Iraq/foreign firms, mostly of US origin. The privatization of Iraqi assets is only one component in a long list of colossal failures in the occupation of Iraq.

Another failure was Paul Bremer's decision to fire all 400,000 members of the Iraqi military in the summer of 2003. Did he expect these trained soldiers who suddenly lost their incomes and their pensions to sit quietly at home and wait for "democracy"? Naturally, the Iraqis are doing the same thing they did during the 1920s when they perceived their colonial British occupiers to be plundering their nation's wealth — resist.[126] For many Iraqis, American troops are today's colonial occupiers. Naomi Klein's powerful article, "Baghdad Year Zero," revealed the sentiments inside Iraq — utter frustration and a loss of dignity. Her article included interviews with Iraqis, including Haider al-Abadi, minister of communication, who summarized the problems: "We know that there are terrorists in the country, but previously they were not successful, they were isolated. Now because the whole country is unhappy, and a lot of people don't have jobs ... these terrorists are finding listening ears.[127]

In June 2004 the Bush administration "transferred Iraq's sovereignty" by installing Ayad Allawi as the interim leader, the choice of US/UK governments and the CIA, with no democratic input from the Iraqi people. As an Iraqi exile he spent many years in Britain, including a long history with the CIA-supported Iraqi National Accord. According to a *Guardian* article, in the 1970s he had "close links" to Saddam Hussein's Mukhabarat intelligence agency and was referred to as a "manipulator and by some accounts a brute."[128] The *Guardian* concluded that Allawi "is a symbol of all that has gone wrong in Iraq."[129]

The international blowback stemming from the doctrine of militant imperialism is bolstered by reports of widespread civilian deaths following US military operations within Iraq. Although the following *Reuters* article did not gain mainstream media follow-up, renowned public health scientists have dramatically illustrated the tragic fallacy of "spreading democracy" via military force and occupation:

> 'Making conservative assumptions, we think that about 100,000 excess deaths, or more have happened since the 2003 invasion of Iraq,' researchers from the Johns Hopkins Bloomberg School of Public Health in Baltimore, Maryland, said in a report published online by The [UK] Lancet medical journal.
>
> 'Violence accounted for most of the excess death and air strikes from [US-led] coalition forces accounted for the most violent deaths .... The risk of death from violence in the period after the invasion was 58 times higher than in the period before the war,' Les Roberts and his colleagues said in the report which compared Iraqi deaths during 14.6 months before the invasion and the 17.8 months after it.
>
> 'Most individuals reportedly killed by coalition forces were women and children,' Roberts added.[130]

No Exit Strategy and Imperial Overstretch

We are the strongest nation in the world today. I do not believe we should ever apply that political, economic, [and] military power unilaterally. If we'd followed that rule on Vietnam, we wouldn't have been there. None of our allies supported us; not Japan, not Germany, not Britain or France. If we can't persuade nations of comparable values of the merit of our cause, we'd better reexamine our reasoning.

> — Robert McNamara, former US Secretary of Defense, 1961–1968, as quoted in the 2003 award-winning documentary film, *The Fog of War* [131]

The creation of a well-functioning local secret police [in Iraq], that in effect is a branch of the CIA, is part of the general handover strategy. If you are in control of the secret police in a country then you don't really have to worry too much about who the local council appoints to collect the garbage.

The presence of a powerful secret police, loyal to the Americans, will mean that the new Iraqi political regime will not stray outside the parameters that the US wants to set. To begin with, the new Iraqi government will reign but not rule.

> — John Pike, expert on classified military budgets, Washington-based Global Security organization, April 2004 [132]

Camp Victory North [is] a sprawling base near Baghdad International Airport .... Over the past year, KBR contractors have built a small American city where about 14,000 troops are living, many hunkered down inside sturdy, wooden, air-conditioned bungalows called SEA (for Southeast Asia) huts, replicas of those used by troops in Vietnam. There's a Burger King, a gym, the country's biggest PX — and, of course, a separate compound for KBR workers, who handle both construction and logistical support. Although Camp Victory North remains a work in progress today, when complete, the complex will be twice the size of Camp Bondsteel in Kosovo — currently one of the largest overseas posts built since the Vietnam War.

Such a heavy footprint seems counterproductive, given the growing antipathy felt by most Iraqis toward the U.S. military occupation. Yet Camp Victory North appears to be a harbinger of America's future in Iraq. Over the past year, the Pentagon has reportedly been building up to 14 'enduring' bases across the country — long-term encampments that could house as many as 100,000 troops indefinitely.

— Joshua Hammer, "Digging in: If the US Government Doesn't Plan to Occupy Iraq for Any Longer than Necessary, Why Is It Spending Billions of Dollars to Build 'Enduring' Bases?" *Mother Jones*, March/April 2005[133]

At the wise age of 85, Robert McNamara, the controversial secretary of defense during the Vietnam War, reflected on those turbulent events and advised that if your allies do not support you, be prepared to "reexamine your reasoning." Regardless of the Iraqi people's quest for self-determination, the neoconservatives plan to keep 100,000 or more US troops stationed *permanently* inside Iraq. The evidence is clear: US contractors were given $4.5 billion to rapidly build 14 large military bases inside Iraq, which the Pentagon refers to in their Orwellian terms as "enduring camps." The neoconservative policy paper published in September 2000, "Rebuilding America's Defenses," explicitly stated their goals regarding new military bases regardless of whether Saddam Hussein remained in power: "While the unresolved conflict with Iraq provides the immediate justification, the need for a substantial American force presence in the Gulf transcends the issue of the regime of Saddam Hussein."[134] The Project for a New American Century further advocated this doctrine: "And even should US-Iranian relations improve, retaining forward-based forces in the region would still be an essential element in US security strategy given the longstanding American interests in the region."[135]

Despite proclamations of progress in Iraq, the escalating levels of violence, massive civilian deaths, and destruction of property (including the complete destruction of Falluja and a significant portion of Najif), the slogans of "spreading democracy" appear to many Iraqis and informed observers as both farcical and hypocritical. Perhaps US policy-makers should heed the warning of another individual tested in times of war, Winston Churchill: "Never, never, never believe any war will be smooth and easy," and that statesman who gives into "war fever [becomes] the slave of unforeseeable and uncontrollable events."[136]

Have we forgotten the history lessons provided by the most recent attempted colonial occupation of central Asia? December 24, 1979, can be viewed as one of the pivotal events that initiated the end of the Soviet Empire. On that Christmas Eve, Soviet soldiers entered Afghanistan to crush what they regarded as anti-Soviet, Islamist "terrorists" who were interfering with its nominally Marxist-Leninist government. Soviet political leaders and military commanders expected that operations in Afghanistan would be over in a "matter of months."

Not surprisingly the unpredictable reality of warfare and its outcomes were once again recorded in the history books. Ten years later, the last of the demoralized soldiers from the Soviet Union withdrew from a completely devastated Afghanistan. While there are different variables, the Soviet experience there provided some unfortunate parallels to what the US military and policymakers are facing in the occupation of Iraq. The facts on the ground in Iraq today suggest that the US-led invasion has produced unforeseeable and uncontrollable events that are replete in the history of modern warfare.

The unraveling inside Iraq was apparent within months of the invasion. In 2003 it was repeatedly claimed that, once Saddam Hussein was captured or killed, the attacks on US troops would dissipate, and the mysteriously missing "vast stockpiles" of WMD material, including evidence of a reconstituted nuclear weapon program, would be found. In reality, after Saddam Hussein's capture in December 2003, attacks by insurgents increased, no WMD stockpiles were found, and the original rationale for war was transferred to a desperate and Orwellian claim of "spreading democracy" — by using military force.

The June 2004 transfer of "sovereignty" fooled no one. According to the *Asia Times*, most Shi'ite voters in the January 2005 election "thought they were voting for the US to leave, for good."[137] Considering that polls show 80 percent of the Iraqi people want US troops and associated contractors to leave immediately, a *real* democracy in Iraq would not likely sign any SOFA (Status of Force Agreement) that allows permanent US basing in Iraq.[138] As of early 2005 this politically explosive issue of the legal status of US garrisons inside Iraq remains unresolved, but the Pentagon seems determined to keep 120,000 troops there "until 2007" even if a new Iraqi government demanded withdrawal.[139]

Presumably a democratic Iraq would also have some say in economic issues and naturally seek to keep much of Iraq's oil industry nationalized in an effort to retain the critical profits, thereby facilitating the reconstruction of its infrastructure, healthcare, and education systems. However, this is the exact *opposite* of what the Bush administration and its major campaign contributors vigorously pursued under the tenure of Paul Bremer, former pro-consul of the Coalition Provisional Authority (CPA).[140]

Therein lies the paradox for the United States: in a *true democracy* Iraq's leader would be expected to do what is in the best interest of the majority of Iraqi citizens, regardless of whether they are Shi'ite, Sunni, or Kurdish. From a purely objective perspective, it would have been economically advantageous for a sovereign Iraqi government to request oil sales in the currency that provided the most purchasing power for rebuilding its country — which, given valuations now and into the foreseeable future, implies the euro.

Fatefully, US military personnel are currently facing the same bleak situation that Soviet forces faced in their 10-year occupation of Afghanistan. US policy-makers must begin taking into account the harsh reality on the ground in Iraq, which includes the emergence of a vast resistance movement, ongoing guerilla warfare in most population centers, and the complete loss of "moral legitimacy" in the fallout of the Abu Gharib prison scandal.

Without a fundamental change in US leadership and global strategy, historians may ultimately regard March 19, 2003, as a tragic event that ended the admiration and prominence of America. The only way to prevent this would require the US government to immediately change current foreign policies, energy policies, and domestic fiscal policies. The US military's "imperial overstretch" and associated budget and trade deficits clearly preclude the pursuit of continued occupation of Iraq without the support of the international community.

Contributors to this book believe that unless drastic actions are taken immediately to reverse the policies of the neoconservatives, the ultimate outcome of Operation Iraqi Freedom may be the same as Operation Ajax — an oppressive US-puppet government that radicalizes the population and produces a rigid, quasi-theocratic government that becomes staunchly anti-Western. The imperial conquest of Iraq may turn what was previously the most secular society of the Middle East oil-producing states into a modern-day Islamic theocracy.

This analysis was echoed during a meeting at the New American Foundation in Washington. Brent Scowcroft, national security advisor under President George H.W. Bush, and Zbigniew Brzezinski, President Carter's national security advisor, both stated in January 2005 that the Iraq crisis required a completely new strategy. Scowcroft recommended that Iraq be turned over to NATO or the UN, because they would not be "so hostilely viewed" by Iraqis. Brzezinski bluntly stated, "I do not think we can stay in Iraq in the fashion we're in now. If it cannot be changed drastically, it should be terminated."[141] He also said it would take 500,000 troops, $500 billion, and the resumption of a (US) military draft to ensure "adequate security" in Iraq. I concur with Brzezinski's analysis: the most "optimistic outcome" in Iraq at this point will be a Shi'ite-dominated theocracy.[142] At present, only enlightened US leadership willing to engage in concessions with the other industrialized nations, along with a multilateral handover to the UN and NATO, could possibly mitigate the US quagmire in Iraq. Considering Bush's unique inability to admit to making mistakes, this compromise appears rather doubtful.

The only way Washington can safely extract itself and the US troops from Iraq is by multilateral compromise on a broad scale. This would likely involve negotiations concerning some of the prewar oil exploration contracts and a carefully crafted compromise regarding the petrodollar

The only way Washington can safely extract itself and the US troops from Iraq is by multilateral compromise on a broad scale.

versus petroeuro currency issue. To begin salvaging the Iraq crisis, the US government will likely need to concede several prewar oil exploration and lease contracts to the French, Russian, and Chinese oil companies. In exchange these countries' governments would need to formally commit significant financial and technical resources to a large UN-sponsored alternative energy consortium, discussed in subsequent chapters.

Some will describe these recommendations as strategic capitulation, but pragmatic compromise is required at this junction, given the US debt levels and near-universal antagonistic feelings toward the US military presence in Iraq. The facts before, during, and after the Iraq War show that the real victims of this tragic hubris are the US and UK soldiers and Iraqi civilians — who have all suffered terribly under misguided geostrategic policies and the untenable dream of a US global empire.

> It is the absolute right of the State to supervise the formation of public opinion.
>
> If you tell a lie big enough and keep repeating it, people will eventually come to believe it.
>
> The lie can be maintained only for such time as the State can shield the people from the political, economic and/or military consequences of the lie. It thus becomes vitally important for the State to use all of its powers to repress dissent, for the truth is the mortal enemy of the lie, and thus by extension, the truth is the greatest enemy of the State.
>
> — Joseph Goebbels, German Minister for Public Enlightenment and Propaganda, 1933–1945

> If tyranny and oppression come to this land, it will be in the guise of fighting a foreign enemy.
>
> — James Madison, United States Congressman

Five

Dollar Dilemma: Why Petrodollar Hegemony Is Unsustainable

'In the future the euro is (going to be) taking a place in the international markets in general as the money of exchange.' Asked if a switch to pricing oil in euros was possible, 'Of course, in the oil market and in any market. It's a stable and a strong currency, the role of the euro is going to be increased step by step. It's normal.'

— Loyola de Palacio, European Energy Commissioner,
June 2003[1]

Prewar Momentum toward a Petroeuro

The [Iraqi] cabinet has decided to assign a committee of economists with the task of seriously studying the possibility of using the euro or any other currency instead of the dollar in the commercial transactions of our foreign contracts. The dollar is one of the levers of our enemy's influence and power on both regional and international levels.

— The Iraqi News Agency, quoting a statement by the
cabinet after a meeting chaired by President Saddam Hussein,
September 14, 2000[2]

On Sept. 24, 2000, the regime of Saddam Hussein stunned the world after a routine cabinet meeting by announcing that it would no longer accept dollars for oil being sold under the UN Oil for Food program. All oil sales were to be paid for in euros. A government statement said the move was to confront the "daily American-Zionist aggression," an apparent reference to support for UN sanctions. The Iraqi move did little to hurt the US economy. It paid off for Iraq when the euro appreciated by 30%.

— Robert Block, the *Wall Street Journal*, April 15, 2003[3]

The European Parliament ... calls on the EU, in dialogue with the OPEC and non-OPEC countries, to prepare the way for payment for oil in euros.

— European Parliament resolution on the Communication
from the Commission on the European Union's oil supply,
June 14, 2001[4]

In May 1999, the EU and Russia began discussing the adoption of the euro for oil and gas sales.[5] While discussions at that time did not result in formal policy changes, by 2004 Russia had agreed to sell its natural gas to Germany priced in the euro and is considering the possibility of a petroeuro pricing arrangement with the EU nations.

EU leaders on Thursday made an audacious bid to lure Russia away from its reliance on the greenback, calling on Moscow to start accepting euros instead of dollars for its exports, dangling the attractive carrot of a boom in investment and trade .... Russia currently receives dollars for its European oil and gas exports, but the EU wants to switch to euros instead. A joint communique has been signed by both sides agreeing to discuss the issue in further detail.[6]

Dollar hegemony and, by extension, petrodollar recycling are not unstainable given the economic and political forces created early in this new century.

The euro has become accepted as a global competitor to the US dollar for rather straightforward reasons: the US trade and budget deficits are inferior to the EU's; the US savings rate is abysmally low when compared to the EU; and the enlarged EU represents an economy almost as large as that of the US. Lastly, in general, the European Central Bank (ECB) pursues monetary policies that control the expansion of the money supply, whereas the Federal Reserve continues to print dollars with wild abandonment. Subsequently, the euro is valued higher than the dollar.

Given the continuing devaluation of the dollar, pressure is building within OPEC to switch to the euro. The central impediment is that all three internationally traded crude oil pricing "markers" are currently denominated in dollars. Despite this technical obstacle, news stories before the Iraq War portrayed an active debate regarding the plausibility of a euro-denominated oil transaction system.

In 2002 Iran introduced a proposal to receive payments for crude oil sales to Europe in euros instead of US dollars. According to Iranian sources, this decision was "based primarily on economics, but politics are still likely to be a factor in any decision ... as Iran uses the opportunity to hit back at the US government, which recently labeled it part of an 'axis of evil.'"[7] An Iranian parliamentary representative was quoted as saying "There is a very good chance MPs will agree to this idea .... Now that the euro is stronger, it is more logical."[8]

Interestingly, Venezuela's ambassador to Russia, Francisco Mieres-Lopez, floated the idea of switching to the euro as their oil currency standard approximately one year before the April 2002 coup attempt against Hugo Chavez.[9] Although the coup collapsed after two days with Chavez being restored to power, various reports suggested that the CIA, and a rather embarrassed Bush administration, had met with civilian and military coup plotters and had likely supported Chavez's overthrow.[10]

Following the 2003 Iraq War, several articles appeared on European, Canadian, and Asian media websites that illustrated active discussion within OPEC concerning the possibility of pricing oil in a basket of currencies, including the dollar and the euro. While present on the Internet, these stories about a potential petroeuro were again conspicuously missing from the five corporate-controlled US media conglomerates.

OPEC Statements Regarding a Petroeuro

In the long-term, perhaps one question that comes to mind is could a dual system operate simultaneously? Could one pricing system apply to the Western Hemisphere in dollars and for the rest of the world in euros .... Should the euro challenge the dollar in strength, which essentially could include it in the denomination of the oil bill, it could be that a system may emerge which benefits more countries in the long-term.

— Javad Yarjani, Head of OPEC's Petroleum Market
Analysis Department, in a speech to Spanish officials,
April 2002[11]

In April 2002 Javad Yarjani gave a speech entirely devoted to the dollar and the euro in the international oil trade business. He candidly provided insights into the conditions that would create additional momentum within OPEC to include the euro as an alternative transaction currency in the international "oil bill."

Yarjani's words warrant careful consideration given that two of the variables required for a currency switch have taken place since 2002. Too many US economic pundits have imprudently dismissed the idea of the petroeuro; however, as Yarjani said:

> The question that comes to mind is whether the euro will establish itself in world financial markets, thus challenging the supremacy of the US dollar, and consequently trigger a change in the dollar's dominance in oil markets. As we all know, the mighty dollar has reigned supreme since 1945 …. Having said that … in the long run the euro is not at such a disadvantage versus the dollar when one compares the relative sizes of the economies involved, especially given the EU enlargement plans. *Moreover, the Euro-zone has a bigger share of global trade than the and while the has a huge current account deficit, the euro area has a more, or balanced, external accounts position [sic] … looking at the statistics of crude oil exports, one notes that the Euro-zone is an even larger importer of oil and petroleum products than the US.*
>
> From the EU's point of view, it is clear that Europe would prefer to see payments for oil shift from the dollar to the euro, which effectively removes the currency risk …. There is also very strong trade links between OPEC Member Countries (MCs) and the Euro-zone, with more than 45 percent of total merchandise imports of OPEC MCs coming from the countries of the Euro-zone …. Of major importance to the ultimate success of the euro, in terms of the oil pricing, will be *if Europe's two major oil producers — the United Kingdom and Norway join the single currency ….* This might create a momentum to shift the oil pricing system to euros.
>
> In the short-term, OPEC MCs, with possibly a few exceptions, are expected to continue to accept payment in dollars …. In the long-term, perhaps one question that comes to mind is *could a*

dual system operate simultaneously? Could one pricing system apply to the Western Hemisphere in dollars and for the rest of the world in euros? .... Should the euro challenge the dollar in strength, which essentially could include it in the denomination of the oil bill, it could be that a system may emerge which benefits more countries in the long-term .... Time may be on your side.[12] [emphasis added]

Indeed, OPEC's move toward the euro will likely continue, considering the EU's successful expansion in May 2004. The inclusion of ten additional member states resulted in an aggregate GDP increase from approximately $7 trillion to $9.6 trillion. The EU is now an oil-consuming purchasing population 33 percent larger than the US', and it is projected that over half of OPEC crude oil is now exported to the EU–25. This excludes other potential EU/euro entrants, such as the UK, Norway, Denmark, and Sweden. Additionally, since late 2002 the euro has been trading above the US dollar, with predictions that the dollar will continue its downward trend relative to the euro in 2005 and beyond. Current US trade and budget deficits will not be quickly reversed, especially given the ideological tax cuts passed by the Bush administration.

OPEC and US Dollar Devaluation

[Dr. Mojarrad implied] the switch to the euro, which as done during the last few months had helped [Iran] to negate the effects of a depreciating dollar and falling international oil prices. He said that if the country had continued its receipts in dollars, it would have meant large losses, which would have translated into domestic inflation.

This was because large volumes of its imports are ... sourced from Europe. The Iranian central bank was keen to avert that situation and had consequently adopted the euro-denominated payments to ensure that the losses were minimised. The country had also resorted to managing its reserves to minimize the effects of the depreciating dollar.

— C. Shivkumar, the *Hindu Business Line*, June 2003[13]

Oil exporters have sharply reduced their exposure to the dollar over the past three years, according to data from the Bank for International Settlements. Members of [OPEC] have *cut the proportion of deposits held in dollars from 75 per cent in the third quarter of 2001 to 61.5 percent* [by the 3rd quarter of 2004].

Middle Eastern central banks have reportedly switched reserves from dollars to euros and sterling *to avoid incurring losses*

*as the dollar has fallen and prepare for a shift away from pricing oil
exports in dollars alone.* [emphasis added]

— Steve Johnson and Javier Blas, *Financial Times*,
December 2004[14]

A particularly distinctive analysis of OPEC oil-pricing trends was provided by
James Turk, founder of www.goldmoney.com. Using data from the US
Department of Commerce's report, "US International Trade in Goods and
Services," he calculated the euro's average exchange rate with the dollar from
2001 to 2003 in relation to oil prices. While certainly not conclusive, his analysis implied that OPEC may be, at least *tacitly*, pricing oil in the euro due to
its relative stability. The following table is from Turk's article.

Column (4) illustrates that from 2001 to 2003 the price of imported oil
rose from $21.40 to $26.97. This 26-percent increase is commensurate with
the dollar's decline relative to the euro over the same period. This analysis's
most fascinating aspect is that column (6) showed the price of crude oil in
terms of the euro had remained essentially unchanged during this time. Based
on this simple chart, it appears that OPEC may have used an implicit policy
to price crude oil around €24 per barrel during 2001 to 2003. Perhaps this
is a coincidence, or perhaps a conspiracy within OPEC to maintain their purchasing power given the dollar's decline. However, as Turk stated:

> It does not seem logical that this result is pure coincidence. It is
> more likely the result of purposeful design, namely, that OPEC is
> mindful of the dollar's decline and increases the dollar price of its
> crude oil by an amount that offsets the loss in purchasing power
> OPEC's members would otherwise incur. In short, OPEC is pro-
> tecting its purchasing power as the dollar declines.[16]

US Imports of Crude oil					
(1)	(2)	(3)	(4)	(5)	(6)
Year	Quantity (thousands of barrels)	Value (thousands of US dollars)	Unit price (US dollars)	Average daily US$ per € exchange rate	Unit price (euros)
2001	3,471,066	74,292,894	$21.40	0.8952	€23.91
2002	3,418,021	77,283,329	$22.61	0.9454	€23.92
2003	3,673,596	99,094,675	$26.97	1.1321	€23.82

5.1: *US imports of crude oil — 2001–2003*
Source: James Turk, "OPEC Has Already Turned to the Euro."[15]

Figure 5.1 also shows that US imports of crude oil rose by $25 billion from 2001 to 2003, adding to the US trade deficit. In 2004 the US trade deficit was $665 billion, a staggering increase over 2003's trade deficit of $489 billion. In 2003 crude oil imports represented 20.2 percent of the deficit. If other energy-related petroleum products are included, this grows to 26.5 percent.[17] Moreover, these trends are accelerating. Through November 2004 US oil imports were already $119 billion, a whopping rise of $20 billion over 2003. The huge price increase of imported oil contributed in large part to the $176 billion rise in the US trade deficit from 2003 to 2004.

Turk's analysis has important implications, as it shows that a weakening dollar has actually *increased* the US trade deficit due to our excessive energy consumption. As long as the US continues to consume enormous levels of petroleum imports, it is not plausible that a weakened dollar will significantly reduce its trade deficit. Secondly, the dollar's supremacy for oil pricing is now at risk. In other words, for the first time since World War II, US consumers are no longer immune to effects of *currency risk* regarding international oil/ energy purchases.

This information provides further evidence that momentum away from the dollar since 2002 reflects the world's growing dissatisfaction with the Bush administration's ideologically driven economic and tax policies. Despite the quasi-mystical claims from "economic fundamentalists" such as Vice President Cheney, who after being informed by former US Treasury Secretary O'Neill that a growing budget deficit for 2003 was threatening the US economy, cut him off and proclaimed, "Reagan proved that deficits don't matter."[18] Based on an analysis of the dollar's steep declines in the wake of huge tax cuts from 2001 and 2003 — obviously *US deficits do matter*.

Likewise, many US economic commentators and the media punditry in general seem to fall into the *non sequitur trap* of assuming the benefits of both an appreciated and a depreciated US dollar without accounting for the drawbacks of either. One cannot assume the benefits of a weak dollar (trade advantage, modest inflation) while retaining those of a strong dollar (asset values, buying power). One must acknowledge the drawbacks of a declining dollar — capital flight and reduced consumption — alongside the benefits. The idea that a cheaper dollar significantly helps US trade exports is more mythical than realistic. The reason is simple: considering that trade now accounts for less than 10 percent of the American economy, declines in the US dollar are quite marginal from a macro perspective and do not result in comparable declines in imports.

In 2004 several surprising stories appeared in the foreign media that addressed the complex issues of OPEC's momentum toward a potential petroeuro, giving further credence to Turk's theory that OPEC may be tacitly pricing oil in the euro. The following commentary from February 2004 reinforced this assertion:

The average price for the Organization of Petroleum Exporting Countries' basket of seven benchmark crudes slipped by 8¢ to $30.44/bbl Thursday.

'The value of the OPEC basket has been above the $22–28 target range for 108 trading days over the past 8 months,' Horsnell noted. 'Over the same period, the value of the OPEC basket in euros has stayed within a 22–28 euros band on all but 2 trading days, and on those 2 days it was below the band.'

He said, 'This is of course just a rather bizarre statistical coincidence. It certainly does not imply that the target band has been secretly switched into euros or that the dollar has lost its primacy in the oil market.'[19]

Whether this observation was a "bizarre statistical coincidence" or purposeful design, it is clear that OPEC members are trying to maintain their purchasing power in the face of a devalued dollar. The question is, can OPEC be motivated to continue pricing oil exclusively in dollars if under threat from neoconservative unilateralism, or will they gradually move toward a formal euro pricing mechanism? The likely answer to that question was addressed in the following excerpt from a Toronto newspaper, the *Globe and Mail*, in January 2004:

OPEC is considering a move away from using the US dollar — and to the euro — to set its price targets for crude oil, the highest-profile manifestation of the debilitating effect of depreciation on the greenback's standing as the currency of international commerce.

Several members of the Organization of Petroleum Exporting Countries are seeking formal talks on using the euro, as well as the US dollar, when determining price targets for crude, a senior oil minister within the cartel said Monday. 'There are countries that are proposing this,' Venezuela's Oil Minister Rafael Ramirez said in Caracas. 'It's out there, under discussion.'

Mr. Ramirez did not specify which OPEC members are pushing the proposal, but much of the impetus is believed to come from Persian Russian Gulf producers.[20]

As a follow-up to Turk's analysis, I conducted a similar currency comparison of the average price of crude oil for 2004 (through November 2004, using the most current data).

Based on this estimation from 2003 to (November) 2004, the average US price of imported oil increased by 27 percent (from $26.97 to $34.27 per barrel), which is greater than the dollar's 17-percent drop in value relative to the euro during this period (a drop of 20 percent by December 2004). Note that the average price of imported oil for the first 11 months of 2004 was

2004 US Imports of Crude oil					
Year * (*through November)	Quantity (thousands of barrels)	Value (thousands of US dollars)	Unit price (US dollars)	Average daily US$ per € exchange rate	Unit price (euros)
2004	3,499,471	119,939,861	$34.27	1.3007	€26.35

5.2: US imports of crude oil — 2004 Source: United States Census[21]

€26.35 per barrel, representing a 30-percent lower price relative to the average price in dollars. Despite its agreement in 2000 for $22 to $28 per barrel pricing band, OPEC may be attempting to retain its purchasing power by using an *undeclared* euro pricing band of approximately €24 to €28. In essence, it appears the euro might have gained primacy in the oil market due to its relative *stability* over the dollar.

Additionally, the November 2004 Center of American Progress's study of the dollar, euro, and price of crude oil illustrated that oil prices and the dollar's valuation are now moving in the *opposite direction*. The economist who analysed this reached the same conclusion previously noted:

> To compensate for this loss of buying power, [oil producers] may have raised the dollar price for oil. As a result, *while oil prices in dollars rose by 162 percent from their low point in January 2002, they climbed by less than half that rate measured in euros, 77 percent.* At that rate, oil prices would have only risen to $34 per barrel in October 2004, instead of the actual $52, without changes in the dollar's value.[22][emphasis added]

Since 2002–2003, American energy consumers have felt the effects of higher oil prices far more than EU consumers. This is the opposite of what one would expect if OPEC were pricing oil trades solely on the US dollar. While it is very doubtful that all ten OPEC countries (excluding Iraq) would voluntarily choose to abandon the dollar completely, it is increasingly likely that they, along with Russia, will continue to pursue methods to retain their holdings by shifting currencies in their central banks, increasing the price within the pricing band, or formally denominating oil sales in a basket of currencies.

OPEC contemplated this last option early as the 1970s, following the collapse of the Bretton Woods Agreement, and ongoing macroeconomic trends will result in a formal announcement to price oil in a basket of currencies.[23] The dollar's accelerating decline makes this inevitable. This is yet another reason why reducing excessive consumption and subsequently the level of imported energy is in the long-term economic and national security interests of the US.

International Blowback Against the Dollar?

> The Saudis are holding the line on oil prices in OPEC and should they, for example, go along with the rest of the OPEC people in demanding that oil be priced in euros, that would deal a very heavy blow to the American economy.
>
> — Yosef Ibrahim, Managing Director of the Strategic Energy Investment Group in Dubai and member of the US Council on Foreign Relations, as reported in the *Observer* (UK), February 2003[24]

> There is no pressing need to replace the dollar with the Euro but those countries that lose out when the dollar is weak might want to have an alternative to a 100% exposure to US dollars. However, the complex system of trading and pricing that is already in place is not going to be revolutionized on a whim. Anti-American sentiment might equally be a spur to change, *especially if some of the major producers and exporters begin to see the US as an unsafe pair of hands with rogue unilateral policies. Threatening a switch might become a novel way of limiting the worst excesses of neo-conservatism.* [emphasis added]
>
> — Allison Mitchell, "OPEC and the Euro," February 2004[25]

> "Down with America .... Euro yes! Dollar no!"
>
> — Chants of an anti-war street protest in Nigeria, as witnessed by Robert Block, reporter for the *Wall Street Journal,* 2003[26]

This broad movement away from the dollar does not appear to be based purely on the structural imbalances of the US economy, as it has carried a trade account deficit every year since 1989. Massive deficit spending was tolerated in the early years of the Reagan administration — but of course, the US was still the world's largest creditor then. It is now the world's largest debtor.

Tragically, the arrogance of the current Bush administration with its strange avocation for unilateral warfare, along with the dismissal of various international accords and apparent disregard for international law, have created tremendous international blowback. This rapid deterioration of US international stature is apparent in global surveys of both "friendly" and "hostile" nations.[27] The consequences of this blowback is likely manifested with the systemic drawback from the dollar. During 2003 governments in Asia, Russia, and Canada all significantly reduced their dollar holdings.[28, 29, 30] Despite the lack of media coverage, these dramatic movements away from the US dollar on the eve of the Iraq War were widespread. Joseph Quinlan, a global economist with John Hopkins University, summarized these risks just before the outbreak of the war:

"Today if you have the US acting [in Iraq] against world opinion, there could be an even faster pullback out of dollar-denominated assets .... How we go to war influences the rate of decline of the dollar."[31]

Unlike 1991's Desert Storm, the early tactical "victory" in Iraq has not led to any increases in the dollar's value. In fact, the war accelerated its downward trend — especially among the OPEC oil producers. History has shown that opposing geopolitical alliances will form when an empire begins excessive military adventurism, and the openly stated neoconservative goal of US global domination will naturally be resisted by other powerful nations. The following quote summarized the risks inherent to neoconservative doctrine:

> Unlike 1991's Desert Storm, the early tactical "victory" in Iraq has not led to any increases in the dollar's value.

> One of the dirty little secrets of today's international order is that the rest of the globe could topple the United States from its hegemonic state whenever they so choose with a concerted abandonment of the dollar standard. This is America's preeminent, inescapable Achilles Heel for now and the foreseeable future.
>
> That such a course hasn't been pursued to date bears more relation to the fact that other Westernized, highly developed nations haven't any interest to undergo the great disruptions which would follow — but it could assuredly take place in the event that the consensus view coalesces of the United States as any sort of 'rogue' nation — in other words, if the dangers of American global hegemony are ever perceived as a greater liability than the dangers of toppling the international order. The Bush administration and the neoconservative movement have set out on a multiple-front course to ensure that this cannot take place, in brief by a graduated assertion of military hegemony atop the existent economic hegemony.
>
> — Anonymous former US government employee[32]

In April 2003 *Bloomberg News* reported that Indonesia, a small non-OPEC oil exporter with a Muslim majority, was evaluating a petroeuro. As the article below illustrated, the political fallout from the Iraq invasion was not limited to Europe.

> Pertamina, Indonesia's state oil company, dropped a bombshell recently. It's considering dropping the US dollar for the euro in its oil and gas trades.
>
> Other Asian countries may not be far behind any move in Indonesia to dump the dollar. The reasons for this are economic and political, and they could trigger a realignment that undermines US bond and stock markets over time.[33]

Additional articles have suggested that other countries such as Malaysia may drop the dollar in favor of the euro. Incidentally, the final "axis of evil" country, North Korea, officially dropped the dollar and began using euros for trade, effective December 7, 2002.[34] Unlike OPEC producers, North Korea's switch will have negligible economic impact, but it illustrated the geopolitical fallout of Bush's harsh rhetoric. In fact, it appears that a disconcerting "anti-dollar" movement could be spreading in Asia and perhaps Africa. Indeed, in 2003 a *Wall Street Journal* reporter witnessed an unusual anti-war protest in Nigeria, an OPEC member that could become another target in the "war on terror" if the euro were adopted as their oil export currency.

> "European countries," preached Shiek Ibrahim Umar Kabo, the head of Nigeria's Council of Muslim Scholars, "have refused to be fooled by America" and support the war. "We should therefore encourage transactions with the euro and stop patronizing the American dollar."
>
> The sheik's advice was met with cries of "Down with America." The enthusiasm spilled out into the streets with the faithful shouting, "Euro yes! Dollar no!"
>
> Shiek Ibrahim said the dollar boycott was, in his opinion, "the most effective means of peaceful protest available to bring the US back to its senses." He insisted that the ploy could slow down the American economy and "may even lead to its collapse."[35]

Certainly one of the most troubling pieces of news regarding the dollar/euro issues and the political fallout from the Iraq War relates to Russia. In mid-October 2003, after meeting with German Chancellor Schroeder, Russian President Putin mentioned that Russian oil sales could be redenominated in euros.

> "We do not rule out that it is possible. That would be interesting for our European partners," Putin said.
>
> A move by Russia, as the world's second largest oil exporter, to trade oil in euros, could provoke a chain reaction among other oil producers currently mulling a switch and would further boost the euro's gradually growing share of global currency reserves.[36]

Yosef Ibrahim, the managing director of the Strategic Energy Investment Group in Dubai and a member of the US Council on Foreign Relations, stated that Saddam Hussein's switch to the euro for Iraqi oil trades '*was another reason [why the US attacked]* . There is a great political dimension to this. Slowly *more power and muscle is moving from the United States to the EU, and that's mainly because of what happened in Iraq.*'[37][emphasis added]

Further evidence that Russia is gravitating toward a petroeuro system was provided by Lukoil vice president Leonid Fedun, who stated that the transaction cost for the switch would be minimal at just 0.08 percent.[38] Fedun said,

'There is no problem .... If the state decides to do this, then we will support this initiative. From the point of view of the [Russian] economy, there's no difference.'[39]

This *Moscow Times* article included comments from Yevgeny Gavrilenkov, chief economist at Troika Dialog, stating that debate is growing on a move toward the euro as Russia mulls siding with the EU: "Such an idea is really possible. Why not? More than half of Russia's oil trade is with Europe. But there will be great opposition to this from the United States."[40]

The proposition that Russia, the second-largest oil exporter in the world, switching to the euro will be met with "great opposition" from the US is an understatement. Nevertheless, according to the same article, from a purely monetary and trade perspective this Russian switch appears logical. Obviously the US government would prefer that Russia sell its oil in dollars or a dual currency arrangement, as opposed to a single currency, petroeuro oil-trading system.

The Saudi Question: The Sword of Damocles

Damocles — in classical mythology, courtier at the court of Dionysius I. He so persistently praised the power and happiness of Dionysius that the tyrant, in order to show the precariousness of rank and power, gave a banquet and had a sword suspended above the head of Damocles by a single hair. Hence the expression "the sword of Damocles" to mean an ever-present peril.

— Columbia Encyclopedia, Sixth Edition, 2005.

Though it was less concerned with the secrecy of Arab investments, the CIA concurred that OPEC money continued to have a great potential for disrupting markets if an Arab government became displeased with US policy. [The CIA report stated] 'Temporary dislocation of international financial markets would ensue, if the Saudi Arabian government ever chose to use its accumulated wealth as a political weapon.' [emphasis added]

— CIA memo "Saudi Arabian Foreign Investment", marked "Secret, Not Releasable to Foreign Nationals," reviewed for declassification in May 1985, as noted in David Spiro's book, *The Hidden Hand of American Hegemony*[41]

Saudi Arabia's Prince Muhammad Bin-Turki Bin-Abdallah Bin-Abd-al-Rahman said ... rather than resorting to an [oil] embargo ... he argues that a more effective punishment for the United States, Israel's principal source of financial and political support, *would be to change the currency in which oil is traded from the dollar to the euro, something that Iraq has already done.* This option, he said, is a strategic and rational one, compared with cutting off production, and it is purely commercial. The Arab countries have the right to choose the currency, just as it is the right of consumer countries to choose to deal with oil-exporting countries. [emphasis added]

— "Protest by Switching Oil Trade from Dollar to Euro,"
Oil and Gas International, (US), April 15, 2002[42]

In the aftermath of the September 11, 2001 attacks, several little-noticed news stories appeared in which former FBI counterterrorism agents publicly stated that investigations into Al Qaeda-financed terrorism had been systematically thwarted under both the Clinton and George W. Bush administrations.[43] The FBI showed the principal financiers of Osama bin Laden to be wealthy members of the Saudi elite. The first foreign leader to meet with Bush after 9/11 was French President Chirac, who handed him a detailed French report of Osama bin Laden's financial network. It was "The Economic Network of the bin Laden Family" by Jean-Charles Brisard.[44]

According to Brisard, who interviewed FBI agent John P. O'Neill just two months before the 9/11 attacks, FBI investigations of Osama bin Laden's network were thwarted due to bin Laden's close ties to "high-ranking personalities and families of the Saudi Kingdom."[45] Following the 1998 East African Embassy bombings, O'Neill became the FBI's foremost Osama bin Laden hunter, and he reportedly told Brisard that "All of the answers, all of the clues allowing us to dismantle Osama bin Laden's organization, can be found in Saudi Arabia," emphasizing the "inability of American diplomacy to get anything out of King Fahd" concerning terrorist networks. The reason? There was only one: *corporate oil interests.*[46] [emphasis added] Other FBI agents, including Robert Wright and Sibel Edmonds, also claimed that their blocked investigations showed the principal financiers of Osama bin Laden were often in the Saudi elite.[47]

Since at least 1996, the evidence suggests that the Radical Fundamentalist Unit and its associated UBL (Usama bin Laden) unit at the FBI headquarters systematically blocked various FBI field agents from pursuing links between Islamist terrorists and their Saudi financiers.[48] The question remains: why did successive US administrations block FBI investigations into bin Laden? Perhaps because, in essence, Saudi Arabia *is the principal enabler* of the petrodollar recycling system — thus it holds the sword of Damocles over dollar supremacy.

As the CIA memo warned, OPEC money flows, and in particular the Saudi Arabian government, could use its "accumulated wealth as a political weapon [if it] became displeased with US policy."[49] A Saudi strategy of showing its displeasure at the

> Since at least 1996, the evidence suggests that the Radical Fundamentalist Unit and its associated UBL (Usama bin Laden) unit at the FBI headquarters systematically blocked various FBI field agents from pursuing links between Islamist terrorists and their Saudi financiers.

US would likely be conducted economically, not via the often-mentioned, but illogical, claim of an oil embargo. We learned from the oil shocks of the 1970s that oil is a tangible asset and its price depends on overall supply, not necessarily determined by a particular supplier. A more likely "anti-US" strategy could include pulling the monetary plug on the petrodollar system. Statements by the former US ambassador to Saudi Arabia hint that some may question why they should be "so kind" to the US in pricing oil exclusively in the dollar.

> One of the major things the Saudis have historically done, in part out of friendship with the United States, is to insist that oil continues to be priced in dollars. Therefore, the US Treasury can print money and buy oil, which is an advantage no other country has. With the emergence of other currencies and with strains in the relationship, I wonder whether there will not again be, as there have been in the past, people in Saudi Arabia who raise the question of why they should be so kind to the United States.[50]

It is doubtful that US Congress members at this committee meeting missed the subtle warning that was carefully articulated about petrodollars versus petroeuros. In December 2004 the Bank of International Settlements (BIS) stated that, in spite of oil prices increasing 85 percent from 2001 to 2004, overall OPEC bank deposits barely rose. The BIS report noted this unusual phenomenon, "Oil reserves have not been channeled into the international banking system in the most recent cycle."[51]

In January 2005, an article on a Middle East Finance and Economy website was succinctly entitled, "Saudi Sees Stronger Euro Role."[52] This one-paragraph story hinted that Saudi Arabia's central bank expects the euro to "play a greater role in currency reserves in the future." In somewhat cryptic language, it reported that Hamad Saud Al Sayyari, the governor of the Saudi Arabian Monetary Agency, implied it did not matter which currency oil is priced in, but he wanted stability in prices.[53]

If true, this nuanced statement may confirm an active discussion within Saudi Arabia regarding a potential switch to a petroeuro. If the regime made such a transition, the neoconservatives would likely transfer the "war on terror" directly to Saudi Arabia. Equally foreboding are significant monetary shifts in reserve funds away from the dollar toward the euro in various industrialized nations. Economist Hazel Henderson outlined the potential outcomes of the current US strategy of global domination. She cited US military overreach and a domestic failure to effectively switch to renewable energy sources, among other factors, concluding:

> The result of this scenario? The USA could no longer run its huge current account trade deficits or continue to wage open-ended

global war on terrorism or evil. The USA ceases pursuing unilateralist policies. A new US administration begins to return to its multilateralist tradition, ceases its obstruction and rejoins the UN and pursues more realistic international cooperation.[54]

If OPEC and other governments continue to perceive the euro as a highly appreciated and more stable currency due to the EU's balanced budget and trade accounts, why would the US dollar retain its World Reserve status if, and when, US deficits cause significant disruption to the value of the dollar? Statements by the ECB and some OPEC members about a petroeuro indicate the possible outcome. I suspect that by 2010 we will witness a graduated approach entailing a replay of the 1974 Saudi agreement that established the petrodollar recycling phenomenon — but this time, a basket of currencies including the dollar and euro.

Iran's Oil Bourse: Introducing a Euro-denominated Oil Marker

The decision-making in connection to the continuation of [oil] transactions in dollars is being considered in a committee set up by the Central Bank of Iran.

> — Seyyed Mehdi-Mir-Moezzi, Managing Director of the National Iranian Oil Co., August 2002[55]

Iran is to launch an oil trading market for Middle East and OPEC producers that could threaten the supremacy of London's International Petroleum Exchange. A contract to design and establish a new platform for crude, natural gas and petrochemical trades is expected to be signed with an international consortium within days .... *Some industry experts have warned the Iranians and other OPEC producers that Western exchanges are controlled by big financial and oil corporations*, which have a vested interest in market volatility. [emphasis added]

> — Terry Macalister, "Iran Takes on West's Control of Oil Trading," the *Guardian*, (UK), June 2004[56]

Newsweek has learned that the CIA and DIA have war-gamed the likely consequences of a US pre-emptive strike on Iran's nuclear facilities. No one liked the outcome. As an Air Force source tells it, '*The war games were unsuccessful at preventing the conflict from escalating.*' [emphasis added]

> — "War-Gaming the Mullahs," *Newsweek*, September 2004[57]

In my interviews [with former high-level intelligence officials], I was repeatedly told that the next strategic target was Iran. Everyone is saying, 'You can't be serious about targeting Iran. Look at Iraq,' the former [CIA] intelligence official told me. But the [Bush administration officials] say, 'We've got some lessons learned — not militarily, but how we did it politically. We're not going to rely on agency pissants.' No loose ends, and that's why the C.I.A. is out of there.

— Seymour Hersh, "The Coming Wars," *New Yorker*, January 2005[58]

Current geopolitical tensions between the United States and Iran extend beyond the publicly stated concerns about Iran's nuclear intentions, and likely include a proposed Iranian petroeuro system for international oil trades. The Iranians are about to commit a far greater "offense" than Saddam Hussein's conversion to the euro for Iraq's oil exports in the fall of 2000. In 2006, the Tehran government plans to begin competing with New York's Mercantile Exchange (NYMEX) and London's International Petroleum Exchange (IPE) in international oil trades — using a euro-based international oil-trading mechanism.

One of the more difficult technical obstacles to a euro-based oil-transaction system has been the lack of a euro-denominated oil pricing standard, or oil "marker" as it is known in the industry. The current oil markers are US dollar-denominated: the West Texas Intermediate crude (WTI), UK Brent crude, and UAE Dubai crude.

In June 2004 a significant news development occurred when Iran announced its intentions to create an Iranian oil Bourse. (The word "bourse" means a stock exchange for securities trading, and is derived from the Paris stock exchange, the Federation Internationale des Bourses de Valeurs.) This announcement portended competition between the Iranian oil Bourse and the Atlanta-based InterContinental Exchange (X.IEX), which owns London's IPE and the NYMEX.

Since 1979 the US sanctions against Iran, similar to those against Iraq, have blocked US petroleum interests from conducting business deals there. One article noted that "Washington may frown on any involvement by the US-owned IPE" in the Iranian oil-trading platform.[59] Obviously a successful euro-denominated alternative for international oil trades would challenge the domination that financial centers in London and New York currently enjoy, a factor not overlooked in the following article:

The Tehran oil bourse is scheduled to open in 2005, according to its architect, Mohammad Javad Asemipour, who is a personal adviser to the Iranian energy minister .... [Mr Asemipour] played down the dangers that the new exchange could eventually pose for the IPE or NYMEX, saying he hoped they might be able to cooperate in some way.

The IPE, bought in 2001 by a consortium that includes BP, Goldman Sachs, and Morgan Stanley, was unwilling to discuss the Iranian move yesterday. 'We would not have any comment to make on it at this stage,' said an IPE spokeswoman.[60]

The macroeconomic implications of a successful Iranian Bourse are note-worthy. Considering Iran's switch to the euro for oil payments from its EU and Asian Clearing Union (ACU) customers in mid-2003, it is logical to assume that their proposed Bourse will usher in a fourth crude oil marker — denominated in the euro.[61] That would remove the main technical obstacle for a broad-based petroeuro system for international oil trades. Acknowledging that many of the oil contracts for Iran and Saudi Arabia are linked to the UK's Brent crude marker, the Iranian Bourse could create a significant shift in the flow of international commerce into the Middle East.[62]

It is unclear if this Bourse will be successful, or if it could prompt an overt US military intervention — thereby signaling the second phase of petrodollar warfare in the Middle East. Regardless, the emergence of an oil exchange market in the Middle East is not entirely surprising given the peak and decline of oil exports from the US and UK, in comparison to the remaining oil reserves in Iran, Iraq, and Saudi Arabia.

According to Mohammad Javad Asemipour, an adviser to Iran's energy ministry and the individual responsible for this new oil exchange, "[it] should be trading crude, natural gas, and petrochemicals by the start of the new Iranian year, which falls on March 21, 2005."[63] He also stated that Saudi Arabia and various non-OPEC oil producers from the Caspian region would eventually participate in the exchange. (Note: In December 2004 Iran announced its petroleum exchange will become operational by March 2006, implying a one-year delay).[64]

These foreign news items suggest that, sometime between 2005 and early 2006, international buyers will have a hypothetical choice of buying a barrel of oil for either $50 on the NYMEX/IPE or for €37 to €40 on the Iranian Bourse, (assuming the euro maintains its current 20 to 25 percent appreciated value relative to the dollar — and that covert "interventions" are not under-taken to disrupt the oil exchange). A successful Iranian oil-trading platform will introduce petrodollar versus petroeuro currency hedging and fundamen-tally new dynamics to the biggest market in the world, global oil and gas trades.

These facts further illustrate why petrodollar recycling is unsustainable. The proposed Iranian Bourse signifies that without some sort of intervention, the euro will soon establish a firm foothold in the international oil trade.

Given US debt levels and the stated neoconservative project of US global domination, Tehran's objective constitutes an obvious encroachment on US dollar supremacy in this market. News reports in the autumn of 2004 revealed active "war gaming" within the Bush administration concerning Iran.

> Deep in the Pentagon, admirals and generals are updating plans for possible US military action in Syria and Iran. *The Defense Department unit responsible for military planning for the two troublesome countries is 'busier than ever,' an administration official says.* Some Bush advisers characterize the work as merely an effort to revise routine plans the Pentagon maintains for all contingencies in light of the Iraq War. More skittish bureaucrats say the updates are accompanied by a *revived campaign by administration conservatives and neocons for more hard-line US policies toward the countries ....*
>
> *Administration hawks are pinning their hopes on regime change in Tehran — by covert means, preferably, but by force of arms if necessary.* Papers on the idea have circulated inside the administration, mostly labeled 'draft' or 'working draft' to evade congressional subpoena powers and the Freedom of Information Act. Informed sources say the memos echo the administration's abortive Iraq strategy: oust the existing regime, swiftly install a pro-US government in its place (extracting the new regime's promise to renounce any nuclear ambitions) and get out. *This daredevil scheme horrifies US military leaders,* and there's no evidence that it has won any backers at the cabinet level.'[65] [emphasis added]

These Pentagon leaks indicate that a second Bush term could produce a confrontation with Iran. Then Secretary of State Powell had moderated neo-conservative military designs for attacking Iran, but when Powell left after Bush's first term, this moderating force dissipated. Of course if Senator Kerry had been elected president in January 2005, he might have pursued a similar military strategy. However, most commentators thought Kerry would have more likely pursued multilateral negotiations on the Iranian/EU/OPEC issues.

The immediate concern for Americans and the world is whether the neo-conservatives will attempt to intervene covertly and/or overtly in Iran during Bush's second term in an effort to prevent a euro-denominated crude-oil pricing mechanism. Commentators in India are correct in their assessment that a US intervention in Iran would likely prove disastrous for America, making international terrorism issues worse, not to mention potential retaliatory effects on the US economy.

> The giving up on the terror war while Iran invasion plans are drawn up makes no sense, especially since the previous invasion

and current occupation of Iraq has further fuelled Al-Qaeda terrorism after 9/11 …. It is obvious that sucked into Iraq, the US has limited military manpower left to combat the Al-Qaeda elsewhere in the Middle East and South Central Asia … and NATO is so seriously cross with America that it hesitates to provide troops in Iraq, and no other country is willing to bail out America outside its immediate allies like Britain, Italy, Australia, and Japan.

There is a better way, as the constructive engagement of Libya's Colonel Muammar Gaddafi has shown …. Iran is obviously a more complex case than Libya, because power resides in the clergy, and Iran has not been entirely transparent about its nuclear programme, but the sensible way is to take it gently, and nudge it to moderation. Regime change will only worsen global Islamist terror.[66]

Clearly there are numerous risks regarding neoconservative strategy toward Iran. First, unlike Iraq, Iran has a robust military capability. Secondly, a repeat of any 'shock and awe' tactics is not advisable given that Iran has installed sophisticated anti-ship missiles on the island of Abu Musa, therefore controlling the critical Strait of Hormuz.[67] In the case of a US attack, any shutdown of the Strait of Hormuz — which Persian Gulf-bound oil tankers must navigate — could easily trigger a market panic with oil prices skyrocketing to $100 per barrel or more. World oil production is reportedly to be now flat out with no spare capacity, and a major interruption would escalate oil prices to a level that would set off global economic turmoil with an unpredictable outcome.

> A successful Iranian Bourse will solidify the petroeuro as an alternative oil transaction currency, thereby ending the petrodollar's status as the monopoly oil currency.

A successful Iranian Bourse will solidify the petroeuro as an alternative oil transaction currency, thereby ending the petrodollar's status as the monopoly oil currency. Therefore, a graduated approach is needed to avoid precipitous US economic turmoil. Multilateral compromise with the EU and OPEC on oil currency is certainly preferable to a CIA-attempted coup — such as another Operation Ajax Part II. Even worse would be a desperate overt "Operation Iranian Freedom," at which US military leaders would be rightly horrified.

The December 2004 *Atlantic Monthly* included detailed PowerPoint slides used during high-level US military war games against Iran.[68] These sessions were led by Sam Gardiner, a retired Air Force colonel who for more than two decades ran war games at the National War College and other military institutions. Of the three scenarios simulated, Option No. 3 involved a ground invasion of Iran and a forced "regime change." This operation was projected to last 30 days, but it had been "modeled carefully on the real assault on Iraq, and all five advisers were appalled by it."[69]

The hard lessons unfolding in Iraq were viewed by the war-game participants as a forewarning should the Bush administration pursue its goal of "regime change" in Iran. Gardiner summarized the war games: "After all this effort, I am left with two simple sentences for policy-makers: *You have no military solution for the issues of Iran. And you have to make diplomacy work.*"[70] [emphasis added]

The geopolitical stakes for the Bush administration were raised dramatically on October 31, 2004, when Iran and China signed a huge oil and gas trade agreement valued at $70 billion or £38 billion.[71] The nullification of previous oil contracts by the US-administered Coalition Provisional Authority (CPA) after the Iraq invasion likely created political tensions between the U.S and China over oil supply. The Chinese government may fear the same fate awaits their oil investments in Iran if the US were able to topple the Tehran government. However, the neoconservative strategy of "regime change" in Iran now appears uncertain. Despite the US' desires to enforce petrodollar hegemony, the geopolitical risks of a US attack on Iran's nuclear facilities would surely create a serious crisis between Washington and Beijing.

Without doubt, a unilateral American attack on Iran would further isolate the US government, and it is conceivable that such an overt military operation could provoke some developed nations to abandon the dollar en masse and/or create additional pressure within OPEC or Russia or both toward a petroeuro system. Another risk factor was outlined by Michael Ruppert, who warned of the potential monetary response that China could undertake in the event of an unprovoked US attack on Iran: "The moment China starts selling dollars the rest of the world will crash down the doors of the bank to get rid of theirs as quickly as possible. The run on the dollar will be short, bloody, and catastrophic."[72]

The reasons for any such drastic reaction by other governments are straightforward: the global community is dependent on the oil and gas energy supplies found in the Persian Gulf. Industrialized nations would likely move in tandem on the currency exchange markets to thwart the neoconservatives' desperate strategy to dominate the world's largest hydrocarbon energy supply. Any such efforts that resulted in a dollar currency crisis would be undertaken — not to cripple the US dollar and economy as punishment toward the American *people* — but rather to thwart further unilateral *warfare* and its potentially destructive effects on the current oil production and shipping infrastructure in the Persian Gulf. Logically, the most appropriate US strategy is compromise with the EU and OPEC toward a dual-currency system for international oil trades.

Despite the impressive power of the US military and the ability of US intelligence agencies to facilitate "interventions," it would be perilous for the US to intervene in Iran, given the dire situation in Iraq. The Monterey Institute of International Studies provided an extensive analysis of the possible consequences of a preemptive attack on Iran's nuclear facilities, including this warning:

> Considering the extensive financial and national policy investment Iran has committed to its nuclear projects, it is almost certain that an attack by Israel or the United States would result in immediate retaliation.
>
> An attack on Iranian nuclear facilities ... could have various adverse effects on US interests in the Middle East and the world. Most important, in the absence of evidence of an Iranian illegal nuclear program, an attack on Iran's nuclear facilities by the US or Israel would be likely to strengthen Iran's international stature and reduce the threat of international sanctions against Iran. Such an event is more likely to embolden and expand Iran's nuclear aspirations and capabilities in the long term ... one thing is for certain, *it would not be just another Osirak.*[73] [italics in original]

Pentagon sources confirmed that the Bush administration could undertake a desperate military strategy to thwart Iran's nuclear ambitions while simultaneously attempting to prevent the Iranian Bourse from initiating a euro-based system for oil trades. However, both China and the EU will certainly move to protect their own interests in preserving the free flow of Iran's oil exports and thwart any US-sponsored UN Security resolution advocating the use of military operations, thereby forcing any US actions to be totally unilateral. Realistically, the postwar debacle in Iraq has shown that a similar strategy toward Iran would likely lead to a catastrophic failure.

Alternatively, perhaps a more enlightened US administration could undertake multilateral negotiations with the EU and OPEC regarding a dual oil-currency system, in conjunction with global monetary reform. Either way, US policy-makers will soon face two difficult choices: monetary compromise or continued petrodollar warfare.

The final three pivotal conditions for creating OPEC's transition to euros will occur (1) if and when Norway's Brent crude marker is re-dominated in euros, (2) if and when the UK adopts the euro, and (3) whether or not Iran's proposed Bourse is successful and utilizes the euro as its oil transaction currency. In the meantime, the UK remains uncomfortably juxtaposed between the financial interests of the US banking nexus (New York/Washington) and the EU financial centers (Paris/Frankfurt).

The UK's Prime Minister Blair has lobbied to adopt the euro, seemingly by 2010. After that, there will likely be a concerted effort to quickly establish the euro as an international reserve currency. In view of the UK's uncomfortable juxtaposition between the financial interests of the US and the EU, the realization of this hypothesis would represent a monumental realignment of the transatlantic relationship.

America's Achilles Heel: Lessons from the Suez Crisis of 1956

> One day, some time soon, one way or another, the House of Saud is coming down.
>
> — Robert Baer, Former US Central Intelligence Agency analyst, *Atlantic Monthly*, May, 2002[74]

> The US approach has been unilateralist here as everywhere else: it does what it likes as it likes, a policy that is now showing its limits. Bush needs badly to change course, which Tony Blair should be urging on him. The UN process needs to be respected and reinforced, not least to reassure the markets, and better systems of economic governance need to be put in place. The US' military capacity may allow unilateralism; its soft economic underbelly, we are discovering, does not.
>
> — Will Hutton, "Why Bush Is Sunk Without Europe," *Guardian*, January 2003[75]

> A multilateral approach to these core problems is the only way to proceed. The US is strong enough to dominate the world militarily. Economically it is in decline, less and less competitive, and increasingly in debt. The Bush people's intention appears to be to override economic realities with military ones, as if there were no risk of economic retribution. They should be mindful of Britain's humiliating retreat from Suez in 1956, a retreat forced on it by the United States as a condition for propping up the failing British pound.
>
> — Peter Dale Scott, author and professor at the University of California Berkley, May 2003[76]

The petrodollar recycling system is now under pressure from a competing currency, exacerbated by political tensions arising from the Iraq War and from US neoconservative ideology. The Bush administration probably believed that the occupation of Iraq and the installation of large and permanent US military bases in Iraq would thwart remaining OPEC producers from even considering switching the denomination of their oil sales from dollars to euros. It would appear that any attempt by OPEC members in the Middle East or Latin America to do so shall be met with either overt US military actions or covert US intelligence agency interventions.

Regrettably, Bush and his neoconservative advisers chose to apply a military option to a US economic problem that ultimately requires a multilateral treaty. Under the guise of the perpetual "war on terror" the Bush administration deceived the American people about the unspoken, but very real, economic reasons for the invasion of Iraq. While doing so, this administration sent an authoritarian message to other OPEC members: "You are either with us or against us."

However, the blowback against US foreign policies, including nuanced statements by foreign observers, reveals that blowback against the dollar and the ongoing tragic quagmire in Iraq have exposed the limitations of the unilateral *hard power* politics of US military interventions that lack international support. The lesson is clear: the US cannot unilaterally overthrow sovereign nations at will under the pretext of an expanding "war on terror" without considering the potential economic retaliation from the world community by abandoning the dollar.

> Current US geostrategy of achieving global dominance has not surprisingly resulted in unprecedented levels of international blowback against America.

Current US geostrategy of achieving global dominance has not surprisingly resulted in unprecedented levels of international blowback against America. Despite the early tactical victory of toppling the regime of Saddam Hussein and restoring the petrodollar system in Iraq, the strategic outcome of a US military occupation in Iraq has exposed the tragic hubris behind neoconservative doctrine.

If Washington continues to pursue this doctrine, it would not be surprising if covert operations were pursued in an attempt to overthrow the Iranian government and thwart the emergence of the Iranian Bourse. Then again, the pursuit of these unilateral covert or overt strategies would likely result in disaster for the US. It is hard not to argue that the "war on terror" has scared foreign investors willing to carry American debt.[77] This blowback extends not only to the elite money handlers who have publicly stated that the US dollar is not secure, but also to the widespread anger against the invasion and ongoing war in Iraq. The Pentagon itself officially noted that anti-American sentiments created in the Arab world have reached unprecedented levels. In effect, the US has lost the "hearts and minds" of the Arab world.[78]

There are important historical parallels in which currency warfare proved decisive in thwarting military operations in the Middle East. In July 1956 Egyptian President Nasser, a staunch nationalist, took over the Suez Canal Company, 44 percent of which was British-held, and nationalized the Suez Canal.[79] Despite public opposition to the use of force, the British, French, and Israelis developed a plan in secret at Sèvres, France, in which the Israeli army would invade Egypt, and then under the guise of intervention, British and French troops would retake the canal. On November 5, 1956, the Israelis attacked, and a joint Anglo-French force landed at Port Said. British and French paratroopers attacked Canal Zone 5, killing approximately 1000 Egyptians, mostly civilians.

This invasion of the Suez Canal caught President Eisenhower by surprise. He was furious when he learned this invasion had been arranged by the British and French governments. Subsequently, Eisenhower suspended aid to Israel and thwarted the British military operations by refusing to loan money to Britain, blocking its application for a loan from the IMF, and *threatening to sell US holdings of the British pound.*[80] Due to US pressures, a fiscal crisis erupted in the UK as the value of the pound sterling plummeted. Diplomatically isolated, the foreign troops were withdrawn from the Suez Canal. Shortly thereafter, British Prime Minister Eden resigned in disgrace. Devastating currency devaluation ended the Suez Crisis and marked the final episode of British imperialism in the 20th century.

Perhaps US leaders who espouse the neoconservative strategy of global dominance should take heed in the history lessons provided by the 1956 Suez Crisis. The events before, during, and after the 2003 Iraq War suggest that the global community will not tolerate an imperialist US empire that ignores international law while engaging in unilateral military operations against sovereign nations that do not pose an imminent security threat to the US.

The obvious danger to US power and prestige is that neoconservative strategy has created geopolitical tensions that could result in several oil-producing states acting collectively to pull the monetary plug on the US empire by moving to a *monopoly* petroeuro system. This would be a devastating development. Regardless, news reports of the internal discussions within OPEC suggest that the emergence of a petroeuro is probably inevitable.[81]

While neither the industrialized nations nor OPEC wish to drop the sword of Damocles on the dollar, considering the resulting economic dislocations, such actions would take place as a desperate effort to thwart additional belligerent US military conflicts in the Persian Gulf region. Attempting to hinder US imperialism here is conceivable considering that the euro has become a viable alternative as a World Reserve Currency — and petrocurrency. Furthermore, as the global community quietly awakes to the realities of Peak Oil, the industrialized nations will attempt to prevent any further unilateral US actions to "restructure" the Middle East via destructive force. The risks of disrupting the global oil supply or physically damaging the associated oil pumping and shipping infrastructure are simply too ominous.

Any such decision by the Bush administration to intervene overtly or covertly in Iran could result in the realization of the "rogue nation hypothesis" — a collective abandonment of the dollar to thwart US imperialism. Although unlikely, if this fateful event were to occur, it would create the historical irony of a new Suez Crisis scenario similar to President Eisenhower's actions that ended British imperialism 50 years ago. Certainly from the perspective of OPEC and the industrialized nations, preserving the critical oil production infrastructure in Iran, Saudi Arabia, and elsewhere would likely outweigh the allegiance to the dollar's supremacy and the desire for stability within the current international economic order. Additionally, from China's viewpoint, its huge oil and gas deals established in October 2004 effectively drew a line in the sand around Iran. Hence it is doubtful that American military operations can be conducted against Iran without fear of China divesting itself of US debt instruments.

Recognizing our structural debt levels, overstretched military, and international isolation, could the US economy withstand a massive divestiture of dollar-denominated assets? The answer is obvious. Consequently, if US policymakers continue pursuing unilateral, unprovoked wars in an effort to gain military control over the world's energy supplies while toppling sovereign governments, the US should not expect the industrialized nations or the global community to continue purchasing its debt, thereby funding this type of military imperialism.

The final two chapters offer numerous suggestions for domestic reform within the US media and political arenas, both of which are required to pursue the recommendations in the last chapter. These include various multilateral policy alternatives in an effort to foster a more balanced global economy and bold suggestions concerning international energy reform.

> Breaking US hegemony in the Arab world by using oil revenues to promote the currency of an alternative, and more friendly, power might be a sensible move. It would make US interference in Arab affairs less effective.
>
> Perhaps a new bipolar economic system, between the US and EU is set to emerge in the early part of the twenty-first century, and Arab nations can play a vital part in creating this new world order by switching oil payments from the dollar to the euro. In the process Arab nations will create a world order far more in line with their own interests. At the moment the US has it all its own way, something the EU is strong enough to correct.
>
> — Peter J. Cooper, Middle East Finance and Economy,
> AME Info, October 2000[82]

> Facts are stubborn things; and whatever may be our wishes, our inclinations, or the dictates of our passions, they cannot alter the state of facts and evidence.
>
> — John Adams, 2nd US President, 1770

Six

Saving the American Experiment

We hold these Truths to be self-evident, that all Men are created equal, that they are endowed by their Creator with certain unalienable Rights, that among these are Life, Liberty and the Pursuit of Happiness .... That to secure these Rights, Governments are instituted among Men, deriving their just Powers from the Consent of the Governed, that whenever any Form of Government becomes destructive of these Ends, it is the Right of the People to alter or to abolish it, and to institute new Government, laying its Foundation on such Principles, and organizing its Powers in such Form, as to them shall seem most likely to effect their Safety and Happiness.

— Thomas Jefferson, Declaration of Independence, 1776

We believe no more in {France's Napoleon} Bonaparte's fighting merely for the liberties of the seas than in Great Britain's fighting for the liberties of mankind. The object is the same, to draw to themselves the power, the wealth and the resources of other nations.

— Thomas Jefferson, US President 1801–1809

Those willing to give up a little liberty for a little security deserve neither security nor liberty.

— Benjamin Franklin, US Founding Father

US Media Consolidation: Threat to Our Republic

> There's really five companies that control 90 percent of what we read, see and hear. It's not healthy.
>
> — Ted Turner, vice chairman of AOL Time Warner and founder of CNN, April 24, 2003[1]

> If media moguls control media content and media distribution, then they have a lock on the extent and range of diverse views and information. That kind of grip on commercial and political power is potentially dangerous for any democracy.
>
> — Chuck Lewis, executive director of the Centre for Public Integrity, March 20, 2004[2]

> Most of the media was on the bandwagon or intimidated. Cheney himself called the president of the corporation that owned one of the networks to complain about an errant commentator. Political aides directed by Karl Rove ceaselessly called the editors and producers with veiled threats about the access that was not granted in any case. The press would not bite the hand that would not feed it.
>
> — Sidney Blumenthal, the *Guardian* (UK), June 24, 2004[3]

> This government lies .... I think we have a government that absolutely is ignoring the truth and a press that is ignoring the truth.
>
> — Helen Thomas, 57-year-veteran correspondent for United Press International, quoted during a speech on the George W. Bush administration, July 8, 2004.[4]

> All journalists make mistakes .... But the falsehoods reproduced by the media before the invasion of Iraq were massive and consequential: it is hard to see how Britain could have gone to war if the press had done its job.
>
> — George Monbiot, the *Guardian* (UK), July 20, 2004[5]

> The CIA owns everyone of any significance in the major media.
>
> — Former CIA Director William Colby[6]

Thomas Jefferson rightly insisted that a *free press is vital* — it is the best, and often the only, mechanism for protecting democracy. Americans seem largely unaware of the issues outlined in this book because the mass media has been reduced to a few mega-media conglomerates responsible for approximately 90 percent of the information flow within the US. Naturally this level of consolidation in the press has resulted in filtering of TV and radio broadcast news, as well as printed media. Since 1980 deregulation of media ownership has resulted in independent US news sources shrinking from 50 in

1983 to roughly 10 sources in 1997.[7] By 2004 the major broadcast media had been further reduced to only five conglomerates. Mark Crispin Miller, media critic and professor of media studies at New York University, provided a listing of the five conglomerates in *Censored 2004*

- **AOL Time Warner:** CNN and related networks; Home Box Office; Warner Brothers movie and television studio, WB television network and affiliated record labels; AOL Internet service; and Time Inc. magazines, such as Time, Fortune, Sports Illustrated, People, and Entertainment Weekly.

- **News Corporation:** Fox broadcast television network and cable news channel, 20th Century Fox movie studio, New York Post and several foreign newspapers and television networks in Europe and Australia. Conglomerate also includes extensive radio network of 34 owned and operated stations, 9 duopolies, 188 affiliated stations, several book publishers, sports franchises, and satellite companies, such as Hughes Electronics Corporation.

- **Walt Disney Company:** ABC television network, ESPN cable sports network, 10 stations/226 local affiliates, 62 radio stations/4600 affiliates, several publishing companies, and Internet portals. As well as Disney amusement parks and related resorts, Miramax and Hollywood Pictures, etc.

- **Viacom:** CBS and UPN television networks; Infinity radio network, with nearly 200 stations; cable television networks MTV, Showtime, and BET; Paramount movie and television studios; and Blockbuster Video movie rental chain, etc.

- **Vivendi Universal:** Large Internet portal in the US and Europe, cable and Satellite TV, Universal Studios, Music, Film, Telecom, and non-media corporations, etc.[8]

In the case of the Iraq War, the corporate-owned US media failed to provide coverage of basic information that was widely available elsewhere. A cursory analysis of European, Indian, Asian, Latin American, and Canadian media reporting provided a considerably more informative and objective analysis of the issues surrounding the war.

Foreign media sources, such as the UK's *Observer*, discussed Iraq and related petroeuro issues before the war, but the US media completely failed to mention this noteworthy item — preferring instead, incessant coverage about alleged WMD threats and imaginary links between Saddam Hussein, 9/11, and the Al Qaeda network.

FOX News played a key role in forming domestic opinion, as it parroted — uncritically — the prewar claims of the Bush/Cheney administration. This trend did not go unnoticed in other countries; British Broadcasting Corporation (BBC) Director-General Greg Dyke expressed grave concerns about the impartiality of both TV and radio broadcast media in the US. He warned policy-makers that corporate control and the adoption of an American- style media would be detrimental to the health of Britain's democracy.

> Personally, I was shocked while in the United States by how unquestioning the broadcast news media were during this war. If Iraq proved anything, it was that the BBC cannot afford to mix patriotism and journalism. This is happening in the United States and, if it continues, will undermine the credibility of the US electronic news media. For the health of our democracy, it's vital we don't follow the path of many American networks.[9]

Although Dyke's opinion regarding media bias and censorship in the US might surprise uninformed Americans, it is a concern well known to those who advocate media reform. While it is comforting to believe that we still have a free media, when compared to news coverage in other industrialized nations, the disparity of information available to American viewers and listeners provides evidence that a free and open media in the US is a myth, not reality. In the first worldwide press freedom index, the US was ranked 17th by an international journalists group, Reporters Without Borders. All top ten rankings were European, with the exception of Canada (ranked 5th).[10] The US' stifling corporate influence was reiterated by PBS commentator Bill Moyers upon his retirement after 30 years in TV journalism. He warned of the transformation he witnessed:

> You don't get rewarded in commercial broadcasting for trying to tell the truth about the institutions of power in this country .... I think my peers in commercial television are talented and devoted journalists, but they've chosen to work in a corporate mainstream that trims their talent to fit the corporate nature of American life. And you do not get rewarded for telling the hard truths about America in a profit-seeking environment ....
>
> We have got to nurture the spirit of independent journalism in this country, or we'll not save capitalism from its own excesses, and we'll not save democracy from its own inertia.[11]

Today, Americans must rely almost exclusively on Internet-based news sources to learn about important stories that ultimately have far greater impact on our lives than the latest sex/murder/drug scandals that serve as our daily infotainment from the five conglomerates. Truthfully, in the US, the Internet is currently the last, and only, bastion of free speech and unfiltered news.

Frankly, this book could not have been written if the research were solely based on information provided by the US corporate media. The crucial research revealed in this book was provided mostly by European, Asian, and Canadian news sources, and some independent US outlets. Despite a year of debate in which the American people learned plenty of details about Saddam Hussein's 1980s WMD program and the brutality of his regime, the US corporate media *never* discussed the crucial economic issues about Iraq's oil transaction switch to the euro, nor was sufficient coverage provided on Iraq's numerous international oil agreements.

Had the US broadcast and print media been diligent in their reporting of foreign news stories in the lead-up to the war, perhaps the reasons why nations such as France, Germany, Russia, and China did not support the Iraq War would have been debated in our society. Undeniably, until the US media conglomerates are reformed into more independent and free media outlets, the American people will continue to be at risk for extensive manipulation by their political leaders on a broad range of important subjects that require public knowledge and debate, most especially those decisions that involve sending young American soldiers into harm's way.

> Our liberty depends on the freedom of the press, and that cannot be limited without being lost.
> — Thomas Jefferson, US President 1801–1809

Campaign Finance Structure and Corporate Personhood: Elements of Proto-Fascism

> Few men have virtue to withstand the highest bidder.
> — George Washington, US President 1789–1797

> I hope we shall crush in its birth the aristocracy of our moneyed corporations, which dare already to challenge our government to a trial of strength and bid defiance of the laws of our country.
> — Thomas Jefferson, US President 1801–1809

> Every special interest is entitled to justice full, fair and complete ... but not one is entitled to a vote in Congress, to a voice on the bench or to representation in any public office.
> — Theodore Roosevelt, US President 1901–1909

> The liberty of a democracy is not safe if the people tolerate the growth of private power to a point where it becomes stronger than their democratic State itself. That, in its essence, is Fascism - ownership of government by an individual, by a Group or by any controlling private owner.
> — Franklin D. Roosevelt, US President 1933–1945

> In the councils of government, we must guard against the acquisition
> of unwarranted influence, whether sought or unsought, by the
> military-industrial complex. The potential for the disastrous rise of
> misplaced power exists and will persist. We must never let the weight
> of this combination endanger our liberties or democratic processes.
>
> — Dwight Eisenhower, US President 1953–1961

From Washington's warning of political corruption in the 18th century to
Eisenhower's warnings of "unwarranted influence;" the observations of generals turned presidents are just as relevant. For decades the links between the
US government and the major military–industrial–petroleum conglomerates
have grown into a nearly seamless revolving door: former US Congress members
and even former presidents leave office and become lobbyists for some of the
largest of these conglomerates, creating a proto-fascist military–industrial
–petroleum–*congressional* complex.[12] Alarming enough is the emergence from
this complex of "no-bid" multi-billion-dollar contracts; even more troubling is
the correlation between political campaign contributions and postwar contract
awards. In 2003 the Center for Public Integrity report, "Winning Contractors:
US Contractors Reap the Windfalls of Postwar Reconstruction," stated:

> Companies awarded $8 billion in contracts to rebuild Iraq and
> Afghanistan have been major campaign donors to President Bush,
> and their executives have had important political and military con-
> nections, according to a study released Thursday. The study of
> more than 70 US companies and individual contractors turned up
> more than $500,000 in donations to the president's 2000 campaign,
> more than they gave collectively to any other politician over the
> past dozen years.[13]

Defense spending for the "endless war" against an obscure group of non-
state actors has morphed into a feeding frenzy of the public treasury. Forgotten
and useless Cold War era projects have suddenly been approved for billions in
funding under the fraudulent guise of being necessary for the new "war on
terror," despite the commonsense observation that many of these projects
will be utterly useless against terrorism (i.e., Cold War weapon programs such
as the $13 billion Crusader artillery piece[14]).

One glaring example is the absurd promotion of a National Missile Defense
(NMD) system. The Bush administration attempted to justify constructing an
$800 billion to $1.2 trillion missile defense system as an appropriate response
to what was in effect a complex kamikaze attack using hijacked commercial
jets.[15] The bizarre justifications for this massive project were Orwellian non-
answers using fear-invoking language, suffering from the same illogic used to
"justify" the preemptive war in Iraq.

Mr. Russert: What about the debate over missile defense? Many Democrats are saying this now proves that our focus should be on terrorism and counterterrorism and preparedness, and that the primary threat is not something the missile defense could take care of.

Vice Pres. Cheney: Well, I just fundamentally disagree. I mean, there's no question but what there's a threat on the terrorist front, and we've got to deal with that. We've been working it. We'll continue to work it. But this does not, in any way, diminish the threat with respect to ballistic missiles down the road. A ballistic missile equipped with a weapon of mass destruction, a nuke, for example, a nuclear weapon would be far more devastating than what we just went through. If one of those was to hit one of our cities or to hit a major base overseas where US forces are deployed, the casualty list would be higher. The consequences would be even greater than the terrible tragedy we've just been through.

— *Meet the Press* with Tim Russert, September 16, 2001[16]

First, it is *not plausible* for any terrorist group — a non-state-supported actor — to have access to the billions of dollars required to amass the essential technical staff to design, build, test, or otherwise construct a nuclear warhead in conjunction with an Intercontinental Ballistic Missile (ICBM) program. Obviously such an undertaking requires the *full support* of a nation's government, treasury, and military.

Secondly, given that the US satellite system has the capability to detect and pinpoint any ballistic missile launch against us, why would any nation follow such a self-defeating/suicidal course of action? Why spend tens of billions to build an ICBM and then invite your own destruction by using it? Obviously a "terrorist-based" ICBM is a ridiculous scenario, yet immediately after September 11th, the Bush administration and certain members of Congress repeatedly suggested that those terrorist attacks reinforced the need for a national missile defense system.

Remarkably, the Pentagon now manages 93 percent of the international relations budget, whereas the Department of State controls only 7 percent.[17] Furthermore, private sector military suppliers now include the major campaign contributors for both political parties. These military contractors in Iraq include Halliburton, Kellogg Brown and Root, Vinnell, Military Professional Resources, DynCorp, Science Applications Corporation, BDM (now TRW), Armor Holdings, Cubic, DFI, and International Charter.

> Remarkably, the Pentagon now manages 93 percent of the international relations budget, whereas the Department of State controls only 7 percent.[17]

They are not subject to congressional oversight, nor do they have any loyalty to taxpayers, despite being subsidized by billions of tax dollars.

It appears to be nearly impossible for US politicians to cancel any significant defense project without suffering losses to their re-election campaign coffers. Politicians seeking campaign contributions continue to feed the military–industrial–petroleum–banking complex — despite these behaviors being ultimately self-defeating to the US' economic welfare and harmful to its international reputation.

Some believe that the Iraq War was justified so that the US can continue to enjoy "cheap" gasoline. Americans think that their gasoline prices are far lower than elsewhere, partly because they believe their gasoline taxes are "lower." This false construct does not withstand careful analysis. When the indirect/hidden taxation for our empire of military bases is included, the fully loaded price of gasoline for a US consumer *equals or exceeds the prices in other industrialized nations.* In 1998 the International Center for Technology Assessment computed that Americans indirectly pay a *minimum* of $5.60 per gallon, and potentially much higher based on current tax subsidies to US energy companies, defense department expenses, environmental costs, and other externalities.[18] In 2003 the conservative National Defense Council Foundation's study debunked this powerful myth of "cheap" gas. The truth is much more complex, stemming from the real taxpayer cost of the US' empire of bases. Their study, which revealed the true cost to be over $5.20 per gallon reported:

- Almost $49.1 billion in annual defense outlays to maintain the capability to defend the flow of Persian Gulf Oil — the equivalent of adding $1.17 to the price of a gallon of gasoline

- The loss of 828,400 jobs in the US economy

- The loss of $159.9 billion in GNP annually

- The loss of $13.4 billion in federal and state revenues annually

- Total economic penalties of from $297.2 to $304.9 billion annually[19]

The root cause exasercbating these problems lies in the deeply flawed concept of "corporate personhood." *Unequal Protection: The Rise of Corporate Dominace and the Theft of Human Rights,* by Thom Hartmann, performed a tremendous public service by carefully explaining the full ramifications of corporate personhood and it adverse effects on the state of the union.[20] Corporations gained personhood through aggressive court maneuvers by the former railroad industry, culminating in the 1886 Supreme Court case *Santa Clara County v. Southern Pacific.*[21] Until then, only "We the People" were protected by the Bill of Rights, and the government the people elected could regulate corporations as they deemed necessary.

However, armed with the Constitutional rights of personhood, corporations have steadily gained ways to weaken government restraints on their behavior via campaign contributions under their "right" to freedom of speech. Ironically, this concept is entirely based on the Fourteenth Amendment, which was about protecting ex-slaves, but has been twisted to give artificial entities the legal equivalent of rights and privileges of natural persons — but without accountability.

This decades-long process has inextricably led to what I perceive as American proto-fascism. In 1944 the *New York Times* asked Vice President Wallace to "write a piece answering the following questions: What is a fascist? How many fascists have we? How dangerous are they?" His answers appeared in the April 9, 1944, issue. Draw your own conclusions and compare his analysis to the situation we find ourselves in today.

> The dangerous American fascist is the man who wants to do in the United States in an American way what Hitler did in Germany in a Prussian way. The American fascist would prefer not to use violence. His method is to poison the channels of public information. With a fascist the problem is never how best to present the truth to the public but how best to use the news to deceive the public into giving the fascist and his group more money or more power ....
>
> The American fascists are most easily recognized by their deliberate perversion of truth and fact. Their newspapers and propaganda carefully cultivate every fissure of disunity, every crack in the common front against fascism. They use every opportunity to impugn democracy .... They claim to be super-patriots, but they would destroy every liberty guaranteed by the Constitution. They demand free enterprise, but are the spokesmen for monopoly and vested interest. Their final objective toward which all their deceit is directed is to capture political power so that, using the power of the state and the power of the market simultaneously, they may keep the common man in eternal subjection.[22]

Corporations do not receive a ballot, but with their own interests, they have political positions on certain issues. So instead of having one vote per individual, they make massive donations to politicians. The scale of these donations/bribes far outweigh all personal donors and, not surprisingly, corrupt the democratic process away from the expressed interests of voters, especially on issues directly relevant to the corporate donors' trading interests. Environmental, energy, tax, and foreign policies represent the principle abuses that run contrary to the interests of the common citizenry — and contradictory to basic US principles. During each election cycle most Congress members raise more than $1 million from business interests, and this influence on the political process is getting worse. According to the nonpartisan Political Money Line campaign finance tracking service, in 2004 lobbyists set a new record of spending more than $2 *billion* to promote their positions to the president and Congress.[23] (Lobbyist spending in 2003 was $1.9 billion, $1.7 billion in 2002, $1.5 billion in 2001 and $1.5 billion in 2000).

Most troubling is a new, and profoundly grotesque, example of how corporate influence has placed our entire democratic process at risk. Private corporations such as Diebold, ES&S, and Sequoia run our state and federal elections with electronic voting machines that indefensibly *do not allow any viable paper audit capability* — despite the fact that Diebold makes millions of similar machines, such as ATMs, that produce a paper trail. The recent unexplained divergence of exit-poll data that curiously coincides with the proliferation of "e-voting" machines is highly disconcerting.[24] It is shocking to learn that every other Western nation uses voting systems that can be audited, whereas the US uses an unauditable and fundamentally flawed system.

> It is shocking to learn that every other Western nation uses voting systems that can be audited, whereas the US uses an unauditable and fundamentally flawed system.

In contrast, Germany's elections are still counted by hand because of the fascism of the Third Reich. Mussolini said that fascism should more appropriately be called "corporatism" because it is the merger of corporate and governmental power. It is no wonder that present-day Germans don't let corporations count their votes. The US has been letting corporations and their computers count its votes — potentially confounding the 2000, 2002, and 2004 elections in many states.

Computer scientists at Johns Hopkins University reviewed the proprietary source code used in Diebold e-voting machines and concluded, "Our analysis shows that this system is *far below even the most minimal security standards applicable in other contexts* .... We conclude that *this system is unsuitable for use in a general election.*"[25] [emphasis added] A later test by a private computer information security firm produced similar results. During their tests of a simulated election, the users were able to remotely dial up the voting tabulator computer using a laptop — and transparently access the vote totals — without the legitimate users ever knowing they had manipulated the election.[26] Concerned computer security experts have posted websites showing how easy and transparent it would be to hack into a US election.[27] I can not think of anything more fascist (using Mussolini's definition) than having partisan corporations secretly count the votes and run our national election machinery — while simultaneously blocking any public scrutiny under the guise of "trade secrets." Why do Americans allow fraud-prone voting with these e-voting machines?

The cumulative effects of corporate personhood have become disastrous for the US by irreconcilably corrupting its political process and thwarting its ability to make the necessary reforms before the onset of global Peak Oil. Meanwhile the ruling elites are pursing a desperate struggle to maintain global hegemony by creating unsustainable national debt and economic conditions that will eventually bankrupt the nation. In his book, *The Sorrows of Empire*, Chalmers Johnson stated that America has started down the path "already taken by its erstwhile adversary in the Cold War, the former Soviet Union."[28] He claimed that the US' refusal to dismantle its empire of military bases following the demise of the Soviet Union, combined with a clearly inappropriate response to September 11th, created worldwide blowback and made our decline virtually inevitable. Johnson offered these sobering words:

> The US still has a strong civil society that could, at least in theory, overcome the entrenched interests of the armed forces and the military-industrial complex. I fear, however, that the US has indeed crossed the Rubicon and that there is no way to restore Constitutional government short of a revolutionary rehabilitation of American democracy. Without root and branch reform, Nemesis awaits. She is the goddess of revenge, the punisher of pride and arrogance, and the United States is on course for a rendezvous with her.[29]

From founders such as James Madison to generals such as George Washington and Dwight Eisenhower, enlightened US leadership has repeatedly warned of the dangers to democracy posed by the merging of the state and unlimited corporate power. Failure to heed this wisdom will indeed ensure our rendezvous with Nemesis.

> But besides the danger of a direct mixture of Religion & civil Government, there is an evil, which ought to be guarded against in the indefinite accumulation of property from the capacity of holding it in perpetuity by ... corporations. The power of all corporations ought to be limited in this respect. The growing wealth acquired by them never fails to be a source of abuses.
>
> — James Madison, US President 1809–1817

> Corporations have been enthroned and an era of corruption in high places will follow, and the money power of the country will endeavor to prolong its reign by working upon the prejudices of the people until all wealth is aggregated in a few hands and the Republic is destroyed.
>
> — Abraham Lincoln, US President 1861–1865

US Occupation of Iraq: The Unraveling of Neoconservative Geostrategy

> Sixty years of western nations excusing and accommodating the lack of freedom in the Middle East did nothing to make us safe, because in the long run, stability cannot be purchased at the expense of liberty. As long as the Middle East remains a place where freedom does not flourish, it will remain a place of stagnation, resentment, and violence, ready for export.
>
> — President George W. Bush, November 6, 2003[30]

> Arabs want democracy. They hate their corrupt regimes more than they hate the United States. But, they are not going to listen attentively to the speech of the American president, first, because the consecutive American administrations, in the past 50 years, supported those regimes ... and because all true democracies in the world came as a result of internal struggle, not due to foreign intervention, particularly American.
>
> — Abdul Bari Atwan, editor-in-chief, London-based Arabic daily *Al-Quds Al-Arabi*, November 2003[31]

> No individual, or group, has ever commissioned Mr. Bush to safeguard their rights. And basically, keeping in mind the dark record of the United States in suppressing the democratic movements around the globe, he is not in a position to talk about such issues.
>
> — Iranian Foreign Ministry spokesman Hamid-Reza Asefi[32]

> How can we believe that the one who is biased in favor of Israel ... can bring acceptable democratic projects to the people of the region?
>
> — Imad Fawzi al-Shueibi, Syrian political analyst[33]

> If they want to export democracy through wars, we do not want it. Let them keep it to themselves.
>
> — Ali Rida, 37 year-old worker, Damascus, Syria[34]

Perhaps 50 years ago the people of the Middle East might have believed President Bush's November 2003 speech about the need for democracy in that volatile region, but as the above reactions to his speech attest, it is unrealistic to expect the people in the Middle East to accept the notion that the US is suddenly interested in "spreading democracy," especially through warfare.

The highpoint of US leadership in the Middle East was in 1956 when President Eisenhower ordered the British, French, and Israelis to end their aggressive military action in the Suez against Egypt. To the Middle East, this was a very welcome symbol of America's anti-colonial position and a reflection of human decency. However, over the following half century, the US transformed itself from a heroic, anti-colonial power into a colossal villain, described by the Iranian mullahs as the Great Satan.

US interference in foreign governments regarding Western oil interests in the Persian Gulf, along with the overtly biased treatment of Israel, has contributed to anti-American sentiments in the region. Much of the current "anti-Americanism" in the Middle East is based on the perceived hypocrisy of US foreign policies. While claiming to stand for democracy, US leaders have a long history of selling weaponry and propping up "stable," but oppressive and anti-democratic, regimes including Saddam Hussein during the 1980s. As Ayman al-Zawahiri, an Egyptian terrorist and Osama bin Laden's chief deputy, stated on a Council of Foreign Relations (CFR) website:

> America claims to be the champion and protector of human rights, democracy, and liberties, while at the same time forcing on Muslims oppressive and corrupt political regimes. [America] is responsible for everything that happens in Egypt and responsible for human rights violations there, and in other countries as well.[35]

While al-Zawahiri is undoubtedly a fanatical Islamic militant, it is unfortunate that his claim concerning US support of oppressive Middle East regimes, such as Egypt, Saudi Arabia, Iran, and Iraq, is well documented in history. Most Americans have very little appreciation of the history of colonialism in this area. However, this region's people have very acute memories of foreign interference and oppression throughout the past century. Given this unsavory history, the neoconservative geostrategy of "democratic imperialism" in the Middle East is much more likely viewed by most of its people as "militant imperialism."

The invasion and occupation of Iraq to "disarm" Saddam Hussein's nonexistent WMD have exacerbated these sentiments, especially considering the level of destruction during the military occupation of Iraq. An Iraqi insurgent in Falluja, Khairullah Ibrahim Abbas, summarized the conundrum facing US policy-makers: "At the beginning we thought the Americans came for humanitarian reasons, but now we see they came for destruction."[36] Tragically for American troops serving in present-day Iraq, it seems that neoconservative strategists collectively ignored the history lessons provided by former colonial occupiers. During the 1920s Iraqi Sunnis and Shi'ites joined forces to rebel against their British occupiers. In the 1950s the French learned hard lessons about their colonial occupation of Algeria, and in the 1980s the Soviet Union paid a very heavy price for their devastating occupation of Afghanistan. The US military is not immune to the blowback that stems from colonial occupation.

In addition, we must note that the emergence of US military bases in Saudi Arabia after the 1991 Gulf War created hostility toward both the Saudi regime and US government. Osama bin Laden claimed this was one of the core reasons for his acts of terrorism against the US. Do we want to perpetuate animosity from the Iraqi citizenry over similar perceptions of US imperialism? The stated neoconservative plan of establishing permanent bases in Iraq must be abandoned if the US wishes to create any semblance of democratic rule in Iraq. In fact, gaining a commitment from the international community to help restore stability in Iraq will likely require that the US military vacate the 14 bases that were established during the occupation.

There is little reason to believe that US bases in Iraq will be any more welcome by the Iraqi people than by the Saudis. It is highly likely that these bases, even if somewhat secluded from the major population areas, will be viewed by the average Iraqi as a constant imperial irritant. The history lessons of Mesopotamia are unambiguous — foreign troops are considered occupiers — and will be not be welcomed.

Therefore, Washington needs to negotiate a very small American footprint and pursue realistic options that include multinational UN peacekeeping forces that rotate out of Iraq as conditions allow, with Americans comprising hopefully less than 20 percent. Moreover, US peacekeeping deployments should be limited to Iraq's northern areas where the Kurdish population is generally receptive to the presence of US troops.

Foreign soldiers wearing the distinct light-blue helmets or berets worn by UN peacekeepers will be much better tolerated by the world community, including the average Iraqi citizen. The UN's command of such a force would be correctly perceived by the Iraqis as a *temporary measure*, and many lives — both American and Iraqi — might be spared if such a policy were implemented. In addition, monetary reform regarding an OPEC dual dollar-euro oil pricing mechanism should be negotiated with the UN and European Central Bank, thereby providing the EU nations with sufficient financial motivation to commit both troops and vital resources in a multinational effort to stabilize and rebuild Iraq's infrastructure. Although these suggestions will be rejected by the US military–industrial–petroleum–banking conglomerate, an objective analysis shows the US is running out of options in postwar Iraq.

In an interview with *Prospect* magazine, Emmanuel Todd, French author of *After the Empire: The Breakdown of the American Order* (*Après l'Empire*) prophesized the decline of American hegemony.[37] Todd provided insights into the widespread global concerns of US foreign and monetary policies. He argued that while the global community is fully cognizant of US military superiority, it does not mask our economic vulnerabilities, which are most apparent in the dollar's steady devaluation since 2002. Todd implied that the cumulative economic and geopolitical stresses created by the neoconservatives' drive for global supremacy will ultimately undermine US national finances.

> Until recently, [the US] was the most important factor in maintaining international order. But now it is a factor for instability. The industrial core of the US has been hollowed out. The American trade deficit amounts to $435bn a year. The country needs $1.5bn a day in foreign capital. The US is no longer self-sufficient. Europe, with its strength in exports, is .. . As far as the balance sheet and financial flows are concerned, the US has long been a drain on the whole world. The Europeans can no longer react to this in a friendly manner; they must counter America with industrial and financial methods.[38]

Similar commentary has also appeared in Asian media sources, suggesting that the Chinese government is making a concentrated effort to create bonds and other financial vehicles to facilitate credit expansion in the region, which will soon reduce their purchase of US Treasuries. Additionally, the European Central Bank (ECB) is also creating monetary debt vehicles in an effort to absorb the eventual influx of surplus petroeuros — should Russia convert to a petroeuro system.

Imprudently, domestic observers continue to assume that the US economy will remain the *only* engine for global economic growth into the foreseeable future, assuming that European and Asian countries will be either unable or unwilling to reduce their dependency on the US consumer demand, given the potential economic disruptions that would occur if they pursue alternative economic strategies. This assumption on behalf of the current US policymakers may turn out to be one of the fatal flaws inherent to neoconservative geostrategy.

The Bush administration believes it can continue to create divisions within the EU and Asia, but this may not be the case. Either way, the Bush administration overplayed its hand and exposed the weakness of US hegemonic status in the aftermath of the Iraq invasion. Before the war, the neoconservative strategists failed to recognize the effectiveness of soft power within the United Nations, and following the war and its aftermath of an increasingly chaotic occupation of Iraq, they clearly overestimated the abilities of hard power.

This has exposed the limits of US hegemony to the world community. One of the reasons the US was such a successful hegemonic power for the first 50 years after WW II was the general perception, with the exception of the Vietnam War, that America was an often self-restrained superpower. Indeed, hegemonic power is most effective and long-lasting when it is kept in reserve, always creating the perception that it is actively limiting itself even when displaying its strength.

Neoconservatives abandoned the postwar strategy of multilateral restraint and pursued hard power politics. Apparently Colin Powell tried to warn President Bush about invading Iraq, telling him, "It's nice to say that you can do it unilaterally, except you can't. A successful military plan would require we need allies .... International support has to be garnered."[39] The Bush administration did not heed this advice. They recklessly forfeited US hegemony by violating international law and exposing the inherent weaknesses of unilateral military action. To many observers, the US military's chaotic occupation of Iraq now symbolizes imperial overstretch and has created deep divisions amongst the US' traditional allies. Indeed, the full cost of the Iraq War is not yet known, but the history of empires is unambiguous: they always end with military overextension and subsequent economic decline.

Regrettably, the following analysis concerns a scenario that could potentially trigger a major US monetary crisis. This assessment of Osama bin Laden's reported interest in certain US mainland targets is meant not to create anxiety, but rather to *reinforce the necessity of a strong US/EU partnership* — and the desirability of dollar-euro parity valuation and a dual-currency OPEC transaction option.

Osama bin Laden's Offensive: Economics Not Religion

> Therefore, I am telling you, and God is my witness, *whether America escalates or de-escalates the conflict, we will reply to it in kind*, God willing. God is my witness, the youth of Islam are preparing things that will fill your hearts with fear. They will *target key sectors of your economy* until you stop your injustice and aggression or until the more short-lived of us die. [emphasis added]
>
> — Statement by Usama bin Laden, October 6, 2002[40]

> Bin Laden dwelled on al-Qaida's economic strategy against the United States in portions of an 18-minute video aired Friday on the Arab television station al-Jazeera .... [Bin Laden] credited the religiously inspired Arab volunteers who he fought with against the Soviets in Afghanistan with having "bled Russia for 10 years, until it went bankrupt and was forced to withdraw in defeat." He suggested the same strategy would work against the United States. "So we are continuing this policy in bleeding America to the point of bankruptcy."
>
> — "Bin Laden Says He Wants to Bankrupt America,"
> *Chicago Sun-Times*, November 2, 2004[41]

On September 11, 2001, Al Qaeda terrorists attacked a major economic symbol of US financial power in New York — the World Trade Towers. On

August 2, 2004, the Office of Homeland Security instigated heightened security alerts at five US specific locations. Bizarrely, the following day the media revealed that these "urgent" warnings were based upon evidence collected "two or three years" ago and that there was "no evidence of recent surveillance" by members of Al Qaeda.[42] Not surprisingly, various commentators suggested political motivations behind these dated "terror alerts" as they occurred just after the Democratic National Convention. Regardless of the political aspects, this alert provided valuable insight into several identified targets as part of bin Laden's "offensive" against the US economy:

- International Monetary Fund in Washington
- World Bank headquarters in Washington
- New York Stock Exchange in New York
- Citigroup Center in New York
- Prudential Financial building in Newark, New Jersey[43]

Based on this list, Osama bin Laden is evidently not interested in attacking US civilians in shopping malls, schools, apartment buildings, vacation areas like Disneyland, or historic monuments like the Statue of Liberty, but rather Al Qaeda had *specifically targeted the centers of US financial power*. This strategy is not surprising considering that, as a young man, bin Laden studied economics. His stated grievances are based on specific US foreign policies — most of which relate to the projection of military power in the Persian Gulf and central Asian regions, including the financial/military subsidy of Israel, Egypt, Saudi Arabia, Qatar, and Kuwait.

Supporting assertions that bin Laden and his small band of followers are motivated by US foreign policies can be found in *Imperial Hubris: Why the West is Losing the War on Terror*.[44] It provided an exceptionally candid appraisal of bin Laden's grievances and those of much of the Muslim world, which the author stated have been specifically and consistently repeated as relating to US foreign policies. This "anonymous" author was later identified as Michael Scheuer, a 17-year-veteran of the CIA, and former chief of the Usama bin Laden Unit, Counterterrorist Center, 1997–1999. Scheuer makes the important point that al Qaeda's intentions follow Clausewitz's principle of attacking one's foe at their "center of gravity."[45] In late 2002 Abu-Ubayd al-Qurashi, an Al Qaeda operative, wrote an essay clearly stating that Al Qaeda's goal is to "direct all available force against the [US'] center of gravity during the great offensive."[46] Moreover, this essay indicated that Al Qaeda had identified America's center of gravity as its *economy*.

> A conviction has formed among the mujahedin that American public opinion is not the center of gravity in America. The Zionist

lobbies, and with them the security agencies, have long been able to bridle all the media that control the formation of public opinion in America. *This time it is clearly apparent that the American economy is the American center of gravity* ....

This is what Shaykh Usama Bin Laden has said quite explicitly. Supporting this penetrating strategic view is that the Disunited States of America are a mixture of nationalities, ethnic groups, and races united only by the "American Dream," or to put it more correctly, *worship of the dollar, which they openly call "the Almighty Dollar."* [emphasis added]

— Abu-Ubayd al-Qurashi, "A Lesson in War," *Al-Ansar* (Al Qaeda's Internet website), December 19, 2002[47]

Statements by Osama bin Laden in conjunction with the August 2004 "terror warning" of previously "cased" targets exposed his political goals as having a strong economic component. Targeting the massive World Trade Center Towers and the Pentagon coincide with his stated goals, both figuratively and literally. Therefore, it is logical to deduce that Al Qaeda may seek to create a panic on the US dollar by attacking certain financial centers. Perhaps that strategy presumes that a currency collapse and subsequently crippled economy could no longer finance a global military empire, nor could Washington continue to provide annual multi-billion subsidies in money and advanced US weaponry to Israel, Saudi Arabia, Egypt, Qatar, and Kuwait. Why else would Osama bin Laden *specifically case or target* the east coast's five principle financial centers?

Based on this analysis, the risks of not achieving a compromise on the global monetary system could create very adverse effects on US national security. Could Al Qaeda eventually succeed in a terrorist attack upon US financial centers in an effort to create a dollar crash and global monetary crisis? Could events unfold and cause a domestic uprising against the Saudi monarchy that results in "regime change"? Either of these events could result in a massive divestiture of Saudi assets from the US, a currency collapse, potentially leading to a formal accord creating a *monopoly petroeuro* system within OPEC — as opposed to the preferred dual-currency oil transaction standard.

Considering that these risk factors will only become more salient in the post-Peak Oil environment, Washington policy-makers should begin negotiations with the EU and OPEC regarding the plausibility of a dollar-euro trading band with $1.00 to €1.00 parity valuations, along with a formal dual-currency oil transaction standard. In theory, such an arrangement would protect the dollar from a potentially catastrophic devaluation; provide the European community with a stabilized oil bill, and build the foundation for a strong economic partnership between the US and the EU.

Realistic Campaign against International Terrorism: INTERPOL and the International Criminal Court (ICC)

Al-Qaida's numbers were grossly exaggerated by the Bush administration and US media. Hardcore al-Qaida members never numbered more than 200–300. Claims that there were 5,000–20,000 al-Qaida fighters in Afghanistan were nonsense. These wild exaggerations came from lumping Taliban tribal warriors with some 5,000 Islamic resistance fighters from Kashmir, Uzbekistan, Tajikistan, the Philippines and Chinese-ruled Eastern Turkistan, none of whom were part of al-Qaida.

— Eric Margolis, "Anti-US militants showing up all over,"
Toronto Star, June 2002[48]

Senior FBI officials believe there are now no more than 200 hardcore Al-Qaeda members worldwide. *"Al-Qaeda itself, we know, is less than 200,"* said an FBI official, referring to those who have sworn allegiance to Osama bin Laden, the alleged mastermind behind the Sept. 11 terrorist attacks .... That figure — far fewer than recent press reports have suggested are in the US alone — is based on evidence gathered by the FBI and CIA. It includes Al-Qaeda members who are now in custody at Guantanamo Bay. [The FBI official stated,] *"There was a recent report suggesting that Al-Qaeda is about 5,000 strong. It is nowhere near 5,000 strong."* [emphasis added]

— Rebecca Carr, "Only 200 Hard-core Qaeda Members,"
Palm Beach Post, July 2002[49]

The terrorist attack on the United States could have been treated as a crime against humanity rather than an act of war. Treating it as a crime would have been more appropriate. Crimes require police work, not military action .... The war on terrorism as pursued by the Bush administration cannot be won. On the contrary, it may bring about a permanent state of war. Terrorists will never disappear. They will continue to provide a pretext for the pursuit of American supremacy. That pursuit, in turn, will continue to generate resistance. Further, by turning the hunt for terrorists into a war, we are bound to create innocent victims. The more innocent victims there are, the greater the resentment and the better the chances that some victims will turn into perpetrators.

— George Soros, "The Bubble of American Supremacy,"
Atlantic Monthly, December 2003[50]

According to international polls, much of the world community perceives the Bush administration's "war on terrorism" not as a legitimate response to international terrorism, but as a cynical strategy to pursue global domination by seizing control over the world's largest oil supply. This current geostrategy has weakened the US' security in the fight against terrorism and created international blowback against the US after the ill-fated Iraq invasion. A completely revamped US strategy is warranted if the fight against international terrorism is to be seen as a legitimate campaign in the eyes of the world community.

To facilitate global cooperation, a clear distinction must be established between international terrorist groups, such as Al Qaeda, and non-international groups whose political grievances are geographically specific. For example, the Irish Republican Army (IRA) of the 1970s and 1980s engaged in terrorist tactics, but like today's Hamas and Hezbollah, they limited their activities to specific regional/political conflicts. Additionally, and despite the claims of certain political leaders, it is critically important to realize that the US and UK governments have failed to report on the actual size of the Al Qaeda terrorist network. Although buried by our subservient media, the number of dedicated Al Qaeda members who have shown allegiance to Osama bin Laden is reportedly very small. According to senior FBI officials, as of 2002 there were *only about 200 hard-core Al Qaeda members still at large.*

Al Capone's infamous Chicago mafia had two to three times as many members as Al Qaeda. However, the FBI did not bomb Sicily in the 1930s during our "war against organized crime."

In comparison, Al Capone's infamous Chicago mafia had two to three times as many members as Al Qaeda. However, the FBI did not bomb Sicily in the 1930s during our "war against organized crime." Likewise we cannot stop Al Qaeda with bombs or "regime change." The Orwellian ambiguity of the current global "war on terrorism" should be replaced with a more defined, and winnable, "*Campaign against Al Qaeda.*" While the 200 members represent a threat that must be eliminated via intelligence operations, evidence strongly suggests that Al Qaeda is not a global menace that supposedly operates in 60 countries but is actually *very small* and now disorganized.

A powerful three-part BBC documentary series, *Power of Nightmares,* argued that while Osama bin Laden is a threat, much of what we have been told about a centralized, international terrorist threat "is a fantasy that has been exaggerated and distorted by politicians. It is a dark illusion that has spread unquestioned through governments around the world, the security services and the international media."[52] Is it possible that the "war on terror" is being used as the Straussian mechanism to forcefully exaggerate an external threat — thereby masking geostrategic maneuvers regarding domination over the globe's oil supplies? Is it merely coincidental that the US' expanding "war on terror" is directly correlated to areas where hydrocarbons reserves or pipelines exist?

Rarely discussed in Western media is Osama bin Laden's resentment based on what he perceives as the "transfer of wealth" from the corrupt Saudi monarchy to the US. He stated that oil should be priced at $144 per barrel — which he may view as a form of punitive reparation for the world's 1.2 billion Muslims. A careful analysis by author Michael Mann suggested that bin Laden may accurately be described as a violent "anti-Imperialist militant Islamist."[53] In *Imperial Hubris*, Michael Scheuer deftly argued that bin Laden perceived his acts of terrorism as part of a "defensive jihad" against US policies:[54]

> Bin Laden's center of gravity ... lies in the list of current US policies toward the Muslim world because that status quo enrages Muslims around the globe — no matter their view of al Qaeda's martial actions — and gives bin Laden's efforts to instigate a worldwide anti-US defensive jihad virtually unlimited room for growth .... Until those [foreign] policies change, the United States has no option but increasingly fierce military response to the forces marshaled by bin Laden, an option that will prolong America's survival but at as yet undreamed of costs on blood, money and civil liberties.[55]

According to Scheuer, we should dispense with the absurd notion that Osama bin Laden "hates our freedoms." Bin Laden hates our ongoing foreign policies, most especially the positioning of US troops on the Arabian Peninsula, the birthplace of Islam, which he views as offensive to Islam. Scheuer contended that Al Qaeda-sponsored terrorists attacks will not end unless either the US pursues a total genocidal war against numerous Muslim countries in the region — killing millions in the process — or US policy-makers change foreign policies and align them with US principles, not the interests of the military–industrial–petroleum–banking conglomerate.

The US military, like all others, is a very blunt instrument that is well equipped and trained to destroy physical assets and defeat foreign military forces. Not surprisingly, it is simply not suited for hunting down terrorists, nor should it be used for such. Indeed, the presence of US troops and the "collateral damage" that occurs with large-scale military operations only serve to create more hatred and individuals sympathetic to bin Laden. In truth, defeating Al Qaeda-sponsored terrorism will require not only changes in US foreign policy, but also considerable international cooperation via joint intelligence/police operations between the US, EU, Africa, central Asia, and the Middle East. Recognizing the limitations of the US military's hard power, and its potential economic blowback, the most logical alternative is the realignment of US foreign policies in these areas with true American ideals.

A more logical approach would consist of a highly empowered INTER-POL operation, working in conjunction with the International Criminal Court (ICC).[56] Such a recalibrated global strategy should produce the least amount of blowback in a worldwide anti-terrorism campaign.

We must acknowledge that terrorism will exist as long as man walks the earth, so we must live in dignity, not in fear. Reducing ignorance and oppression that breeds fear and hatred will reduce future recruits for terrorist groups. We must frame international terrorism not as an abstract war, but as a specific *crime against humanity*. Western nations need to adjust their perceptions accordingly and work diligently together within the international framework to round up these few criminals. The campaign against worldwide terrorism is not a war between nation states; it is a war of ideas over foreign policies and the self-determination of nations. The US ultimately won the Cold War because it won the hearts and minds of those who were oppressed under the former political system of the Soviet empire. Likewise, if Americans truly practiced the values in the Declaration of Independence, Constitution, and Bill of Rights, the US would have the world's respect and admiration, not the world's fear and loathing.

Rising above the current anti-Americanism will require a complete restructuring of current campaign finance laws in an effort to remove the unwarranted political power of the military–industrial–petroleum–banking conglomerate, an honest and balanced foreign policy regarding Israel, non-interference in the internal politics of oil producing states, and a viable national energy strategy that permits the end to support for Middle Eastern repressive regimes. The key to any semblance of peace and global stability in the 21st century will revolve around multilateral accords designed to reduce hydrocarbon consumption, and a US policy of *sustained energy reform* — thereby allowing more enlightened foreign policies — just as the founding fathers envisioned.

Realigning US Foreign Policies: Rebuilding Good Will Towards America

Despite an initial outpouring of public sympathy for America following the September 11, 2001, terrorist attacks, discontent with the United States has grown around the world over the past two years. Images of the US have been tarnished in all types of nations: among longtime NATO allies, in developing countries, in Eastern Europe, and, most dramatically, in Muslim societies."

The American public is strikingly at odds with publics around the world in its views about the US role in the world and the global impact of American actions. In contrast to people in most other countries, a solid majority of Americans surveyed think the

US takes into account the interests of other countries when making international policy.

US image problems are not confined to Muslim countries. The worldwide polling conducted throughout the summer and fall finds few people, even in friendly nations, expressing a very favorable opinion of America, and sizable minorities in Western Europe and Canada having an unfavorable view. Many people around the world, especially in Europe and the Middle East/Conflict Area, believe the US does not take into account the interests of their country when making international policies.

> In contrast to people in most other countries, a solid majority of Americans surveyed think the US takes into account the interests of other countries when making international policy.

— *What the World Thinks in 2002: How Global Publics View Their Lives, Their Countries, The World, and America.*
Pew Global Attitudes survey, December 2002[57]

There are numerous strategies and policies that could be pursued to reduce global tensions and begin restoring international goodwill toward the US. Fundamentally speaking, reducing geopolitical tensions in an era of depleting resources will require US policy-makers to revisit multilateral traditions — in a world ruled by law, not by military might. Multilateral strategies providing immediate benefits to US leadership would begin with adopting numerous international accords, including the acceptance of the legitimacy of the ICC, signing the treaty banning anti-personnel mines, strengthening as opposed to weakening the Biological Weapons Convention, and accepting the Comprehensive Test Ban Treaty on nuclear weapons.

Most of the world community has rejected the regional policies of the Bush administration, and as such, a drastic reorientation of US strategy is required if the economy and international stature is to be restored under new leadership. The following regional policies outline a more enlightened approach to US foreign policy.

Europe

The US does not need to maintain the current level of military forces in Europe. The institutions of NATO should be transferred to the European Defense Force (EDF), and the Atlantic Alliance should be relegated to a basic mutual-defense pact. NATO's historical mission ended with the 1991 collapse of the Soviet Union, and other than the 1999 Kosovo campaign, it would appear difficult to invent a new mission for this structure. The EU on its own initiative seeks to gradually extend the supranational European economic and governmental constructs across eastern Europe, and their accession guidelines (along with those of NATO which would be transferred to the EDF) are more than sufficient to eventually create a uniformly prosperous and peaceful zone at least to the borders of Russia. The damaged US relationship with Turkey, although not generally regarded as part of Europe, over the Iraq War could be mitigated by the next US administration if it provided political support for Turkey's acceptance into the EU.

Russia

The US should follow the EU's lead by formally recognizing the Russian Federation as a market economy that currently impedes Russia's accession to the World Trade Organization. Otherwise, the US government needs to become fully committed to reducing the former Soviet WMD systems, implying a significant increase in funding to dismantle them. Additionally, it should reverse its opposition to mutual supervisory access toward monitoring nonproliferation and disarmament agreements, which presents the greatest obstruction to properly accounting for and dismantling Russian WMD.

Furthermore, the G–8 nations should adopt measures to disrupt the massive organized crime, financial laundering operations which have funneled at least $200 billion into private accounts since the fall of the Soviet Union. Undoubtedly, Russia presents an array of daunting obstacles to economic development and political reform after a chaotic decade of inept privatization schemes. A more appropriate development plan would entail a clear framework of incentives with progressive accession to European institutions (the EU and EDF). Lastly, the US should withdraw the many current military deployments in various Caspian region states that are unnecessarily antagonizing the Russia government and its military leadership.

Korea

Resolving the Korean peninsular dispute requires at the very minimum the reinvigoration of the Sunshine Policy rapprochement and ending this administration's rather irrational antagonism of North Korea. A German-style reunification should become the ultimate target of US foreign policy, with UN involvement for the reassimilation of North Korea's disastrous economy. Furthermore, the $13 billion South Korean military budget alone is larger than North Korea's entire $9 billion governmental budget. Negotiations should entail blanket amnesty for Kim Jong Il as well as all North Korean officialdom, a concrete US military withdrawal timeline (as a concurrent de-escalation), and an economic revitalization development plan could easily include $8 billion of the current South Korean annual military expenditure bolstered with $2 billion of US assistance ($100 billion/10 years).

To gain amnesty, the North Korean government would be required to forfeit all 8,000 spent uranium fuel rods, transferable technology, and related nuclear material to the UN or International Atomic Energy Agency (IAEA).

Additionally, in exchange for massive economic, food supplies, and agricultural development, the North Korean government should agree to cease all exports of advanced missile technology. For this, the US and world community should fulfill the earlier pledge to build two light-water nuclear power plants for North Korea's energy needs. In effect, the proposed reassimilation of North and South Korea, along with general amnesty for the current North Korean regime, should remove the impetus for such weaponry.

China

The US' current belligerent policy of military containment around China's periphery survives as a pointless anachronism from the Cold War, and this should end. Moreover, the Theater Missile Defense System, notable for its uselessness and excessive cost, also symbolizes this posture's illogic and should be cancelled immediately. The divided-China problem persists as the only real exacerbating factor in Sino-American relations that largely involves US support for abandonment of the 1993 Singapore agreement.

A cooperative framework accord with a commonwealth arrangement that ensures Taiwan's free-market democracy under a sovereign One China principle should be advocated by the US. Bilateral regime interactions (including sequential rule compliance guidelines) should be implemented in the areas of infrastructural networking. This should facilitate Taiwanese foreign policy dismantlement and the demilitarization of the Taiwan Straits with the stated objective of a coordinated federation treaty, ensuring Taiwan autonomy while repudiating use of force.

Middle East

The Israeli-Palestinian conflict, the central flashpoint for all Middle Eastern affairs, facilitates broad anti-American sentiments and potentially facilitates the recruitment of Al Qaeda members. The outline of a viable peace plan is understood by the majority of the world community and includes issues discussed during the last meaningful negotiations in Taba, Egypt (January 2001). The US should leverage its massive subsidization of the Israeli economy to compel a resolution based on 1967 borders, full diplomatic relations with the Arab states, and binding regional cooperative frameworks. A symbolic "right of return" for a few Palestinians to the newly created state would seem advisable, along with a large refugee settlement fund for the majority of Palestinians who remain in their host countries. This fund should be under UN supervision, funded by members of the international community, especially the wealthy G–7 nations.

Subsequently, the US should normalize relations with Iran and Syria based on resolving particular grievances. For the most part, a resolution to the Arab–Israeli conflict would itself eliminate both the rationale for the international terrorist substructure, which underlies the Western–Arab hostility and the primary outlet that enables various Arab regimes to maintain their popular mandate and militant police states. Finally, the US should withdraw all atypical financial and military support of the dictatorial Persian Gulf regimes (i.e., Saudi Arabia) and cease covert operations, thereby implicitly endorsing democratization by internal processes, including internal uprisings to remove oppressive regimes (without covert interference by the CIA or other clandestine organizations).

Africa

The Western nations should establish a debt cancellation protocol under the auspices of the UN that includes an explicit resolution of the reparations issue with a further grant transfer component. Assistance qualification should require the resolution of outstanding regional and internal disputes, human rights guarantees under pluralistic democracy, and adoption of sustainable growth policies. Implementation should remain contingent on progress toward demilitarization, ongoing adherence to fiscally responsible guidelines, and establishing a framework of intracontinental conventions.

One option would be incremental grants targeted to specific infrastructural improvements under contractual obligation, as well as material humanitarian goods and services as opposed to block cash handouts. While the specific parameters of the protocol can be designed as appropriate, it is more important that it entail all these elements in a comprehensive, enduring African solution. The Bush administration's initiative regarding AIDS should be continued and expanded in this decade.

Latin America

The strategies surrounding the perpetual war on drugs need to be objectively evaluated and likely overhauled. The current policies seem to be creating nothing but endemic "Narco Wars" that fuel the cycle of transience, poverty, exploitation, and victimization. Furthermore, the most beneficial strategy would facilitate overthrowing the drug overlords while also ending the oppressive concentration of wealth and influence in the landed aristocratic elite.

Additionally, the US government should cease any ongoing covert activities in the internal affairs of the democratically elected president of Venezuela and other democracies in Latin America. The US government has more than enough blowback from other regions, and it does not need to create adversarial relationships in its own hemisphere. Negotiations on residual energy issues should be performed via the normal diplomatic apparatus. Washington should also prepare for normalized diplomatic and trade relationships with Cuba. The end of the Cold War rendered the five-decade-old trade embargo as another anachronism of the past, counterproductive for future relationships with Cuba. Given the exceptionally warm waters off Cuba, it would also be mutually beneficial to pursue a joint US/Cuba Ocean Thermal Energy Conversion (OTEC) plantship to further evaluate this renewable energy.

International

The World Trade Organization (WTO) and the International Monetary Fund (IMF) should be reorganized to specifically redress the imbalances of existing trade agreements between the Heavily Industrialized Countries (HIC) and the Less Developed Countries (LDC), provide developing nations with equitable access to industrialized markets, and develop an enforceable structure for differential provisions that guarantee development policies are not undermined by trade liberalization. Oxfam's website describes the goals of "Fair Trade:"

- To improve the livelihoods and well-being of producers by improving market access, strengthening producer organizations, paying a better price and providing continuity in the trading relationship.

- To promote development opportunities for disadvantaged producers, especially women and indigenous people, and to protect children from exploitation in the production process.

- To raise awareness among consumers of the negative effects on producers of international trade so that they exercise their purchasing power positively.

- To set an example of partnership in trade through dialogue, transparency and respect.

- To campaign for changes in the rules and practice of conventional international trade.

- To protect human rights by promoting social justice, sound environmental practices and economic security.[58]

The US should work toward joining the global community, becoming a full participant in multilateral nonproliferation accords and environmental conventions, including ratification of the Kyoto Climate Treaty and a renegotiated ABM agreement. Most essential to US security and global security is an international energy strategy based on aggressive domestic energy reforms as well as global cooperation pursuant to the same goals. Ideally the US should resolve that all international institutions be redesigned on the prerequisite conformance with, and advancement of, the Universal Declaration of Human Rights, revised with interpretive authority granted to the International Court of Justice.[59, 60] These efforts would do much to reduce feelings of anti-Americanism and, if successfully pursued, allow America to rebuild its international stature as a leading proponent of human rights, democracy, and international cooperation.

Preserving Freedom at Home: Protecting the Charters of Freedom

> The Patriot Act makes it able for those of us in positions of responsibility to defend the liberty of the American people.
>
> — President George W. Bush, quoted by the National Committee Against Repressive Legislation, May 2004[61]

> The objective of the Patriot Act [is to make] the population visible and the Justice Department invisible. The Act inverts the constitutional requirement that people's lives be private and the work of government officials be public; it instead crafts a set of conditions that make our inner lives transparent and the workings of government opaque.
>
> — Elaine Scarry, "Acts of Resistance," *Harper's Magazine*, May 2004[62]

> More than two centuries ago, the patriots of Brewster [Massachusetts] shut down the Colonial courts on Cape Cod in one of the first acts of resistance against the tyrannical rule of King George III. Now, deliberately evoking its Revolutionary history, Brewster Town Meeting has formally condemned the antiterrorist USA Patriot Act.
>
> — Nat Hentoff, "Declarations of Independence," June, 2004[63]

> I believe there are more instances of the abridgement of the freedom of the people by gradual and silent encroachments of those in power than by violent and sudden usurpations.
>
> — James Madison, US Founding Father

> What country can preserve its liberties, if its rulers are not warned from time to time that its people preserve the spirit of resistance.
>
> — Thomas Jefferson, US Founding Father

The founding fathers of the United States were astute observers of not only history, but also human behavior. They saw that seeking an empire abroad would result in tyranny at home. Jefferson, Madison, and Washington understood that democracies are incompatible with empires and that imperial pursuits abroad invariably lead to sacrifices in democratic principles, and the diminishment of liberty and freedom. For these reasons the founders warned against the temptation of seeking to be the next Rome, and correctly sought to limit the federal government's ability to engage in imperial wars.

As an American proud of the many noble accomplishments of this nation, I found this chapter was the most difficult to write. The "politics of fear" that have been vigorously pursued by US policy-makers over the last few years have placed this nation and our liberties and freedoms at risk. If they were alive today, Thomas Jefferson, James Madison, George Washington, and the other founders would undoubtedly be appalled at the USA Patriot Act (USAPA), provisions within the Homeland Security laws, various Executive Orders, the consolidation and apparent censorship of the news, and the perpetual state of war that has been declared by the executive branch. We have entered a perilous period when the media has become uncritical and fearful of reporting facts that are contrary to the official narrative yet widely reported in the foreign media and on the Internet.

Nat Hentoff, a writer and longtime civil liberties commentator, noted that just as the colonists rebelled against tyranny when this country was founded, today's patriots are rebelling against provisions of the Patriot Act I (and aspects of Patriot Act II that were covertly passed under the 9/11 Commission laws). Jefferson would be proud to know that over 300 municipalities in 41 states have declared themselves immune to federal law concerning certain provisions of the Patriot Act and Homeland Security. They regard themselves as "Patriot Act-Free Zones."

The outrage of these informed citizens is largely based on two provisions within the original Patriot Act. One is section 215 that gives the government new power to search people's homes without notification.[64] This is known as a "sneak and peak" warrant; the old standard was called "knock and announce." Another controversial section gives the government and the FBI new power to look into people's library, business, and medical records.[65]

Furthermore, the framers of the Constitution would consider debate over the rationales for the Iraq War not as unpatriotic, but as absolutely necessary. Authoritarians refer to anti-war protestors as anti-American, and allies or experts who raised objective questions about the rationales for war were either bribed (Turkey), threatened (Old Europe), dismissed as "irrelevant" (Hans Blix and his UN weapons inspection team), had their character impugned (former weapons inspector Scott Ritter), or even had their careers ruined (outed CIA asset Valarie Plume, the wife of former ambassador Wilson, who disputed the claims that Saddam Hussein attempted to purchase yellowcake uranium from Niger). Indeed, authoritarian media pundits and partisan politicians proclaimed that mere criticism of the president's policies amounted to "political hate speech."

This ideological rigidity concerning the serious subject of engaging in an unprovoked war of choice indicates a significant deterioration of societal discourse. David Domke, a professor of communication at the University of Washington and former journalist, analyzed the "strategic communications" of the Bush administration in his illuminating book, *God Willing? Political Fundamentalism in the White House, the "War on Terror," and the Echoing Press.* In the wake of 9/11 until the March 2003 invasion of Iraq, Domke undertook a scholarly analysis of hundreds of White House communications and associated news stories to dissect the current political environment, which he has termed "political fundamentalism."[66]

This construct described the purposeful communication strategy that "capitalized" on Americans' fears, along with the subservient US media who uncritically echoed this mixing of religion and governance. Domke found the Bush administration's governing patterns included the following elements of political fundamentalism:

- Binary, or simplistic, conceptions of the political landscape, such as good vs. evil and "Either you are with us or you are with the terrorists."

- Calls for immediate action on administration policies as a necessary part of the nation's "calling" and "mission" against terrorism.

- Declarations about the will of God for America and for the spread of US conceptions of freedom and liberty.

- Claims that dissent from the administration is unpatriotic and a threat to the nation.[67]

Domke effectively warned that this form of intolerant political fundamentalism is damaging our basic democratic and political process:

> Blind faith in US governmental leadership to act with integrity and on behalf of the mass public does not work, has never worked. The lessons of McCarthyism in the 1950s, the Vietnam War in the 1960s, Watergate in the 1970s, and Iran-Contra in the 1980s are being learned anew in the United States.[68]

Most of this dilemma is that the press is not fulfilling its historical role of offering critical analysis, while the authoritarians quickly denounce any criticism of the president's policies as un-American. This includes false rationales, such as "supporting the troops" is somehow interchangeable with "supporting the president." But they are not the same: it is the politicians who start the wars, not the warriors.

According to previous US presidents, to not criticize the federal government in times of war if one disagrees with its policies is not only unpatriotic, but un-American. For example, during WW I Teddy Roosevelt stated, "To announce that there must be no criticism of the president, or that we are to stand by the president, right or wrong, is not only unpatriotic and servile, but it is morally treasonable to the American public."[69] Just after Pearl Harbor, conservative Republican Bob Taft reiterated these sentiments in December 1941:

> I believe, there can be no doubt that criticism in time of war is essential to the maintenance of any kind of democratic government .... Too many people desire to suppress criticism simply because they think it will give some comfort to the enemy .... If that comfort makes the enemy feel better for a few moments, they are welcome to it as far as I am concerned, because the maintenance of the right of criticism in the long run will do the country maintaining it a great deal more good than it will do the enemy, and it will prevent mistakes which might otherwise occur.[70]

Roosevelt and Taft were both right; the concept of dissent — even during the 20th century world wars — served to strengthen US democracy. Each member of the US military has sworn to protect this fundamental concept of the Constitution. Sadly, this is often not understood by more reactionary segments of the American population, whom I refer to as authoritarians.

Every American should be concerned with the unprecedented claim that the president has the right to personally designate an American citizen as an "enemy combatant," possibly resulting in their indefinite, or perhaps permanent, detention, without being charged or even having access to legal representation. This claim is thoroughly authoritarian, and this so-called right is clearly *unconstitutional*.

This segues into a subject that has caused much alarm for those Americans, such as me, who believe that our freedom and liberty is sacred and that protection of the Constitution and its ideas is the citizens' highest duty. In an extensive interview for *Cigar Aficionado*, retired General Franks, the former commander of Central Command and the Iraq War, speculated that if terrorists were to successfully use a WMD in the US then our Constitution and Republican government would be in jeopardy.

> The Western world, the free world, loses what it cherishes most, and that is freedom and liberty we've seen for a couple of hundred years in this grand experiment that we call democracy.

It means that the potential of a weapon of mass destruction and a terrorist, massive, casualty-producing event somewhere in the Western world — it may be in the United States of America — that causes our population to question our own Constitution and begin to militarize our country in order to avoid a repeat of another mass, casualty-producing event. Which in fact then begins to unravel the fabric of our Constitution.[71]

It seems heedless that someone who swore to protect the Constitution from enemies both foreign and domestic would openly discuss the possibility of discarding the essence of what their career was dedicated to protect. Many Americans, myself included, found these sentiments both strange and profoundly disturbing. Franks seemed to suggest that a terrorist WMD strike against the American people or anywhere in the "Western world" might cause us to fundamentally question our free and open system of government, unravel our Constitution, and replace it with a militarized government. This would be repeating the German people's grave mistake after the burning of the Reichstag in 1933. Would we too demand "temporary" restrictions on liberty while allowing the militarization of our government in order to supposedly protect us from terrorists?

While the successful detonation of a dirty bomb could produce panic in society and the financial markets, political turmoil, economic damage in the affected area due to the need to decontaminate, and perhaps an economic depression, it would *not* destroy the US. No terrorist attack could destroy our ideas as espoused in the Constitution. After all, the Constitution survived the war of 1812, which included the burning of Washington DC, the Civil War in which over 600,000 Americans died, two world wars, and one Great Depression. The founders spent years carefully deliberating a form of government that could survive the test of time. Lord Hoffman's statements to the British House of Lords illustrated why terrorism does not truly threaten the essence of Great Britain or the US:

This is a nation which has been tested in adversity, which has survived physical destruction and catastrophic loss of life .... I do not underestimate the ability of fanatical groups of terrorists to kill and destroy, but they do not threaten the life of the nation. Whether we would survive Hitler hung in the balance, but there is no doubt that we shall survive al-Qaeda .... The Spanish people have not said that what happened in Madrid, hideous crime as it was, threatened the life of their nation. Their legendary pride would not allow it .... Terrorist violence, serious as it is, does not threaten our institutions of government or our existence as a civil community.[72]

The Charters of Freedom — the Declaration of Independence, Constitution, and Bill of Rights — are far more than pieces of parchment paper; they embody universal truths that define the fundamental principles of the US by boldly proclaiming that all men are created equal — this was, and still is, a revolutionary philosophy that transcends the sovereignty of nations. The Constitution was carefully designed to limit the power of the federal government, thereby protecting the people's rights, and thwart the formation of an oppressive tyranny in the new nation. The only way a terrorist attack could destroy the US is if Americans let it destroy their freedom and liberty.

It is not surprising that many informed citizens, libertarians, and other proponents of civil rights are concerned that a second major terrorist attack on US soil could create the very situation on which Franks pontificated — an unraveling of the Constitution with the passage of draconian powers to the executive branch. Hopefully Americans would instead react with empathy, dignity, and steadfastness should another such attack occur. Regardless, neither a dirty bomb, another anthrax attack, nor even a rogue nuclear bomb justifies the dissolution of our Constitution, our form of government, the postponement of elections as prescribed by the Constitution, or the diminishment of our rights and liberties.

We have entered a disturbingly dangerous period in America history when authoritarians hold the reins of power and imply that the Constitution and its protections are strangely viewed as impediments to our national security. Nothing could be further from the truth. The shift of power to the executive branch based on an ambiguous notion of a "perpetual war" embodies the very threat of despotism and oppression that our forefathers revolted against. The Bush administration stated that this "war on terror" might last decades, thereby implying our Constitutional protections may not apply during this indefinite period. This Orwellian and wholly intolerable situation has become critical in part due to the collective failure of our corporate media conglomerates to fulfill their traditional role as watchdogs against government abuse.

> Of all the enemies to public liberty war is, perhaps, the most to be dreaded because it comprises and develops the germ of every other. War is the parent of armies; from these proceed debts and taxes ... known instruments for bringing the many under the domination of the few .... No nation could preserve its freedom in the midst of continual warfare.
>
> — James Madison, US President, 1809–1817

> It is the duty of the patriot to protect his country from the government.
>
> — Thomas Paine, hero of the American Revolution, author of *Common Sense*, 1776

Seven

Envisioning Progressive Global Reform in the New Century

The significant problems we face can not be solved at the same level of thinking we were at when we created them.

— Albert Einstein

New Realities of the 21st Century: Emerging Tri-Polar World

Let the present America expend what remains of its energy, if that is what it wants to do, on the "war on terrorism" — a substitute battle for the perpetuation of a hegemony that it has already lost. If it stubbornly decides to continue showing off its supreme power, it will only end up exposing to the world its powerlessness. ... what the world needs is not that America disappear, but that it return to its true self — democratic, liberal, and productive.

— Emmanuel Todd, *After the Empire: Breakdown of the American Order*, 2004[1]

The current US predicament in Iraq serves as another example that when a country's superiority psychology inflates beyond its real capability, a lot of trouble can be caused. But the troubles and disasters the United States has met do not stem from the threats by others, but from its own cocksureness and arrogance .... The 21st century is not the 'American Century.' That does not mean that the United States does not want the dream. Rather it is incapable of realizing the goal.

— Qian Qichen, former Chinese minister regarded as one of the "main architects" of China's foreign policy, October, 2004[2]

The US can lose its dominance only as a result of its own mistakes. At present the country is in the process of committing such mistakes because it is in the hands of a group of extremists whose strong sense of mission is matched only by their false sense of certitude.

This distorted view postulates that because we are stronger than others, we must know better and we must have right on our side. That is where religious fundamentalism comes together with market fundamentalism to form the ideology of American supremacy.

— George Soros, *The Bubble of American Supremacy*, 2004[3]

Unfortunately, our country has a problem in far too many parts of the world ... a problem we have regrettably gotten into over many years through both Democrat and Republican administrations, and a problem that does not lend itself to a quick fix or a single solution or a simple plan.

— Margaret D. Tutwiler, in her first public appearance as the State Department's Undersecretary for Public Diplomacy and Public Affairs, February 2004[4]

During the debate over the Iraq War, Senator Robert Byrd stated that the preemptive doctrine is a "distortion of long-standing concepts of the right of self-defense [and] a blow against international law." In what may be prophetic, Senator Byrd also proclaimed that President Bush's politics "could well be a turning point in world history [and] lay the foundation for anti-Americanism" across much of the world.[5]

These observations were also articulated by former president Jimmy Carter: "The restrictions on civil rights in the US and at Guantanamo, cancellation of international accords [illustrates] contempt for the rest of the world," and finally triggered an unprovoked attack on Iraq, "although there [was] no threat to the US from Baghdad .... This entire unilateralism will increasingly isolate the US from those nations that we need in order to do battle with terrorism."[6]

Tragically, the international stature of the US has significantly deteriorated over the past few years, initially due to its various unilateral policies before 9/11, and greatly exacerbated by events surrounding the Iraq War. Tutwiler is quite correct that America's standing abroad has deteriorated to such an extent that "it will take us many years of hard, focused work" to restore our lost stature.[7] Obviously, US foreign policies must change in order to effect this.

Not surprisingly, when the horrific pictures were leaked to the US media of naked Iraqi prisoners being tortured by US intelligence and military forces at Abu Ghraib prison, Tutwiler quit her State Department job and began working on Wall Street. It took her four months to realize her job was "mission impossible." Without a doubt, the failure to immediately hold accountable high officials, such as Donald Rumsfeld, has severely and adversely impacted the ability of the US to repair its standing in Iraq and the entire Middle East.

> The world has been willing to follow the US only when it pursued multilateral policies and adhered to international law. The difference between leadership and domination is that the former relies on persuasion, while the latter relies on coercion. As the war in Iraq demonstrates all too clearly, the US cannot coerce the world community to pursue objectives that are in the interests of the US alone. It's clear that the Bush administration has accelerated the decline of the US' global status. To be sure, even if the US leadership had changed after the 2004 election, the task of regaining America's lost moral standing in the world community would have remained a significant challenge.[8]

While many Americans have unknowingly supported the neoconservative plan for US global domination via the "war on terror," the strategic errors regarding the Iraq War are beginning to expose its inherent paradoxes. The world is now in the process of reorganizing itself into spheres of influence: Europe (to possibly include Russia), the Pacific Rim with China and Japan as its focal point, and North and South America. The US will still be a major nation, but without the overarching threat of the Soviet Union, it is unreasonable to think it can maintain the same global reach and influence that it had during and immediately after the Cold War.

"Old" and "New" Europe as The United States of Europe

> I don't want to see a situation develop in which either Europe or America sees a huge strategic interest at stake and we are not helping each other .... Some want a so-called multi-polar world where you have different centres of power, and I believe [that] will quickly develop into rival centres of power; and others believe, and this is my notion, that we need one polar power which encompasses a strategic partnership between Europe and America.
>
> — Prime Minister Tony Blair, April 2003[9]

> The emergence and growth of the Unites States of Europe as a countervailing power doesn't have to be a nightmare for Americans. In countless ways, the united Europe is a downright boon to the United States .... Beyond the opportunity for profit, Americans can only benefit if an ambitious united Europe begins to take on some of the burdens that necessarily fall to a superpower.
>
> To secure these benefits though, Americans will have to wake up to the revolution. We need to recognize and accept the plain fact that the planet has a second superpower now, and its global influence will continue to increase as the world moves toward a bipolar balance of economic, political, and diplomatic authority. To put it simply, the United States of America has to show respect for the United States of Europe.
>
> — T. R. Reid, *The United States of Europe*, 2004[10]

During the first half of the 20th century, Europe suffered terribly under the imperial hubris of Germany, resulting in two devastating world wars with tens of millions of Europeans killed, followed by a long Cold War with the Soviet Empire. In 1946 Winston Churchill powerfully declared that the "tragedy of Europe" could only be solved if the issues of ancient nationalism and sovereignty could give way to a sense of European "national grouping." He said that the path to European peace and prosperity on the world stage was clear: "We must build a kind of United States of Europe."[11]

This bold path was pursued during the second half of the 20th century when European countries gave up their nationalism in order to create a more peaceful pan-European community. As we enter into this new century Europeans and their governments have largely accomplished this goal from an economic perspective. Robert Mundell, the American Nobel laureate and one of world's experts in currency unions, noted, "The introduction of the euro is one of those epochal events that can only be understood in the context of long periods of history."[12]

Reid's *The United States of Europe* observed that the euro's successful launch was nothing less than a revolutionary act that de facto created a bipolar world from an economic and political perspective.[13] The single euro currency ties their economic fates together, just as the dollar links the 50 US states. Given past centuries of warfare, the Europeans are naturally more interested in their own economic development than militarization of their foreign policies. As Reid argued, the challenge for American policy-makers is to partner with this newly united Europe so that it may share the global "burden" of superpowers.[14]

In order to ensure a "strategic partnership" between an integrated EU and the US as proffered by Prime Minister Blair, a new monetary compromise similar to the Bretton Woods Conference will be required. This chapter offers various suggestions for monetary and energy reform to facilitate development of a strategic partnership, as opposed to a strategic threat. However, before any such policies could be pursued, new approaches toward the EU would be required.

In 2003 Secretary of Defense Rumsfeld created diplomatic consternation amongst the traditional EU centers of power when he referred to the central nations of Europe, many of whom were former eastern bloc (Soviet) nations, as the "New Europe," its new center of power. However as Zbigniew Brzezinski stated in his recent book, *The Choice*, "America must resist the temptation to divide its most important strategic partner. There is no 'old' and 'new' Europe" and that such a slogan has "no geographical or historical content."[15] Despite Rumsfeld's transparent attempts to divide various European governments, the US may be losing not only "Old Europe" but also "New Europe."[16] In fact, these so-called New Europe nations have since transitioned to the euro, and as such their economic and political fates have become inextricably intertwined with the 12 original EU nations of Old Europe. Following the enlargement of the EU–25 in May 2004, the economic destinies of these central European countries are now in the eurozone, not in Washington DC.[17]

In addition, the neoconservatives' "strategic mistakes" have pushed Russia closer to the EU, and the failed attempt to bribe Turkey to participate in the Iraq War has facilitated a new geopolitical alliance between the previously reluctant western European governments regarding Turkey's entry into the EU:

> President Bush and the neocons have made many new enemies;
> old strategic friends, such as France, Germany, and Turkey, are on
> the road to opposition to everything American, this does not

bode well for America's future. Russia is distancing itself from Washington and forming much closer ties with Berlin and Paris, Saudi Arabia has had enough, which is probably good, but the loss of Turkey is really a stupid foreign policy failure.

By treating Turkey like a fifth-rate client state the Bush government has pushed Ankara further into the camp of the benevolent Europeans, and the way Ankara refused to be intimidated by the cowboys in Washington did much to curry favor with Berlin and Paris, which will only serve to help Turkey obtain membership to the European Union.

The Europeans initial balking at Turkey's entry to the Union is quickly being seen by European elites as a strategic mistake; with Iraq now subjugated and under American rule, Turkey has become vital for the Europeans to get a foothold in the Mid East, and Turkey being part of the European Union, the euro would gain substantial legitimacy in the Arab world. As far as Ankara is concerned their economic and strategic future lies with Brussels not Washington.[18]

If this analysis is correct, it is increasingly unlikely the US can maintain its position atop all other nations while attempting to thwart any challenge to its superpower status. The EU is not interested in challenging US military power, but instead in achieving parity status to US economic power. Furthermore, the EU government understands that attempting to challenge the US from a military perspective is not only unnecessary, but unwise, and would likely produce a destabilizing geopolitical environment.

The European Union: Second Pole of Power

Beneath the surface of current security debates, therefore, and in stark contrast to the perceived mismatch of strategic competence and geopolitical power between the US and Europe, lies a sleeping tiger. Despite the many arguments that would question Europe's capacity to take economic and political advantage from such a tectonic shift in monetary realities, the only likely future scenario of change in the realm of currencies is one of greater relative weight for the euro. This is the one area in which long-run dynamics seem to place Europe in a relative structural advantage vis-à-vis the US — despite the appearance of the contrary in the realm of economic productivity and with respect to the current military gap.

— Paul Isbell, "The Shifting Geopolitics of the Euro"[19]

The only way the US has to gain back its currency monopoly would be by destroying the country that is at the heart of the Euro, this is, by waging a Third World War against Germany. But that it cannot do because Germany has been a good girl since 1945, and the nuclear power France is standing at Germany's side, encouraged by Russia and China in the background.

— Germar Rudolf, "On the Brink of World War Three"[20]

From an international trade perspective, the EU economy is much more balanced than that of the US. The EU nations have done a more effective job constraining their debt formation/dependence on foreign capital, while retaining much of their crucial domestic manufacturing base. Because of this past management of its respective economic zones, the EU is poised to become a major pole of global power. Conversely, successive Republican administrations in the US have left themselves little room for error and squandered the opportunity offered by Clinton's surplus economics. Even though much of the surpluses projected in 2000 were bubble-based, they should have been properly taken advantage of to reduce future debt-servicing.

Instead, a policy of tax cuts and massive military spending was pursued. While France and Germany have not been able to strictly adhere to the debt provisions in the Growth and Stability Pact, their external balances are, according to an OPEC executive, much more "balanced" than that of the United States economy.[21]

Furthermore, while European governments have a sometimes stifling policy structure, they have retained a great deal of room for reform when necessary. For example, in 2003 German Prime Minister Schroeder pushed through major reforms of the German economy, Agenda 2010, which is slowly beginning to pay dividends, while in contrast, the US in a similar recessionary phase has no such option.

These structural imbalances suggest that the ongoing bubble distortions of the American economy will ultimately hit a tipping point soon, with a poor prognosis of quick recovery. If this occurs, the euro would serve to increase domestic demand in the EU via expansion of the monetary supply, counterbalanced with a decrease in US domestic demand as its monetary supply contracted. Whether the global impact would be a net increase or net decrease in aggregate demand depends on whether the EU monetary supply expanded more rapidly than the US monetary supply contracted.

The crucial issue at hand is the realization that the EU and the European Central Bank (ECB) will have more monetary flexibility in such an event, which the US no longer has, due to its unbalanced external accounts. This is compounded by foreign holdings of its federal debt, which is now approximately 40 percent of a total $7.6 trillion debt. Ironically, despite the US' history of seeking political and economic independence, its economy and military are simply unable to operate independently of massive foreign investment.

China: Emerging Third Pole of Power

> Something surprising is happening to China's currency.
>
> — "The Renminbi Zone," *Asia Times*, 2003[22]

> In the last century, American people were pioneers of system and technology innovation. However, the interests of a few American financial monopolies now lead this country to war. This is such a tragedy for the American people.
>
> — Wang Jian, Chinese bureaucrat, 2003[23]

> The US dollar is no longer ... in our opinion [seen] as a stable currency, and is devaluating all the time, and that's putting troubles all the time. So the real issue is how to change the regime from a US dollar pegging ... to a more manageable reference, say Euros, yen, dollars — those kind of more diversified systems.
>
> — Fan Gang, director of the National Economic Research Institute, China Reform Foundation, quoted at the World Economic Forum in Davos, Switzerland, January 26, 2005[24]

China deserves special mention given its likely trajectory as a major pole of global power in the beginning of the 21st century. While it may take several more years for China's economy and banking system to undertake the necessary reforms, its regional influence seems assured. The eventual emergence of the Chinese renminbi (RNB), currently being re-valued, as a major currency appears to be well underway, with tacit support of Beijing. As evident in the following article, China's currency is apparently becoming a de facto convertible currency in the Asian Pacific economies.

> Something surprising is happening to China's currency. Although not fully convertible, the renminbi, the 'people's money,' is growing in use as a hard currency outside China — the first sign of its potential role as 'Asia's money.' In Hong Kong and along China's borders with Southeast Asia, an emerging renminbi zone can be traced, fuelled by burgeoning Chinese trade and tourism.[25]

China's membership in the World Trade Organization only accelerates the emergence of a strong, unified Chinese currency. This in turn will increase the desirability of a fully convertible renminbi, both as a way of smoothing the integration of China's economy into the world economy, and as a way for China to exercise its economic might more directly. Full convertibility is a stated goal, but no fixed timetable has been set.

The rising geopolitical influence of China will not only be based upon its economic clout, but its increased demand for sources of hydrocarbons will not transpire with the potential for geopolitical tension with the US. Contrary to stateside US commentary, in 2003, a Chinese bureaucrat, Wang Jian, portrayed a very disconcerting picture of impending geopolitical conflict as we enter the 21st century. His white paper advised China to prepare itself for what he foresaw as an inevitable war between the US and EU — not between the US and China.

> Clouds of war are gathering. Right now, the most important things to do for China are:
>
> 1. Remain neutral between two military groups while insisting on an anti-war attitude.
> 2. Stock up in strategic [oil] reserves.
> 3. Get ready for a short supply of oil.
> 4. Strengthen armament power.
> 5. Speed up economic integration with Japan, Hong Kong, Korea and Taiwan.
>
> War is the extension of politics and politics is the extension of economic interests .... America's wars abroad have always had a clear goal; however, such goals were never made obvious to the public. We need to see through the surface and reach the essence of the matters. In other words, we need to figure out what the fundamental economic interests of America are. Missing this point, we would be misled by American government's shows and feints.[26]

Wang's argument suggesting this conflict is largely based on the structural imbalances endemic to the current US economy. He offered the following warning to Chinese policy-makers:

> While [the dollar's dominance] has been bringing to America economic prosperity and hegemonic power over money, it has its own inborn weakness. In order to sustain such prosperity and hegemonic power, America has to keep unilateral inflow of international capital to the American market .... If America loses its hegemonic power over money, its domestic consumption level will plunge 30-40%. Such an outcome would be devastating for the US economy. It could be more harmful to the economy than the Great Depression of 1929 to 1933.[27]

Assuming that such a major US economic dislocation could occur, every effort should be undertaken to lesson geopolitical tensions that could develop between the US, EU, and China. In any event, the US economy's structural imbalances justify a re-evaluation of fiscal/tax policies as well as foreign policies.

Ultimately we will witness the emergence of a multi-polar world. These trends underline why US policy-makers must quickly begin realigning some longstanding foreign policies in an effort to rebuild its goodwill.

US structural debt levels indicate that its economic security is fundamentally based on the "kindness of strangers," particularly that of Japan and China, who hold a combined $1.4 trillion of US debt. For this reason Washington should cease antagonistic "shows of force" such as the navy's Operation Summer Pulse in July 2004. This massive D-Day-style operation off Taiwan and China's coast marked the first time that 7 of the US' 12 carrier strike groups were all deployed in one place.[28]

The Chinese government was not amused. Despite irresponsible claims in stateside commentary about a potential US "energy war" with China in the coming decade, China may not need to build up its military forces, given its financial leverage over the US economy. Hopefully US policy-makers realize that if China felt threatened by the current belligerent US military encirclement strategy of it — along with the neoconservatives' planned stranglehold over oil supplies in central Asia and the Middle East — China alone has the ability to pull the monetary plug on the dollar by selling off its massive US Treasury holdings.[29]

The most effective method to mitigate such destabilizing global events would be to systematically pursue, through the UN, multilateral reform of the global monetary system, and agreements regarding petroleum and natural gas consumption, access, and pricing mechanisms. Only this approach to cooperatively unwind the current global economic imbalances could provide a desirable outcome for both the US and world community.

The Conundrum: Risk of Widespread US Economic Dislocation

Stephen Roach, the chief economist at investment banking giant Morgan Stanley, has a public reputation for being bearish. But you should hear what he's saying in private. His prediction: America has no better than a 10 percent chance of avoiding economic 'Armageddon' .... Roach sees a 30 percent chance of a slump soon and a 60 percent chance that 'we'll muddle through for a while and delay the eventual Armageddon.' The chance we'll get through OK: one in 10. Maybe.

A source who heard the presentation concluded that a 'spectacular wave of bankruptcies' is possible ... people downtown agree with much of the analysis. It is undeniable that America is living in a 'debt bubble' of record proportions.

— Brett Arends, "Economic 'Armageddon' Predicted,"
November 23, 2004[30]

The US economy is being held together with a prodigious amount of duct tape in the form of massive debt manipulation, excessive consumer spending that is soaking up global investment capital, and a plethora of misleading government statistics about unemployment, productivity, inflation, "GDP growth," and other figures. Various commentators have warned that US economic problems are being exacerbated by unilateral policies that heightened geopolitical risk throughout 2003–2004. These factors all played a significant part in the rising gold price and a falling dollar. If Washington continues to pursue the neoconservative global strategy by threatening countries such as Iran, Syria, or North Korea, this could create a capital flight out of the US and a panic on the dollar.

> The most profound and damaging expression of [US] unilateralism has been through the pursuit of the war on terrorism. The invasion and occupation of Iraq explicitly contravened the United Nations and abrogated international law.
>
> Nearly $1 trillion of foreign capital is funding the US public sector and current account deficits. About $800 billion of this foreign money is invested in US government, agency and corporate bonds .... The weight of foreign investment in the US financing the large twin deficits indicates that the risk of much greater dollar weakness is substantial. Expected dollar depreciation, the large current account and fiscal deficits and increasing geopolitical instability, driven by US electoral politics, make the dollar a very unlikely safe haven for global investors. Foreign capital flight from the US could easily trigger a large dollar devaluation.[31]

Various economic and strategic analysts contend that a major restructuring of the global monetary system is imminent. Additionally, an increasing number of domestic and foreign commentators have warned that an "America in economic crisis would place the world in even greater danger of American military adventures by a government seeking both diversions from its domestic ills while it also sought means to shore up its empire."[32]

Fortunately, the dollar's slide in 2002–2004 was relatively gradual, but appeared to accelerate after the 2004 election. If a dollar "panic" were to occur, Japan alone could not thwart such a crisis. The Japanese government, the largest holder of US Treasury bills, took the unusual step of warning the White House in December 2004 that it will unload its US Treasury/debt holdings if the Bush administration "maintains its laissez-faire approach to the mounting currency crisis."

> The criticism of President Bush's inaction, by a senior member of the ruling Liberal Democratic Party, will be taken as a veiled

threat that Japan could start to sell off its multi-billion-dollar holdings of US Treasuries. 'The Japanese government is going to ask for a strong dollar policy; if it continues to fall, there would be enormous capital flight from the dollar,' said Kaoru Yosano, chairman of the LDP's policy council.[33]

> In order to mitigate a potential monetary crisis, the US government must be in the good graces of the world's industrial nations, in particular the EU.

In order to mitigate a potential monetary crisis, the US government must be in the good graces of the world's industrial nations, in particular the EU. To facilitate that goal, a new US approach that encourages a strong and united EU will be needed, and soon. Therefore, the question becomes: What can the US and EU do to ensure that a strategic partnership develops in the emergence of an integrated EU with a rival currency to the US dollar? Paul Isbell, senior researcher at the Spanish Real Instituto Elcano, offered an alternative approach to US geostrategy — one based on cooperating with the EU to strengthen the US/EU relationship.

> What can Europe do to consciously prepare the way for the day when this tectonic shift in monetary relations becomes undeniably obvious? .... What might Europe do to help insulate itself — and the US — from a potentially cataclysmic jolt to transatlantic relations as the byproduct of such a change? First, Europe should move forward with liberalization and economic reforms in a sensible, integrated fashion .... Second, Ecofin should work to reform the stability pact in a rational way ...
>
> Third, the ECB should stand ready to cooperate with the US Federal Reserve should coordinated currency intervention be called for to halt an excessively rapid fall of the dollar.
>
> Fourth, efforts to integrate and harmonize European capital markets should continue in an effort to drive down transactions costs even further .... Finally, Europe should not abandon its vision of a transatlantic relationship (or a vision of 'the West') based on multilateralism and an international system based on the rule of law.[34]

Isbell illuminated one of the most critical reasons why the US government should seek to maintain a cooperative and strong relationship with the EU. Given the huge structural imbalances in the US economy, heightened possibility of a terrorist attack at a US financial center, along with the risks and expense of US military operations, the likelihood of dollar devaluation is authentic. Isbell stated, the "ECB should stand ready to cooperate with the US Federal Reserve should coordinated currency intervention be called for to halt an *excessively rapid fall of the dollar.*"[35] [emphasis added] I concur with his analysis of why the US must change its macroeconomic policy to accommodate the inevitable ascendancy of a strong euro. As Brzezinski noted, "Only two sides of the Atlantic working together can chart a truly global course that may significantly improve the worldwide state of affairs."[36]

As discussed in chapter 1, the core macroeconomic stresses that have gathered in the global economy are excessive credit expansion with subsequent global overcapacity. The first challenge is economic and requires an increase in global aggregate demand. Any process of sustainable development combined with demographic growth will increase aggregate demand over time. The problem with the current global economy is that excess levels of supply capacity are well beyond those necessary to meet the requirements of aggregate demand. As a general rule, a period of deflationary contraction will simply permit a decline of supply capacity until growth in demand initiates a new expansionary cycle.

To mitigate the depth of a global deflationary contraction, it would seem advisable for the euro to ascend to an International Reserve Currency that should increase domestic demand in the EU via expansion of the monetary supply. This process would have to be counterbalanced with a decrease in US domestic demand as the monetary supply contracted. Managing this type of scenario will be the core monetary challenge for both US and EU finance ministers should a deflationary period occur.

The second major monetary reform revolves around East Asia, but the dollar-euro transition would most likely need to have minimal impact on their supply of capital or rate of demand growth. Asian domestic markets are expanding, and this should be seen as an extension of current development trends. Eventually the demographic and economic trends in Asia should create a consumer base that will eclipse the American consumer base, but this could easily take at least a decade.

Although rarely discussed outside of Internet forums, the US Federal Reserve is quickly facing a financial crisis that may result in some level of debt repudiation. Although unlikely, and assuming any such mechanism could be negotiated, the agreement would require a graduated approach over a decade or more, ideally within the framework of broad international cooperation.

If one agrees with this description of generalized macroeconomic factors, then it is clear that US policy-makers and Americans must accept that some of the following scenarios are irrefutably incompatible with reforms necessary to rebalance the global economy. First, the US does not need any more tax cuts, nor can we afford them. Secondly, we do not need any more "preemptive" wars, nor can we afford them. Thirdly, we cannot continue our excessive oil consumption. Finally, we must not accept any further deterioration of our Constitutional protections, but we must demand that recent legislation be repealed to restore our liberties and freedom.

What Americans do need are exceptionally creative leaders in all government branches and in the private sector with truly Big Ideas — and willing to be honest and yet optimistic with the American people. We need peace and justice in the Middle East to alter the chemistry of the soil in which terrorism grows. Above all, we must reduce our energy consumption and help lead the world in an unprecedented crash program for "energy reconfiguration."

The Global Imperative: International Energy Projects

> We are grossly wasting our energy resources ... as though their supply was infinite. We must even face the prospect of changing our basic ways of living. This change will either be made on our own initiative in a planned and rational way, or forced on us with chaos and suffering by the inexorable laws of nature.
>
> — Jimmy Carter, 1976[37]

> We need an energy bill that encourages consumption.
>
> — President George W. Bush, 2002[38]

> There is no need to belabor the point: the people of this world whose opinions count the most — the people with the power to command armies, economics, and governments — have already made up their minds. The cards are dealt and the bets are on the table. For them, the coming decades will constitute a fatal game of Last One Standing, a brutal contest for the world's remaining resources.
>
> To the interested observer, this may seem patently insane. Even the nation that 'wins' the game will be utterly devastated. In the end, oil, natural gas, and even coal will run out, and not even the wealthy will be able to maintain their current way of life. And in the meantime, hundreds of millions — perhaps billions — will have violently perished. *Why would anyone choose this path?*
>
> — Richard Heinberg, *Powerdown: Options and Actions for a Post-Carbon World*, 2004[39]

Peak Oil is the greatest challenge modern man has faced. Citizens of the world community, especially Americans, must come to accept the fundamental principles of Peak Oil and the fact that energy resource limitations will become evident by 2010. Once this psychological barrier is breached, we must ask, what kind of future do we want, and what are our options?

It is beyond the scope of this book to fully analyze various alternative energy sources and technologies, but more appropriately, it explores the expediency under which this must be pursued.

The US, as the most voracious energy consumer, is the only nation that could provide global leadership in pursuing the development and implementation of energy alternatives. Along with a rejection of the "preventative war" or "Bush doctrine," this would do much to repair its international image. Ideally, such efforts should begin immediately. Robert Freeman eloquently wrote that only "energy reconfiguration" can save America from devolving into despotism. His essay, "Will the End of Oil Mean the End of America?" offered several specific policy recommendations that symbolized the sacrifices we must soon undertake if America is to pursue a concerted effort to enhance our national security, and preserve our freedom:

> Energy reconfiguration means retrofitting all of the nation's build-
> ings, both commercial and residential, to double their energy
> efficiency. It means a crash program to shift the transportation sys-
> tem — cars, trucks — to a basis that uses perhaps half as much oil
> per year. This is well within reach of current technology .... It
> means refitting industrial and commercial processes — lighting,
> heating, appliances, automation, etc. — so that they, too, con-
> sume far less energy than they do today. It means increasing
> efficiency, reducing consumption, and building sustainable, long-
> term alternatives in every arena in which the economy uses oil.[40]

Freeman found optimism in China's 1980s nationwide program to adopt energy efficiency that resulted in a 50 percent reduction in energy intensity while maintaining economic growth. Furthermore, in the 1980s Denmark began a "crash program" in wind-generated electricity that now provides 10 percent of its electrical power, and India's Renewable Energy Development Agency began a program in 1987 to reduce oil-based electricity usage by becoming the largest user of photovoltaic systems in the world.[41] Another renewable energy technology that should be pursued is OTEC. In 2002 the Natural Energy Laboratory in Hawaii successfully deployed a 9,000-foot ocean pipeline that researchers predict will make this electrical production process "far more efficient than previously used technologies."[42] This abundant renew- able technology warrants a massive increase in research and development on a global scale.

As for the US, an aggressive 7-year roll-out of 35 mpg Corporate Average Fuel Efficiency (CAFÉ) standards for all automobiles (including light trucks) would be a tremendous investment enhancing its national security. Writing for the *Austin Chronicle*, Michael Ventura advocated transitioning to a rail-based system, and made the astute observation that our ability — or inability — to quickly dismantle our military empire in exchange for enacting energy recon- figuration, will likely determine the fate of the US dollar in the new century.

> One key to America's future will be: How quickly can we build or
> rebuild heavy and light rail? And where will we get the money to

do it? Railroads are the cheapest transport, the easiest to sustain....
There's only one section of our economy that has that kind of money:
the military budget. The U.S. now spends more on its military than
all other nations combined. A sane transit to a post-automobile
America will require a massive shift from military to infrastructure
spending. That shift would be supported by our bankers in China
and Europe (that is, they would continue to finance our debt)
because it's in their interest that we regain economic viability. What's
not in their interests is that we remain a military superpower. [43]

Americans should harbor no illusions that, with the current campaign
finance structure, it will be exceedingly difficult to enhance national security,
given the powerful military and energy conglomerates who "invest" hundreds
of millions in cash to political campaigns every election in order to purchase
politicians in both parties. This system will have to yield to a more workable
system that places humanity above political ideology and power. Considering
all suppliers report that current oil production is running "flat out," the world
may have arrived at a plateau. Neither the US nor the global community is prepared for such a reality.

Following the peaking of domestic oil production in 1971 and the oil
shocks of the 1970s, the US should have spent much of the past 25 years
preparing for global Peak Oil. A second historic opportunity was lost in the
aftermath of 9/11, when, if under real leadership, the American people could
have become united in the patriotic pursuit of conserving energy and seeking
energy alternatives to strengthen our national security. Unfortunately that
tragedy was exploited to introduce another upon the world — the unprovoked invasion and subsequent occupation of Iraq.

Despite this substantial setback, Americans must have realistic faith in ourselves and believe that we can adjust to the challenges of Peak Oil, or we will
certainly fail. We need a visionary leader to define America's *new role* and
work together toward realizing that vision. Multilateralism and extraordinary
international energy reform in the post-Peak Oil era is the key to global stability in the 21st century. In his book on Peak Oil, Kenneth S. Deffeyes warned
his readers:

> This much is certain: no initiative put in place starting today can have
> a substantial effect on the peak production year. No Caspian Sea
> exploration, no drilling in the South China Sea, no SUV replace-
> ments, no renewable energy projects can be brought on at a sufficient
> rate to avoid a bidding war for the remaining oil. At least, let's hope
> that the war is waged with cash instead of with nuclear warheads.
> — Kenneth S. Deffeyes, retired oil geologist and author,
> *Hubbert's Peak: The Impending World Oil Shortage,* 2001[44]

Crafting a More Balanced Global Economy

Petrodollar recycling was unusual in that it was a severe shock to international economic stability. Yet insofar as the oil shocks were a symptom of US hegemonic decline, similar shocks can be expected in the future. International institutions do not have the capability to handle such threats to stability, and US unilateralism will prevent the strengthening of multilateral cooperative regimes.

Although the relative decline of US hegemony has led to an increase in observable power outcomes, the result ultimately will be worldwide economic instability. When it is in a period of relative decline, it is in the short-term interest of the United States to pursue unilateral exploitation of its dominant position. This interest is increasingly at variance with the international goals of confidence, stability, and cooperation.

— David E. Spiro, *The Hidden Hand of American Hegemony* [45]

This chapter's suggestions are most assuredly audacious and contentious to many observers, but they would provide a broad, and perhaps visionary, framework in which to rebalance the global economy and promote energy conservation and alternative energy sources, while also reducing current "anti-American" sentiments in an effort to restore the US' international stature. If Thomas Jefferson, James Madison, or George Washington were alive today, I suspect they would judge many of these recommendations to be in basic alignment with the nation's founding principles.

Americans must demand that our government begin the long and difficult journey toward energy conservation, the development of renewable energy sources, and sustained balanced budgets that allow real deficit reduction. Repealing large portions of the clearly unaffordable 2001 and 2003 tax cuts could facilitate a balanced budget.

> Americans must demand that our government begin the long and difficult journey toward energy conservation, the development of renewable energy sources, and sustained balanced budgets that allow real deficit reduction.

One the main reasons the US is a waning superpower is its manufacturing base's marked decline. The US was able to propel itself into a dominant role at the end of WW II because of its then massive manufacturing capability. However, this advantage has been lost over the past 30 years. In 1973, the Trilateral Commission stated that for globalization to work, US jobs would have to be transferred to populations with much lower wages than found in the US.

The US has followed this path for the past 30 years, resulting in a huge trade account deficit. Never before in US history have there been such large increases in government spending, tax cuts, federal budget deficits, consumer spending and borrowing, yet without any meaningful job or income growth.

The massive fiscal and monetary stimulus has mostly been spent, with continued excessive military spending as a percentage of GDP, further sapping the ability of the US to do what is absolutely necessary regarding national security — massive energy reconfiguration. Not surprisingly, middle class living standards have stagnated. Addicted to debt and consumption, US society has lost touch with the basic economic reality that domestic savings and implementing the means of production are the mechanisms of wealth creation and social stability.

The Federal Reserve is in the process of slowly raising interest rates in an effort to stem the weakening dollar, but we are in a perilous situation. American corporations and consumers have acquired so much debt that a rate hike might stave off domestic economic growth. A rate increase may cause a lot of pain for average Americans, but we have lived in the fantasy of huge tax cuts, low interest rates, huge budget and trade account deficits for much too long. Military empires have never been cheap. One of the unknown variables is the dollar, which is being rapidly debased. In a best-case scenario, the Federal Open Market Committee would spread this pain over several years, but dollar devaluation will probably occur precipitously.

Hopefully, the US would then begin to restore some of its lost international stature by compromising on the crucial issue of global monetary reform. Responsible leaders are needed who are willing to return to balanced budgets, conservative fiscal policies, and our tradition of engaging in multilateral foreign policies while seeking broad international cooperation. Until the US agrees to negotiate a more balanced global monetary system and embarks on a viable national energy strategy, our nation will continue to pursue a hypocritical foreign policy that is incompatible with the founding fathers' ideals of democracy and liberty.

In order to save the American experiment and stop the slide toward an authoritarian state, Americans must elect an enlightened administration in 2008 and create revolutionary changes in the current political establishment. Both of the major political parties have failed the American people, as the main constituencies of the current governing body are simply different factions of the richest two-percent of the population (the elites who run the military–industrial–petroleum–banking complex). This is a function of our structurally flawed campaign finance structure that renders both Congress and the president incapable of voicing the concerns and interests of the other 98 percent of Americans.

There is no easy way out, and I do not envy the arduous journey that awaits the 44th president, who will likely face a combined economic and energy crisis. Global monetary reform and a compromise with the EU ultimately means the US will have to forfeit its hyperpower status and revert to being a realistic nation as one among equals. Many Americans do want to hear this message, but the US' extraordinary economic imbalances will ultimately unwind. Americans believe the myth that the other G–7 nations' living standards would somehow be unfulfilling if we lived "their way."

In reality their living standards are all excellent relative to the global community, and each of the citizens in those privileged nations should be thankful. Perhaps many of us will have to give up our irrational attraction to gas-guzzling SUVs, but do we really want these excesses to define our "values?" Regardless, we may not have the luxury of choice for much longer, as the dictates of the global economy and physics will soon come to the forefront.

The only solution is international cooperation, real leadership, global monetary reform, and sacrifices by the American citizenry to reduce energy consumption. US politicians are not interested in being truthful with the people, as both parties are more or less in the pockets of the military–energy conglomerates. The US media conglomerates are not serving the public's interest. Consequently, real campaign finance reform and the comprehensive rejection of corporate personhood may be the only way for the US to possibly enact the required energy reforms with the onset of global Peak Oil.

In order to save the American experiment from the shared destiny of all empires — military overextension and subsequent economic decline — I recommend the following suggestions. While these proposals are bold, imperfect, and contentious, it is obvious that adjustments will be required to begin rebalancing the global economy and preparing the world community for the challenges presented by global Peak Oil.

Disavow the Preventative War Doctrine

The unrealistic neoconservative goal of global domination must be quickly discarded by any new US administration if it seeks to reduce current and future geopolitical tensions. The concept of the US openly violating international law with unilateral "preventative wars" in the oil-rich regions of the world will simply *not be tolerated* by most industrialized nations.[46] Hopefully one of the first official acts of the 44th president will be to officially disavow this "Bush doctrine" and state a desire for a multilateral approach to international terrorism. Such a gesture would allow the world community to breathe a collective sigh of relief and extend to the new administration much needed political capital. Multilateral cooperation will be needed for the following issues/ reforms.

US Fiscal Discipline

We must restore some semblance of fiscal responsibility in this country if we want to save the dollar. The Iraq conflict had cost approximately $300 billion by the end of 2004, and estimates of current military expenditures are approximately $1 billion per week. US taxpayers (and their children and grandchildren) will pay for the 2003 Iraq War, unlike the 1991 Gulf War. The credit worthiness of a currency is based upon the ability of the government to collect tax revenue from its citizens. The devaluation of the dollar in 2002–2004 reflected the world community's lack of trust in US economic policies.

International Energy Projects

Washington should propose to the UN that it form an international consortium of energy scientists and researchers to develop alternative fuels for transportation. IHS Energy has stated that least 85 percent of the world's total oil deposits are already in production. The most recent findings of worldwide oil "mega projects" going online from 2004 to 2010 suggest an "unbridgeable supply-demand gap [for oil] opening up after 2007."[47] If alternative fuels for transportation cannot be developed and implemented over the next decade, disastrous consequences will beset the global community. Ideally, the US and UN would immediately advocate investments totaling hundreds of billions to be spent annually on *simultaneous*, international Manhattan Project/Apollo-type energy programs pursuant to global energy reconfiguration.

- Ultra-fuel-efficient gasoline and diesel engines (as a "bridge technology")
- Clean coal technology with mitigation of carbon dioxide emissions
- Geothermal power (retrofitting commercial and residential buildings)
- Hydrogen Fuel cells for mass transit (land, sea, and air)
- Small-scale solar retrofitting of residential and commercial buildings
- Large-scale solar power plants (e.g., 200-megawatt solar "Power Tower")
- OTEC (e.g., fleet of 100-megawatt floating plantships producing liquified hydrogen and potable water)
- Biomass and biodiesel for localized, agriculture-based farm production
- Wind power (rapid deployments in both small- and large-scale settings)
- Thermal deployermization (new technology that warrants more R&D)
- Nuclear fusion (still unproven technology but warrants more R&D)

Advanced Manufacturing to Reduce US Trade Deficit

Alan Greenspan, the chairman of the Federal Reserve, has given Americans the peculiar impression that it does not matter where American products are made, just so long as people can continue to buy them. This is simply not true. The demise of over 2.8 million US manufacturing jobs since 2000 has led to decreased income, growing levels of personal debt, and new records of personal bankruptcies.

A superpower that loses its manufacturing base will not be a superpower for long. One of the most outspoken observers of this truism is Eamonn Fingleton, whose 1999 book *In Praise of Hard Industries: Why Manufacturing, Not the Information Economy, Is the Key to Future Prosperity* was somewhat derided during the "New Economy" frenzy.[48] Following the dot-com/technology bubble, it appeared that he was right: there is no "New Economy paradigm," and real wealth creation requires manufacturing and production.

The US must substantially reinvest in sustainable energy technology, advanced manufacturing, and various other export sectors in order to gradually but earnestly move the economy from a trade account deficit position back into a trade account surplus position. This will take decades, but on a positive note, the imperative for large-scale "energy reconfiguration" and development of alternative energy technologies provides the US workforce with an opportunity to make gains in its advanced manufacturing base, while also enhancing long-term security.

Energy Allocation Accords

The UN should form an international group of scientists and engineers to study energy depletion stemming from global Peak Oil. Under UN supervision, the global community should devise a methodology and formal agreements regarding the distribution of hydrocarbons based on the global depletion rate (i.e., Uppsala Accord).[49] Successful implementation of such a worldwide treaty would undoubtedly be a modern miracle. The incentive to abide by such an accord is the inescapable fact that the alternatives are either oil depletion warfare in the Persian Gulf and/or economic warfare in the international foreign exchange markets. These adverse events can be avoided, but only if the international community can agree to an energy treaty that reflects oil depletion, while also transforming the current economic/monetary system and implementing strict measures to control population growth.

> It is essential that the US uses less energy and immediately improves its infrastructure before the full effects of Peak Oil make any energy reforms excessively painful and expensive.

It is essential that the US uses less energy and immediately improves its infrastructure before the full effects of Peak Oil make any energy reforms excessively painful and expensive. Given that Americans consume 25 percent of all hydrocarbons, we have the most to both gain and lose if energy reforms are not implemented during this decade while we still have the capability to pursue a gradual *Powerdown* scenario.[50]

Global Monetary Reform

The main problem with the current global economy is that excess levels of credit creation (i.e., a credit/derivative bubble) have facilitated the building of supply capacity that is well beyond the requirements of global aggregate demand. As a general rule, a period of deflationary contraction would permit a decline of supply capacity until such time that growth in demand initiates a new expansionary cycle.

Economists, such as Richard Duncan (author of *The Dollar Crisis*), have argued that excessive growth of global credit and subsequent structural problems of the US dollar may unleash a deflationary contraction of the global economy.[50] A depression could occur with a significant devaluation of the dollar, and the downturn will be very long-lasting unless global aggregate demand increases, particularly in the EU and East Asian economies.

Therefore it seems imperative that the US government begins discussions with the G–8 nations (plus China) to reform the global monetary system, ideally, to allow for a controlled expansion of markets in Europe and East Asia. The global economy will be more balanced and better off with three engines of global growth: the US, the EU, and Asia. The great challenge will be to implement a gradual, controlled decrease in the US money supply, while attempting to minimize dislocations in the US and global economy. The first reform should be the euro as the second International Reserve Currency, at parity with the dollar, thereby allowing a dual-OPEC oil transaction currency standard. This should join the US with the EU as two equal "co-hegemons."

While this rebalancing is necessary to create sustainable long-term growth, any broad transition from a dollar to a euro standard or euro/dollar standard with subsequent enormous capital market reorientation will be forcefully opposed by the American elite of the political and business establishment.

Regardless, the ascendance of the euro and ultimately the yuan has likely been fortified given the structural debt, trade, and fiscal imbalances in the US economy. The US consumer cannot go into indefinite debt as the single engine for global growth, nor can the Federal Reserve continue to reinflate bubbles indefinitely.

Both the EU and East Asia will have to recognize that the party is over and they cannot ride the American consumer in perpetuity. Whether or not they wish to confront the challenges of this transition, they will find these imposed by brutal economic realities.

Conclusion

> Guard against the impostures of pretended patriotism.
> — President George Washington, Farewell address, 1796

Peace, commerce, and honest friendship with all nations —
entangling alliances with none.

> — President Thomas Jefferson, Inaugural address, 1801

This great Nation will endure as it has endured, will revive and
will prosper. So, first of all, let me assert my firm belief that the
only thing we have to fear is fear itself — nameless, unreasoning,
unjustified terror which paralyzes needed efforts to convert
retreat into advance. In every dark hour of our national life, a
leadership of frankness and vigor has met with that understanding
and support of the people themselves which is essential to victory.

> — President Franklin D. Roosevelt, Inaugural address, 1933

In the end, the choice of these two alternatives — Grab the Oil
or Energy Reconfiguration — is much bigger than oil alone. It is
a choice about the fundamental ethos and, in fact, the very nature
of the country. Most immediately, it is about democracy versus
empire. In economic terms, it is about prosperity or poverty. In
engineering terms, it is a matter of efficiency over waste. In moral
terms this is the choice of sufficiency or gluttony. From the standpoint of the environment, it is a preference for stewardship over
continued predation. In the ways the US deals with other countries it is the choice of co-operation versus dominance. And in
spiritual terms, it is the choice of hope, freedom and purpose over
fear, dependency and despair. In this sense, this is truly the decision that will define the future of America and perhaps the world.

> — Robert Freeman, "Will the End of Oil Mean the
> End of America?" 2004[52]

This book is intended to inform the readers of the challenges and choices that
lie directly ahead. In my own analysis three decades of US fiscal and energy
policies have placed the nation on a trajectory toward an economic downturn
of considerable depth and duration, and recent US foreign policies are fostering
potentially cataclysmic global warfare that will ultimately leave the so-called
winner in a ruined state of energy deprivation and economic bankruptcy.

This need not be the case, but global Peak Oil is undoubtedly the true test
that will define the human condition during this new century. Freeman ended
his essay on the profound notion that the US' destiny will be based on how willing the American people are to adjust to the realities of hydrocarbon depletion.

The "Greatest Generation" of Americans came of age when America was
not a superpower. They endured hardships under the Great Depression and
made tremendous sacrifices during WW II, both of which served to strengthen
their character. The current generation must also adapt to new realities, just

as the Greatest Generation did, and begin to pursue sustainable fiscal policies and reduced energy consumption levels.

Regrettably, the US political system is flawed under its current funding mechanisms, and the media has become excessively filtered by its large conglomerates. As a result politicians in both major political parties are completely incapable of initiating the needed reforms, while the American people have become largely ignorant and complacent about the world around them. The sad reality is that too many of us resemble Leo Strauss's "vulgar many" who could be "inspired to rise above their brutish existence only by fear of impending death or catastrophe."[53]

Too many Americans are willing to be ruled by fear and lies, rather than by persuasion and truth. We have allowed our government to initiate the dangerous "preventative war" doctrine by waging an unpopular and illegal war in Iraq, while refusing to acknowledge that Saddam Hussein, although a despot, did not pose an imminent security threat to the US.

Now the US military occupies a country where polls indicate 80 percent of the Iraqi people have "no confidence" in US involvement and will feel safer if the US military "occupiers" were to leave immediately.[54] Obviously, only broad UN involvement could possibly restore political stability within Iraq, as the US/CIA-sponsored Iraq leader does not have much popular support, or control, outside the militarized "green zone" within Baghdad.

From a foreign policy perspective, Americans live in a self-censored bubble, too often failing to acknowledge that 50 years of covertly overthrowing governments and replacing them with oppressive puppet-regimes in oil-producing states, in conjunction with our unprincipled support of Israel, is not in the interest of long-term national security. This combination of foreign policies as practiced under both Republican and Democratic administrations has not surprisingly produced blowback in the form of the Al Qaeda terrorist network. Likewise, the recent growth of anti-American sentiments (or more accurately, *anti-Imperialism*) will continue to result in further diplomatic and economic backlash against the US' reckless foreign policies.

Nations that convert to a petroeuro-based transaction currency will not undertake such monetary decisions on the false notion that the US and Europe have fundamentally different values, cultures, or principles, but instead will base them on economic factors and, in some cases, for political considerations. Abandoning international law in the pursuit of imperialist US policies that openly seek global domination and control over the world's energy supply will result in economic catastrophe and international isolation.

The belief in market fundamentalism is inappropriate for energy policy. If Americans make the mistake of letting the "invisible hand of the market" decide this issue, we would be condemning millions of people in our nation and in the world community to a life of poverty, suffering, and death. Simply stated, too much of the US' infrastructure is tied up in oil dependence for a market-based correction. The resulting market failure would create escalations in the price of virtually everything, and certain critical items, such as food, would soon become too expensive for a large segment of society.

Simply stated, too much of the US' infrastructure is tied up in oil dependence for a market-based correction.

Clearly, the imperative of energy reconfiguration, in conjunction with monetary reform, implies that the US' overblown military expenditures of $400 billion per year must be reduced by perhaps 50 percent, which even at $200 billion per year is comparable to the combined expenditures of the EU, Russia, and China (which in aggregate represent about 2 billion people, compared to the US' 300 million). Energy reconfiguration will require *trillions* of dollars in new investment and create new domestic jobs that will be safe from outsourcing. Clearly, the US should use what is left of its capital and taxpayer base toward this goal — and certainly not tax cuts for the wealthiest among us, nor expanding our empire of bases.

A full-scale reallocation of hundreds of billions of tax dollars is immediately required toward essentially draconian government policies of restructuring our energy infrastructure to accommodate a much less energy-intensive existence. We will need to become a fully mobilized society, like the one that made sacrifices during WW II, that is dedicated toward energy reconfiguration. Ironically, reducing military expenditures is in our long-term national security interest. With increasingly limited choices, the US must seek policies that could mitigate this transition into a graduated approach where possible, and a rapid approach where needed.

The fundamental problem is that much of the world feels that the US, and especially the Bush administration, simply does not play fair. This administration's unilateralism, combined with events after WW II and during the Cold War standoff, have consistently stacked the global deck in our favor. Now, we seem to be further solidifying our hegemonic power by seizing control of the Middle East's energy supply, establishing satellite states around Russia and China, undermining the emergence of a cohesive, powerful EU rival, while ignoring international law and abandoning multiple international treaties. Yet from all appearances this strategy is being recklessly pursued without analysis, or even recognition, of the subsequent unfolding economic and geopolitical consequences.

In recent years an interesting conceptual bias has gained prominence in stateside commentary, especially within right-wing ideology, that appears to manifest on two levels. On the one hand, there's a singular fixation with the US military element of geopolitical relations, to the relative disregard for the economic dimension. On the other hand, there's a certain presumption that the US can pursue its geopolitical aims with impunity, while other nations will be restrained by economic considerations.

This segues into the more long-standing assumption that other major powers would be unable to overcome their own rivalries in such manner as to present effective opposition to US interests; America would be able to play one against the other to its own advantage, in perpetuity. Given the events in Iraq before and after the war, this belief may prove to be the key false assumption made by the Bush administration. OPEC's momentum toward a petroeuro or basket of currencies for international oil transactions is well underway.[55] A gradual transition to a petroeuro is likely by 2010, and without active US engagement and compromise, the Iraq War will likely not be this decade's last oil currency/oil depletion war.

As Brzezinski noted, the US has acquired a rather "paranoiac" view of the world.[56] We must throw off such fears and be realistic; it is we who have changed, not the world. Despite this growing paranoia, no industrialized or developing nation wants the American economy to collapse. They admire our technical base, research and development capability, education system, and of course they want us as consumers. In return, we are expected to be good customers, not a militant imperialist power seeking domination over the world's largest energy supply.

My principal concern is that our nation appears to be on a path like that of the German population of the 1930s, on the verge of becoming a highly militarized society that is fearful of shadowy enemies lurking inside every airplane and distrustful of all allies. We must overcome such irrational fear and peacefully make some painful, but necessary, adjustments to both our economy and our society.

First and foremost, we must not allow our government to cynically use the "war on terror" to frighten the citizenry in order to gain our complicity for more unprovoked oil-related warfare. If we allow such imperialist policies to continue, the international community will reluctantly thwart such belligerency in nonviolent "economic warfare" — via abandoning the dollar. This situation would quickly prove devastating given the structural imbalances in the US economy. Failure to pursue multilateral reforms will result in increasing levels of societal disorder, endless warfare with requisite military conscription, ongoing political deception and repression at home, and ultimately economic bankruptcy. Undeniably, the only rational strategy is to compromise our hegemonic status and pursue multilateral treaties. Unfortunately, I remain rather skeptical that the proposed reforms will happen unless a significant global financial crisis occurs.

The real struggle in the US is apparently more internal than external. Can we return to our republican origins and restrain ourselves from seeking empire? Can we rejoin the community of industrialized nations, as an equal to the EU and ultimately China? The ultimate test for the American experiment: *Can we once again begin living within our means,* from both fiscal and energy perspectives? Can the US show global leadership by reducing our oil and gas consumption and pursue what Heinberg called the necessity of engaging in a "Global Powerdown" toward less complexity?[57] If we could rise to that type of enlightened leadership, our problems with today's "anti-Americanism" and tomorrow's terrorist will quickly subside.

The analysis provided in this text proffers that five difficult challenges will await the next US administration: 1) negotiating global monetary reform, 2) broadly re-organizing US fiscal policies, 3) developing a national energy strategy, 4) attempting to repair our damaged foreign relationships with the UN, EU, Russia, and the Middle East by realigning our foreign policies with American principles and human rights, and 5) reigning in the unwarranted power of the military–industrial–petroleum–intelligence branch of our government through comprehensive campaign finance reform and massive reallocation of public funds from military spending toward alternative energies and wide-ranging infrastructure energy reconfiguration.

To conclude, it is not hyperbole to suggest that the destiny of the global community in this new century will be largely determined by monetary and energy developments before 2010 as we enter the post–Peak Oil world. This epoch for the US and the world community requires broad reform of the global monetary system and the imperative of worldwide cooperation pursuant to energy reform.

The beginning of the 21st century will either be a disastrous period of oil-related military and economic warfare, or an unprecedented and noble effort at international cooperation. Either way, the status quo is no longer plausible due to both physics and macroeconomics, nor is it desirable if we wish to preserve our humanity.

As Americans, our political, social, and economic choices will impact this momentous judgment. Will we rejoin the community of nations as an equal among allies and collectively work on future challenges, or will we continue our downward path of militarism and economic ruin in a desperate attempt to maintain superpower status under the guise of the "war on terror?" These desperate attempts to maintain the unsustainable status quo will ultimately damage the essential principles of liberty and freedom that founded the United States 229 years ago.

The American experiment has reached a historic crossroad. Will we be a fleeting empire recklessly pursuing global domination with its potential of generating catastrophic warfare, or are we to be a long-lived enlightened Democratic republic that heeds the wisdom of the founding fathers by resisting the temptation of empire — and compromise for peace, justice, and the rule of law as we enter the 21st century?

America will never be destroyed from the outside. If we falter and lose our freedoms, it will be because we destroyed ourselves.

I am a firm believer in the people. If given the truth, they can be depended upon to meet any national crisis. The great point is to bring them the real facts.

— Abraham Lincoln, US President, 1861–1865

All tyranny needs to gain a foothold is for people of good conscience to remain silent.

I have sworn upon the altar of God eternal hostility against every form of tyranny imposed upon the mind of man.

— Thomas Jefferson, US President 1801–1809

Epilogue

By Lieutenant Colonel Karen Kwiatkowski (retired)

In a lifetime of taking chances, Saddam Hussein's biggest gamble occurred in late September 2000 when he walked out of a government meeting and announced he would henceforth sell his oil in euros, not dollars. This was seen as a political move; the euro had been down, struggling against the dollar and other currencies. Saddam would pay a financial price for this decision.

In return, he would perhaps curry favor with the euro-based suppliers of his Oil for Food imports, France and Germany, in a move not likely to concern the euro-ambivalent, but US-wary, Russia and China. Certainly the currency switch was a slap at the American and British governments. It probably seemed to be not only a cost-effective tactic, but also an efficient one, given the dearth of Iraqi military and economic capacity after over a decade of sanctions and US/UK bombing in northern and southern Iraq.

Saddam Hussein's gamble didn't work out this time. He, his family, the Ba'ath Party that had ruled Iraq since 1968, 24 million Iraqis, France, Germany, Russia, China, Iraq's neighbors, and the United Nations continue to pay dearly for this choice.

Saddam Hussein's decision was ignored, buried in the petroleum business journals and the odd European publication, a blip in the stream from selected wire services. It was disregarded, just as Americans themselves missed the signs that the first part of the 21st century would be known by political scientists as Neoconservatism Ascendant.

William Clark has wisely and patiently explained how and why Saddam Hussein's choice accelerated the current American military quagmire in Iraq. Clark has carefully illuminated how the Washington establishment, unaccountable to citizens and shrouded in arcane motivations, has willfully compromised the ideas of liberty and freedom that we so cherish in this country.

Of course, some of them, particularly the neoconservatives, do understand what global Peak Oil means for the United States' financial house of cards and its military-industrial complex that has become so dangerous to the rest of the world. In order to solve serious structural economic problems and deal with changing international energy supplies and finances, they might have considered the traditional American ethic of working hard, producing value, and living frugally until the nation emerged with honor, a free market, and individual liberty intact, as its founders envisioned.

Instead, the neoconservative prescription, embraced by a panicked Washington establishment, continues to be to print and spend easy money and to harden and spuriously exercise the military empire constructed over the last 65 years. The invasion of Iraq, and very likely the American annexation of the Saudi oil fields, is part of the neoconservative vision as suggested by Richard Perle and David Frum in *An End to Evil: How to Win the War on Terror*.[1] This manifesto is the ultimate neoconservative solution: a cure that kills enemies of the American banking and energy sectors until, presumably, none exist and the economy lives out its remaining days in a bell jar of safety and profit.

As fantastical and paranoid as the neoconservative perspective on America's role and rights in the world may be, those qualities are trumped by its sheer illogic and by its almost robotic contempt for classical liberal values of the individual, liberty, and the binding nature of one's word. Neoconservatives advocate an America that prospers through domination and promotes radical change along these lines. But for neoconservatives, American aggression and contempt for international law and morality is acted out on an unnaturally static stage.

Neoconservatism has hijacked the language of liberalism while clearly repudiating ideas of a decentralized, responsible, and honorable Republic and the value of a well-informed citizenry armed with a Constitution. That President Bush, Vice President Cheney, and their esteemed staff could blatantly lie their way into a long-planned, illegal, and unprovoked invasion of Iraq is an amazing accomplishment. Even after those lies were exposed and thousands of casualties taken, the Bush administration proceeds apace in the Middle East and Caspian oil regions. Free trade with all and entangling alliance with none has been transmogrified into coerced trade and military subjugation of the lesser recalcitrants.

Instead of the promised liberty, human rights, and self-government, neoconservatism delivers a gift of distrust, fear, and hate on a national level, and a bloody spectacle of destruction on a local level. American soldiers and militias once fought for the values of self-government and individual liberty. Our current era of Neoconservatism Ascendent violates that heritage and has made our defenders into mercenaries for a modern Washington establishment with international intentions as closely guarded as the recommendations of Cheney's National Energy Policy Development Group, and for the same reason.

In my 20th year of military service, from May 2002 to February 2003, I was a staff officer in the office of the Secretary of Defense, Undersecretary for Policy, Near East and South Asia Directorate (NESA). Our deputy undersecretary was Cheney's hand-placed acolyte, William Luti. Our undersecretary for policy was the ardently pro-Likud and strikingly dim Douglas Feith; his bosses were Deputy Defense Secretary and neoconservative ideologue Paul

Wolfowitz, and old Cheney pal and establishment insider Defense Secretary Donald Rumsfeld. The machinery for a new kind of American empire was in place with the odd neoconservative at the State Department and a former Chevron board director Condoleeza Rice as national security advisor to George W. Bush, himself quite familiar with the financial vulnerability end of the oil business. Fueled by unchallenged military capability, this group was further energized by the uniquely ignorant hubris that comes from never having worn a uniform. When I came to this assignment, I was unaware that neo-conservatism was our foreign policy impetus. Co-workers told me there was a dangerously politicized environment in this part of the Defense Policy secretariat. I was advised to learn about neoconservatism and Leo Strauss in order to understand these strategy and policy choices and the role of propaganda and misdirection in pursuing them.

As William Clark has pointed out, neoconservative strategy — using overt military actions to pursue energy or financial policies — has two main flaws. First, the enabling political propaganda that may be successfully directed at Americans usually remains transparent to the rest of the world, and the odd American as well. Secondly, the aftermath of our invasion and occupation of Iraq, a country we had militarily humiliated in 1991 and militarily and economically punished since, would predictably provide a complicated environment on the ground. This would be necessarily unsupportive of the known neoconservative objectives of oil production, access, and military presence.

That the Bush administration apparently had no plan to change this environment of predictable resistance to better support our wishes is beyond irresponsible. But it is understandable. The philosophy that calls for American military dominance and *control* of (*not just access* to) global energy stocks, clothed in language of liberation and human rights, truly has little insight into either military strategy or liberation. Compounding the widespread ignorance of its advocates, the philosophy itself is unconstrained by basic morality.

It became clearer to me that the oaths taken by career military officers and NCOs, and similar commitments made by government employees and political appointees, to serve with honor, lawfully, respecting and preserving the Constitution of the United States, had been corrupted. Key neoconservatives, such as Paul Wolfowitz and Abe Shulsky, the director of the Orwellian-named Office of Special Plans (OSP), seemed to spend far more time in creative and urgent justification for the invasion of Iraq than in considering the legalities or moral correctness of propagating fearful falsehoods to the Congress and the people in order to "get" a war.

The recent revelation of an ongoing FBI investigation, since 2001, into possible espionage and other untoward activities in this part of the Pentagon is only one of many red flags indicating that our current foreign policy, particularly our neoconservative policy in Iraq, is defective and unserviceable.

Supporters of Bush's neoconservative remedy for a declining dollar, and those who believe that the invasion and subsequent occupation of Iraq is really about liberation and fighting terrorism have an enduring dilemma, even after they understand the underlying themes and motivations of US foreign and domestic policies as detailed in this book. If not neoconservative militarism, or the more deceptively phrased "democratic imperialism," what then should comprise American foreign and domestic policy? What guiding paradigm gets us safely into the future, our lives and lifestyles and values not cast away like so much jetsam?

The answer lies in our own short history as a nation. When America has behaved beyond the strict confines of her charter as a constitutional republic, she has wasted lives and treasure, and in the long term lost much and gained little. Our early imperial adventure in the Philippines began after Washington and the mainstream media of the day provoked a similarly preemptive war with a weakened Spain in 1898. The result was a 35-year insurgency in the Philippines with tens of thousands dead, its eventual dictatorships, and finally, almost 100 years later, our military withdrawal from that country.

In early 2003 retired lieutenant general and administration insider Jay Garner tried to explain the positive side of the Iraq occupation by comparing it to the Philippine experience.[2] This comparison reeks with truth, but the conclusion Americans draw should be far less comforting than Garner intended.

America's Korean experience likewise contains lessons on the futility of military and political strategies pursued by academics and laypeople in Washington, far from those who pay the price for their ignorance and mistakes. Former US foreign service officer and Korea scholar Gregory Harrison wrote in 1971:

> No [case] is so astonishing in its origin as the division of Korea; none is so unrelated to conditions or sentiment within the nation itself at the time the division was effected; none is to this day so unexplained; in none does blunder and planning oversight appear to have played so large a role .... [3]

Tragically, in 2023, 20 years after the American invasion and occupation of Iraq, historians will draw similar conclusions about that unjustified, costly, and disastrous intervention.

Vietnam is often discussed as a parallel to Iraq these days, but it is a superficial one, with one exception. Then, as now, we witnessed a media too willing to serve as à mouthpiece for Republican and Democratic administrations alike and too able to ignore the history, reality, and hypocrisies of our approach and objectives in Vietnam. Shortly after the Tet Offensive, Walter Cronkite was both commended and scorned for stating on the *CBS Evening News* in February 1968 that "We are mired in stalemate." Any assessment of Cronkite's honesty or venality ignored the fact that, long before 1968, the Pentagon understood the condition of stalemate and politicians were unwilling or unable to withdraw American forces from Vietnam until 1975, seven years after that CBS broadcast and after tens of thousands more American troops had died there.

As we have seen in our recent Iraq experience, the Pentagon's steadfast reliability in the face of amazingly corrupt and incompetent policy-makers and media collusion with the Washington party line are still with us. As a result, men and women still die for the unclear objectives, impossible dreams, and incorrigible greed of those inside the Beltway.

Today two generations of Vietnamese struggle to create their own reality, made possible only after our complete military withdrawal. Today, our administrations encourage trade with, and travel to, an emerging capitalistic and peaceful Vietnam. Could this be an Iraqi future? If we leave now, it indeed could be. But if neoconservatism really is ascendant, we are staying, and thanks to *Petrodollar Warfare*, you can begin to understand why.

The United States is facing crises — an energy crisis, a national fiscal crisis, a petrodollar crisis. A phase in our modern American history is ending, and something new will be either forced upon us or chosen by us, or some combination of both.

Neoconservatives, accepting a zero-sum game and having a startling lack of imagination, believe that we need only reject our classical liberal and republican traditions and forcibly change others, to the extent of taking over foreign oil-rich countries while intimidating fellow oil-importing countries. America is a great nation, but the world is far bigger and far more resourceful than George W. Bush and the neoconservatives can appreciate.

The solid performance of the euro both before and since the invasion of Iraq and the emergence of a competing petroeuro continue to evolve, seemingly unaffected by our adventure in Iraq and, ironically, even encouraged by it. The economic marketplace seeks comparative value in currency, in businesses, in policies, and in countries. Thus the millions of economic and financial transactions worldwide persist and eventually prevail, while Washington neoconservatives nervously finger their beads and seek to implement a global command economy.

Thomas Jefferson clearly envisioned the disaster that would befall America if media were restrained, if citizens were uninformed and too trusting of government proclamations, and if the excessive political influence of big business and special interests were metastasized in the corridors of political power and at the door of the US Treasury.

While Jefferson had some familiarity with the Jacobins in revolutionary France, it is doubtful he envisioned the neoconservative persuasion and its inane and warlike approaches to solving critical problems of excessive debt, decades of a military "subsidy" artificially depressing domestic oil prices, and currency collapse. He might have addressed our current and coming crisis as an oil-dependent nation in terms he knew and loved best — classical liberal values of free speech, free trade, and free action, constitutional restraint of centralized government power, strict limitations on executive power, trust in the creativity and productive power of Americans themselves, and possibly, the occasional usefulness of refreshing "the tree of liberty with the blood of tyrants" — tyrants he fully expected to be hiding out in a city called Washington.

Endnotes

Foreword and Introduction

1. Peter Phillips, *Censored 2004: The Top 25 Censored News Stories*, Seven Stories Press, 2003, pp. 94–97.
2. Chalmers Johnson, *Sorrows of Empire: Militarism, Secrecy, and the End of the Republic*, Metropolitan Books, 2004, p. 283.
3. Association for the Study of Peak Oil and Gas, "Updating the Depletion Model #392," <www.asponews.org/HTML/Newsletter44.html>. Note: The calculation of Peak Oil by the ASPO is updated throughout the year, which can create small shifts in the calculation for the actual peak. Before the mid-2004 revision, APSO predicted the peak production in 2010, but now projects it to be 2008.
4. Association for the Study of Peak Oil and Gas, "Country Assessment: Saudi Arabia," Newsletter #21, September 2002, <www.asponews.org/ASPO.newsletter.021.php#99>. Also see "Country Assessment: Iraq," September 2002, Newsletter 24, December 2002, <www.asponews.org/ASPO.newsletter.024.php#118>.

Chapter 1. The American Century: Post–World War II Period

1. John S. Irons, "Beyond the Baseline: 10 year Deficits Likely to Reach $5.9 Trillion," OMB Watch, August 26, 2003, <www.ombwatch.org/article/articleview/1768/1/202/>.
2. "2003 Job Searches the Longest in 20 Years," *Reuters*, January 9, 2004, <www.foxnews.com/story/0,2933,107945,00.html>.
3. Martin Wolk, "White House Job Comments Touch a Nerve," *msnbc.com*, February 16, 2004, <www.msnbc.msn.com/id/4263244/>.
4. United States Department of Labor, July 2004 employment statistics, August 6, 2004, <www.bls.gov/news.release/empsit.nr0.htm>.
5. "Unemployment Measures Understate Job Slack," Economic Policy Institute (EPI), March 2004 bulletin, <www.jobwatch.org/previous.html>.
6. "Growth in Unemployment and Missing Labor Force," Economic Policy Institute, July 2004 bulletin.
7. Stephen Roach, "Coping with the Global Labor Arbitrage," Morgan Stanley, February 4, 2004, <www.morganstanley.com/GEFdata/digests/20040209-mon.html>.
8. Kevin Phillips, *Wealth and Democracy: A Political History of the American Rich*, Broadway Publishing, 2003.
9. Ibid., p. 153.
10. Administrative Office of the US Courts, "Personal Bankruptcy Filings Continue to Rise in Fiscal Year 2003," news release, November 14, 2003, <www.uscourts.gov/Press_Releases/fy03bk.pdf>.

11. Administrative Office of the US Courts, "Bankruptcy Filings Down in Fiscal Year 2004," news release, December 3, 2004, <www.uscourts.gov/ Press_Releases/fy04bk.pdf>.

12. Roach, op. cit.

13. Richard Duncan, *Dollar Crisis: Causes, Consequences, Cures*, John Wiley & Sons, 2003, p. 3.

14. Brett Arends, "Economic 'Armageddon' Predicted," *Boston Herald*, November 23, 2004, http://business.bostonherald.com/businessNews/ view.bg?articleid=55356.

15. William Keegan, "Sinking US Dollar Could Drag World Under: The Bank of International Settlements Fears a Deflationary Crisis Because the Global Economy is Too Tied to America," the *Observer*, July 6, 2003, <www.guardian.co.uk/recession/story/0,7369,992277,00.html>.

16. International Institute for Strategic Studies (IISS), 2002 International Defense Expenditures table, March 19, 2003, <www.iiss.org/>.

17. Ibid.

18. Stockholm International Peace Research Institute (SIPRI), "The Fifteen Major Spenders in 2003," <www.sipri.org/contents/milap/milex/ mex_major_spenders.pdf>.

19. Ibid.

20. Ibid.

21. Chalmers Johnson, *Sorrows of Empire: Militarism, Secrecy, and the End of the Republic*, Metropolitan Books, 2004.

22. Ibid., pp. 6–7.

23. Zbigniew Brzezinski, speech given at the New American Strategies for Security and Peace conference, October 28–29, 2003, general website <www.newamericanstrategies.org/>. Link to speech <www.newamericanstrategies.org/transcripts/Brzezinski.asp>.

24. Wesley Clark, *Winning Modern Wars; Iraq, Terrorism, and the American Empire*, Public Affairs, 2003, p. 130.

25. Ron Suskind, *The Price of Loyalty: George W. Bush, the White House, and the Education of Paul O' Neill*, Simon & Schuster, 2004, p. 86.

26. Richard A. Clarke, *Against All Enemies: Inside America's War on Terror*, Free Press, 2004, pp. 30–32.

27. US Department of State, press remarks of Secretary Powell with Foreign Minister of Egypt Amre Moussa, Cairo, Egypt (Ittihadiya Palace), February 24, 2001, <www.state.gov/secretary/rm/2001/933.htm>.

28. "Official: US Calls off Search for Iraqi WMDs," *CNN News*, January 12, 2005, <www.cnn.com/2005/US/01/12/wmd.search/>.

29. James Risen and David Johnson, "Threats and Responses: Terror Links; Split at CIA and FBI On Iraqi Ties to Al Qaeda," *New York Times*, February 2, 2003.

30. Michael Klare, *Resource Wars: The New Landscape of Global Conflict*, Owl Books, 2002.

31. F. William Engdahl, "A New American Century? Iraq and the Hidden Euro-dollar Wars," *currentconcerns.ch*, no. 4, 2003, <www.currentconcerns.ch/archive/ 2003/04/20030409.php>.

32. F. William Engdahl, *A Century of War: Anglo-American Oil Politics and the New World Order*, 2nd edition, Pluto Press, 2004.

33. Emmanuel Todd, *After the Empire: The Breakdown of the American Order*, Columbia University Press, 2004, p. 64.

34. Engdahl, "A New American Century?" op. cit.

35. Ibid.
36. Ibid.
37. Ibid.
38. Ibid.
39. Daniel Yergin and Joseph Stanislaw, *The Commanding Heights: The Battle for the World Economy*, 1997, pp. 60–64. Excerpt from "The Commanding Heights, Nixon, Price Controls, and the Gold Standard," <www.pbs.org/wgbh/commandingheights/shared/minitext/ess_nixongold.htm>.
40. David E. Spiro, *The Hidden Hand of American Hegemony: Petrodollar Recycling and International Markets*, Cornell University Press, 1999, pp. 121–123.
41. Ibid, p. x.
42. Ibid, p. 125.
43. Engdahl, *A Century of War*, p. 130.
44. Ibid., pp. 130–138. Engdahl was able to purchase the secret minutes of a May 1973 Bilderberg meeting from a Paris bookseller. His book contains photocopies of the cover page and related text discussed in chapter 1. The cover page is stamped: "SALSJOBADEN CONFERENCE 11–3 May 1973," "PERSONAL AND STRICTLY CONFIDENTIAL" and "NOT FOR PUBLICATION EITHER IN WHOLE OR IN PART"
45. Ibid, p. 140.
46. Duncan, op. cit., pp. 8–9.
47. Engdahl, "A New American Century?" op. cit.
48. Ibid.
49. Ibid.
50. Joseph Nye, *The Paradox of American Power, Why the World's Only Super Power Can't Go It Alone*, Oxford University Press, 2002.
51. John Judis, "History Lesson: What Woodrow Wilson Can Teach Today's Imperialists," the *New Republic*, June 2, 2003, <www.tnr.com/doc.mhtml?pt=TQpQdfYWiSnYPS4TSm45pg==>.
52. George Kennan, document PPS 23 in *Foreign Relations of the United States*, 1948, *I*, pp. 509–529.
53. Gellman Barton, *Washington Post* reporter who covered the March 1992 story on the original version of the Pentagon's "Defense Policy Guide" as prepared by Paul Wolfowitcz, <www.pbs.org/wgbh/pages/frontline/shows/iraq/themes/1992.html>.
54. Project for a New American Century, "Rebuilding America's Defenses: Strategies, Forces and Resources for a New Century," September 2000, <www.newamericancentury.org/RebuildingAmericasDefenses.pdf>.
55. Ibid.
56. Engdahl, op. cit.
57. Ibid.
58. Ibid.
59. Ibid.
60. Robert Block, "Some Muslim Nations Advocate Dumping the Dollar for the Euro," *Wall Street Journal*, April 15, 2003.
61. Engdahl, *A Century of War*, op. cit., p. 135.
62. Oliver Morgan and Islam Faisal, "Saudi Dove in the Oil Slick," *Observer*, January 14, 2001, http://observer.guardian.co.uk/business/story/0,6903,421888,00.html.
63. Spiro, op. cit., p. 110.
64. Engdahl, op. cit., pp. 137–138.

65. Ibid., p. 136.
66. Spiro, op. cit., p. x.
67. Block, op. cit.
68. Charles Recknagel, "Iraq: Baghdad Moves to Euro," *Radio Free Europe*, November 1, 2000, <www.rferl.org/nca/features/2000/11/01112000160846.asp>.
69. Ibid.
70. "UN to Let Iraq Sell Oil for Euros, Not Dollars," *CNN News*, October 30, 2000, http://archives.cnn.com/2000/WORLD/meast/10/30/iraq.un.euro.reut/.
71. Engdahl, "A New American Century?" op. cit.
72. Ibid.
73. Stan Goff, "The War for Saudi Arabia," *freedomroad.org*, August 9, 2004, <www.freedomroad.org/milmatters_30_saudiarabia.html>.
74. California Energy Commission database, "World Gasoline Prices: Average Prices for February 2004," <www.energy.ca.gov/gasoline/statistics/world_gasoline_prices.html>.
75. Davis Wastell, "Bush accuses Clinton of Exploiting Oil Reserves," *Telegraph* (UK), September 24, 2000, <www.telegraph.co.uk/news/main.jhtml?xml=/news/2000/09/24/wpres24.xml>.
76. "German Truckers Fume over Fuel Prices," *CBS News*, September 26, 2000, <www.cbsnews.com/stories/2000/09/15/world/main233748.shtml>.
77. "French Fuel Dispute Escalates," *CNN News*, September 7, 2000, http://edition.cnn.com/2000/WORLD/europe/09/07/france.fuel/.
78. Ed Vulliamy, Paul Webster, and Nick Paton Walsh, "Scramble to Carve up Iraqi Oil Reserves Lies behind US Diplomacy," *Observer*, October 6, 2002, http://observer.guardian.co.uk/iraq/story/0,12239,805580,00.html.
79. "Cheney Energy Task Force Meeting Map of Iraq Oil Fields," Judicial Watch Media Advisory, July 17, 2003, <www.judicialwatch.org/071703.c_.shtml>.
80. Simon Nixon, "What's That in Euros," *Spectator* (UK), October 16, 2003.
81. "The Disappearing Dollar," *Economist*, December 2, 2004, <www.economist.com/printedition/displayStory.cfm?Story_ID=3446249>.
82. Engdahl, op. cit.
83. Todd, op. cit., p. 64.
84. Michael Hudson, *Super Imperialism: The Origin and Fundamentals of US World Dominance*, Pluto Press, 2003.
85. Martin Feldstein, quoted in "EMU and International Conflict," *Foreign Affairs*, November/December 1997, pp. 2, 21.
86. William Drozdiak, "Even Allies Resent US Dominance: America Accused of Bullying World," *Washington Post*, November 4, 1997.
87. Engdahl, op. cit.
88. Ibid.
89. Ibid.
90. Michel Chossudovsky, *War and Globalization: The Truth Behind September 11*, Global Outlook and the Centre for Research on Globalization (CRG), 2002, pp. 109–112.
91. Pepe Escobar, "The Roving Eye: Pipelinestan," *Asia Times*, January 26, 2002.
92. Coilin Nunan, "Petrodollar or Petroeuro? A New source of global conflict," *Feasta Review* 2, 2004, <www.feasta.org/documents/review2/nunan.htm>.
93. "The Strategy Behind Paris-Berlin-Moscow Tie," *Intelligence*, 447, February 20, 2003, <www.intelligence.com>.
94. Ibid.

95. Zbigniew Brzezinski, *The Grand Chessboard: American Primacy and Its Geostrategic Imperatives*, Basic Books, 1998, p. 40.
96. Engdahl, op. cit.
97. Project for a New American Century (PNAC), <www.newamericancentury.org/>.
98. PNAC "Rebuilding America's Defenses: Strategies, Forces and Resources for a New Century," op. cit.
99. Neil Mackay, "Bush Planned Iraq 'Regime Change' Before Becoming President," *Sunday Herald* (Scotland), September 15, 2002.
100. Pat Rabbitte, "Iraq Being Used by the US to Flex Its Political Muscles," *Irish Times*, March 31, 2003, <www.ireland.com/focus/iraq/comment/comment3103b.htm>.
101. "Polls: World Not Pleased with Bush," *Associated Press*, March 4, 2004, <www.cbsnews.com/stories/2004/03/04/world/main604135.shtml>.
102. Will Lester, "Many Think US Wants World Domination," *Associated Press*, March 16, 2004, <www.guardian.co.uk/worldlatest/story/0,1280,-3868046,00.html>.

Chapter 2. US Geostrategy and the Persian Gulf: 1945–2005

1. Franklin D. Roosevelt, letter to Stettinius, February 18, 1943.
2. Miles Ignotus (pseudonym suggested to be Henry Kissinger), "Seizing Arab Oil," *Harper's Magazine*, March, 1975.
3. PNAC, "Rebuilding America's Defenses: Strategies, Forces and Resources for a New Century," September 2000, <www.newamericancentury.org/RebuildingAmericasDefenses.pdf>.
4. Osama bin Laden, "World Islamic Front Statement: Jihad Against Jews and Crusaders," February 23, 1998, <www.fas.org/irp/world/para/docs/980223-fatwa.htm>.
5. Daniel Yergin, *The Prize: The Epic Quest for Oil, Money and Power*, Free Press, 1991, pp. 404–405.
6. Craig Unger, *House of Bush: House of Saud: The Secret Relationship between the World's Two Most Powerful Dynasties*, Scribner, 2004, pp. 14–15.
7. Agence France-Presse, "US World Leader in Arms Sales, Saudi Arabia No 1 Buyer," *spacewar.com*, October 15, 2003, <www.spacewar.com/2003/031015185737.myb78ucw.html>.
8. President Carter, US State of the Union, January 21, 1980, <www.jimmycarterlibrary.org/documents/speeches/su80jec.phtml>.
9. Michael Klare, *Resource Wars: The New Landscape of Global Conflict*, Owl Books, 2002, p. 64.
10. Robert Dreyfuss, "The Thirty Year Itch," *Mother Jones Magazine*, March/April 2003, <www.motherjones.com/news/feature/2003/10/ma_273_01.html>.
11. Ibid.
12. Ibid.
13. Michael Klare, "Bush-Cheney Energy Strategy: Procuring the Rest of the World's Oil," Foreign Policy in Focus (FPIF), January 2004, <www.fpif.org/papers/03petropol/politics_body.html>.
14. Thomas L. Friedman, "A New Mission for America," *International Herald Tribune*, December 6, 2004, <www.iht.com/articles/2004/12/05/opinion/edfried.html>.
15. Yergin, op. cit.
16. CIA Intelligence Memorandum (ER 77–10147), "The Impending Soviet Oil Crisis," March 1977, <www.foia.cia.gov>. In search field, type ER77–10147.

17. Ibid., p. 6.
18. Ibid., p. 3.
19. Richard Heinberg, "Smoking Gun: The CIA's Interest in Peak Oil," *museletter.com*, August 2003, <www.museletter.com/archive/cia-oil.html>.
20. Dick Cheney, then CEO of Halliburton, 1998, cited by Sitaram Yechury, "America, Oil and Afghanistan," *Hindu*, October 13, 2001, <www.hinduonnet.com/thehindu/2001/10/13/stories/05132524.htm>.
21. National Energy Policy Development Group (NEPDG), Report, May 2001, <www.whitehouse.gov/energy/>.
22. Klare, op. cit.
23. Krell Aleklett, "Dick Cheney, Peak Oil, and the Final Countdown," paper presented at Uppsala University, Sweden, The Association for the Study of Peak Oil and Gas, May 12, 2004, <www.peakoil.net//Publications/Cheney_PeakOil_FCD.pdf>.
24. NEPDG, op. cit.
25. F. William Engdahl, "Iraq and the Problem of Peak Oil," *Current Concerns*, no. 1, 2004, <www.currentconcerns.ch/archive/2004/01/20040118.php>.
26. US Energy Department, Iraq Country Analysis Brief, March 2004, <www.eia.doe.gov/emeu/cabs/iraq.html>.
27. Klare, *Resource Wars*, op. cit.
28. Michael Klare, *Blood and Oil: The Dangers and Consequences of America's Growing Petroleum Dependency*, Metropolitan Books, 2004.
29. Klare, "Bush-Cheney Energy Strategy," op. cit.
30. Ibid.
31. Ibid.
32. Barton Gellman, "Keeping the US First: Pentagon Would Preclude a Rival Superpower," *Washington Post*, March 11, 1992, A1. Also see *Der Spiegel*, March 16, 1992, pp. 18–21, <www.yale.edu/strattech/92dpg.html>.
33. PNAC, op. cit., p. 26.
34. Gellman, op. cit.
35. Letter to President Clinton dated January 26, 1998, advising military action for "the removal of Saddam Hussein's regime from power," PNAC, <www.newamericancentury.org/iraqclintonletter.htm>.
36. PNAC, op. cit.
37. Gellman, op. cit.
38. Ibid.
39. Ibid.
40. "The War behind Closed Doors," *PBS Frontline*, excerpts from a 2003 interview with *Washington Post* reporter Barton Gellman on the original 1992 "First Draft of a Grand Strategy," <www.pbs.org/wgbh/pages/frontline/shows/iraq/themes/1992.html>.
41. Joseph Nye, *The Paradox of American Power: Why the World's Only Superpower Can't Go It Alone*, Oxford University Press, 2002.
42. Gellman, op. cit.
43. PNAC, op. cit., p. 8.
44. Mackay, op. cit.
45. PNAC, op. cit.
46. Bernard Weiner, "How We Got into This Imperial Pickle: A PNAC Primer," The Crisis Papers, May 26, 2003, <www.crisispapers.org/Editorials/PNAC-Primer.htm>.
47. Ibid.

48. Engdahl, "A New American Century?" op. cit.
49. PNAC, op. cit.
50. Office of the President of the United States of America, *The National Security Strategy of the United States* (NSS), 2002, p. 29, <www.whitehouse.gov/nsc>.
51. The Crisis Papers (<www.crisispapers.org>) contains a broad compilation of essays by Bernard Weiner and Earnest Partridge. Partridge, a lecturer-consultant in environmental and applied ethics, has a website, *Gadfly* (http://gadfly.igc.org). Partridge is writing a book, *A Progressive Manifesto*.
52. Weiner, op. cit.
53. *NSS*, op. cit.
54. E.J. Currie Duncan, LL.B., LL.M. provided a legal analysis of the 2003 Iraq War, "Preventive War and International Law after Iraq," May 22, 2003, <www.globelaw.com/Iraq/Preventive_war_after_iraq.htm>.
55. "Iraq War Illegal, Says Annan," *AFP/Reuters*, September 16, 2004, <www.abc.net.au/news/newsitems/200409/s1200210.htm>.
56. Julian Darley, *High Noon for Natural Gas: The New Energy Crisis*, Chelsea Green Publishing, 2004, back cover. Transcript of interview of Julian Darley discussing natural gas depletion with Sue Supriano, *globalpublic media.com.*, August 18, 2004, <www.globalpublicmedia.com/INTERVIEWS/JULIAN.DARLEY/>.
57. Victor Mallet, "China Unable to Quench Thirst for Oil," *Financial Times*, January 20, 2004, http://news.ft.com.
58. Gal Luft is executive director of the Institute for the Analysis of Global Security (IAGS), Washington, DC. Anne Korin is its director of policy and strategic planning and the editor of *Energy Security*.
59. Tim Appenzeller, "End of Cheap Oil?" *National Geographic*, June 2004, p. 89.
60. David R. Francis, "China's Risky Scramble for Oil," *Christian Science Monitor*, January 20, 2005, <www.csmonitor.com/2005/0120/p16s01-cogn.html>.
61. Stephen Kinzer, "Pipe Dreams: A Perilous New Contest for the Next Oil Prize," *New York Times*, September 24, 1997, IV–1.
62. Rahul Bedi, "India Joins Anti-Taliban Coalition," *Jane's Intelligence Review*, March 15, 2001, <www.janes.com/security/international_security/news/jir/jir010315_1_n.shtml>.
63. Jean Charles-Brisard and Guillaume Dasquie, *The Forbidden Truth: US-Taliban Secret Oil Diplomacy, Saudi Arabia and the Failed Search for bin Laden*, Nation Books, 2002, p. 43.
64. Ibid.
65. "Agreement on US 3.2 Billion Gas Pipeline Project Signed," Global Policy Forum, December 28, 2002, <www.globalpolicy.org/security/oil/2002/1230pipe.htm>.
66. Dale Allen Pfeiffer, "Much Ado about Nothing — Whither the Caspian Riches?" *From The Wilderness*, December 5, 2002, <www.fromthewilderness.com/free/ww3/120502_caspian.html>.
67. "New Study Says Caspian Oil Reserve Estimates are Exaggerated," *Alexander's Gas & Oil Connections*, 7 (13), June 27, 2002, <www.gasandoil.com/goc/news/ntc22663.htm>.
68. "Kerr McGee Abandons Kazakhstan," *Neftegaz.ru*, November 21, 2002, <www.neftegaz.ru/english/lenta/show.php?id=29666>.
69. "Expert: No Guarantees in Caspian Oil," *Johnson's Russia List*, November 1, 2002, <www.cdi.org/russia/johnson/6529-2.cfm>.
70. "Cheney Energy Task Force Meeting Map of Iraq Oil Fields," Judicial Watch Media Advisory, July 17, 2003, <www.judicialwatch.org/071703.c_.shtml>.

71. Ed Vulliamy, Paul Webster, and Nick Paton Walsh, "Scramble to Carve up Iraqi Oil Reserves Lies behind US Diplomacy," *Observer*, October 6, 2002, http://observer.guardian.co.uk/iraq/story/0,12239,805580,00.html.

72. ASPO, "Iraq Reserves," Newsletter no. 37, January 2004, <www.asponews.org/HTML/Newsletter37.html>.

73. "Maps and Charts of Iraqi Oilfields: Cheney Energy Task Force," Judicial Watch, <www.judicialwatch.org/071703.c_.shtml>.

74. Iraqi Oil Foreign Suitors: List #1: Algeria through Italy, Judicial Watch, <www.judicialwatch.org/IraqOilFrgnSuitors.pdf>.
Iraqi Oil Foreign Suitors: List # 2: Japan through Vietnam, Judicial Watch, <www.judicialwatch.org/IraqOilGasProj.pdf>.

75. Dan Morgan and David B Ottoway, "Iraqi War Scenario, Oil Is the Key Issue; US Drillers Eye Huge Petroleum Pool," *Washington Post*, September 15, 2002.

76. Vulliamy, Webster, and Walsh, op. cit.

77. Ibid.

78. Ibid.

79. Iraq: Country Analysis, Energy Information Administration, November 2004 analysis, <www.eia.doe.gov/emeu/cabs/iraq.html>.

80. Engdahl, "Iraq and the Problem of Peak Oil," op. cit.

81. ASPO, op. cit.

82. Ibid.

83. Thomas L. Friedman, "A New Mission for America," *International Herald Tribune*, December 6, 2004, <www.iht.com/articles/2004/12/05/opinion/edfried.html>.

84. Timothy Burn, "Hunt for 'New' Oil," *Washington Times*, September 28, 2003, <www.washtimes.com/specialreport/20030928-123431-1449r.htm>.

85. Ibid.

86. Ibid.

87. John R. Talbot, *Where America Went Wrong*, Financial Times Prentice Hall, 2004, p. 133.

88. Burn, op. cit.

89. Ibid.

90. Ibid.

91. Thomas I. Palley, *Publish What You Pay: Confronting Corruption and the Natural Resource Curse*, Open Society Institute (OSI), July 1, 2003, <www.soros.org/initiatives/washington/articles_publications/articles/publishpay_20030304>.

92. Daniel Yergin, *The Prize: The Epic Quest for Oil, Money and Power*, Free Press 1991, p. 334.

93. "Behind the Invasion of Iraq" *Aspect's of India's Economy*, 33 and 34, November/December, 2002, <www.rupe-india.org/>. Also available as a book.

94. Michael Klare, "Transforming the American Military into a Global Oil-Protection Service," *Global Policy Forum*, www.tomdispatch.com, October 7, 2004, <www.globalpolicy.org/empire/economy/2004/1007oilprotection.htm>.

95. Yergin, op. cit., p. 183.

96. Ibid., p. 334.

97. Ibid., p. 337

98. Ritt Goldstein, "Defense Redefined Means Securing Cheap Energy," *Sydney Morning Herald*, December 26, 2002, <www.smh.com.au/articles/2002/12/25/1040511092926.html>.

99. Michael Meacher, "This War on Terrorism is Bogus," *Guardian* (UK), September 6, 2003, http://politics.guardian.co.uk/iraq/comment/0,12956,1036687,00.html.

100. Klare, "Bush-Cheney Energy Strategy," op. cit.
101. Ibid.
102. Klare, *Blood and Oil*, op. cit., p. 70.
103. Ibid.
104. Ibid., p. 72.
105. "OPEC Head: We Have No Extra Oil," *Reuters*, as reported on *CNNmoney.com*, August 3, 2004, http://money.cnn.com/2004/08/03/news/international/opec.reut.
106. "Russia May Stop Exporting Energy Sources by 2010: Expert," *mosnews.com*, December 7, 2004, <www.mosnews.com/money/2004/12/07/energyefficiency.shtml>.

Chapter 3. Global Peak Oil: The Millennium's Greatest Challenge

1. Colin J. Campbell and Jean H. Laherrère, "The End of Cheap Oil," *Scientific American*, March 1998, pp. 80–86, http://dieoff.com/page140.pdf.
2. George Monbiot, "Bottom of the Barrel: The World is Running out of Oil — So Why Do Politicians Refuse to Talk about It?" *Guardian* (UK), December 2, 2003, <www.guardian.co.uk/comment/story/0,3604,1097622,00.html>.
3. Chris Skrebowski, "Global Oil Production Now Flat Out," *Energy Institute*, August 2004, <www.energyinst.org.uk/index.cfm?PageID=948>.
4. Inscription at the CIA Headquarters. Almost a direct quote from *The Bible*, John 8:32 "And ye shall know the truth, and the truth shall make you free."
5. John Myers, "The Hard Truth About Crude," *Financial Sense*, January 16, 2004, <www.financialsense.com/editorials/daily/2004/0116.html>.
6. Anthony H. Cordesman, *The US, the Gulf, and the Middle East: Energy Dependence, Demographics, and the Forces Shaping Internal Stability*, Center for Strategic and International Studies, December 2, 2002, <www.csis.org/burke/gulf/us_me_energy_demo.pdf>.
7. Colin J. Campbell, "Peak Oil: An Outlook on Crude Oil Depletion, revised February 2002," Mbendi Information Services Ltd., <www.mbendi.co.za/indy/oilg/p0070.htm>.
8. Kenneth A. Dreffeyes, *Hubbert's Peak: The Impending World Oil Shortage*, Princeton University Press, 2001, p. 4. Also see Newsletter "Hubbert's Peak," January 16, 2004, predicted Peak Oil in 2005, <www.princeton.edu/hubbert/current-events-01-16-04.html>.
9. Ibid., p. 4.
10. ASPO, Newsletter no. 23, November 2002, <www.asponews.org/ASPO.newsletter.023.php#109>.
11. *Fossil Fuels and Human Civilisation*, Institute for Environmental and Legal Studies, July 31, 2004. Source for graph listed as ASPO/Exxon, <www.intnet.mu/iels/Fossil_Fuels.htm>.
12. Ibid.
13. Jeffrey Ball, "As Prices Soar, Doomsayers Provoke Debate on Oil's Future," *Wall Street Journal*, September 21, 2004, A1, A14.
14. Ibid.
15. Michael C. Lynch, "The New Pessimism about Petroleum Resources: Debunking the Hubbert Model (and Hubbert Modelers)," 2003, <www.energyseer.com/NewPessimism.pdf>.
16. *Fossil Fuels and Human Civilization*, op. cit.
17. *New Projects Cannot Meet World Demand This Decade*, ODAC/The Oil Depletion Analysis Centre, November 16, 2004.

18. ASPO, Newsletter no. 44, August 2004, <www.asponews.org/HTML/Newsletter44.html>.
19. Skrebowski, op. cit.
20. Jean H. Laherrère, "Forecasting Future Production from Past Discovery," OPEC seminar, September 28–29, 2001, <www.hubbertpeak.com/laherrere/opec2001.pdf>.
21. Skrebowski, op. cit.
22. Dreffeyes, op. cit., p. 7.
23. Laherrère, op. cit.
24. Ibid., p. 15.
25. "World Oil Reserves: The Coming World Oil Crisis," Figure 3.3, table of reported oil reserves: 1980–1998, <planetforlife.com/oilcrisis/oilreserves.html>.
26. ASPO, <www.asponews.org/>.
27. Campion Walsh, "Canada's Oil Reserves 2nd Only to Saudi Arabia," *Dow Jones Newswires/ Petroleumworld.com*, May 6, 2003, <www.rense.com/general37/petrol.htm>.
28. Michael C. Ruppert, "Paris Peak Oil Conference Reveals Deepening Crisis," *From the Wilderness*, May 30, 2003, report on research presented May 26–27 at the French Institute for Petroleum (IFP), sponsored by ASPO, <www.fromthewilderness.com/free/ww3/053103_aspo.html>.
29. Jean H. Laherrère, "Future of Oil Supplies," Seminar Center of Energy Conversion in Zurich, May 7, 2003, <www.hubbertpeak.com/laherrere/zurich.pdf>.
30. Ibid., p. 12.
31. Ibid.
32. Ibid.
33. Julian Darley, *High Noon for Natural Gas: The New Energy Crisis*, Chelsea Green, 2004.
34. Brad Lemley, "Anything into Oil," *DISCOVER*, 24 (05), May 2003.
35. Richard Heinberg, *The Party's Over: Oil, War and the Fate of Industrial Societies*, New Society Publishers, 2003.
36. Jeff Wright, "Energy and the Free Market," Colorado Free Report, July 12, 2003, <www.freecolorado.com/2003/07/energy.html>.
37. Ibid.
38. Ibid.
39. Heinberg, op. cit.
40. Bill Butler, "The Great Rollover Juggernaut: World Oil Depletion and the Inevitable Crisis," section entitled "Alternate Sources of Hydrocarbon Fuels and Why Most of Them Can't Help." <www.durangobill.com/Rollover.html>.
41. Ibid.
42. Ulf Bossel and Baldur Eliasson, "Energy and the Hydrogen Economy," Methanol Institute, Switzerland, January 8, 2003, <www.methanol.org/pdfFrame.cfm?pdf=HydrogenEconomyReport2003.pdf>.
43. John R. Wilson and Griffin Burgh, "The Hydrogen Report: An Examination of the Role of Hydrogen in Achieving US Energy Independence," TMG/ The Management Group, July 2003, <www.tmgtech.com/images/Energy_Economics_Rev_B.doc>.
44. Richard Heinberg, *Powerdown, Options and Actions For a Post-Carbon World*, New Society Publishers, 2004, pp. 124–129.

45. David W. Keith and Alexander E. Farrell "Rethinking Hydrogen Cars," *Science*, 301, 2003, pp. 315-316, <www.sciencemag.org/cgi/content/full/301/5631/315?ijkey=7l8fYOLX4bkJs&keytype=ref&siteid=sci>.

46. Robert Sanders, "Hydrogen-Fueled Cars Not Best Way to Cut Pollution, Greenhouse Gases and Oil Dependency," *UC Berkeley News*, June 17, 2003.

47. "What Is Ocean Thermal Energy Conversion?" National Renewable Energy Lab reference, <www.nrel.gov/otec/what.html>.

48. William Avery and Chih Wu, *Renewable Energy from the Ocean: A Guide to OTEC*, Oxford University Press, 1994. Search for ISBN: 0195071999 at <www.oup.com>. Also see white paper by Dr. Luis Vega, principal researcher, Natural Energy Laboratory of Hawaiian Authority (NELHA). Ocean Thermal Energy Conversion (OTEC), December 1999, <www.otecnews.org/articles/vega/OTECbyVega_with_photos.pdf>.

49. William Avery and Walter G. Berl, "Solar Energy from the Tropical Oceans," *Issues in Science and Technology*, Winter 1997, <www.issues.org/issues/14.2/avery.htm>.

50. Heinberg, op. cit., pp. 117-137.

51. Robert Dreyfuss, "The Thirty Year Itch," *Mother Jones Magazine*, March/April 2003, <www.motherjones.com/news/feature/2003/10/ma_273_01.html>.

52. George Monibot, "Bottom of the Barrel," *Guardian* (UK), December 2, 2003.

53. "US Using Anti-Terror War to Gain World Oil Reserves - Soviet Intelligence Chief," *mosnews.com*, March 21, 2005, <www.mosnews.com/news/2005/03/21/shebarsh.shtml>.

54. "Revealing Statements from a Bush Insider about Peak Oil and Natural Gas Depletion," transcript of ASPO Conference with comments of Matthew Simmons, Paris, France, May 2003, *From the Wilderness*, June 12, 2003, <www.fromthewilderness.com/free/ww3/061203_simmons.html>.

55. Ibid.

56. Campbell, op. cit., pp. 151–152.

57. "BP Maps out Iraq Strategy: World's No. 3 Oil Company Is Getting Ready to Work on the World's Second-largest Reserves of Crude," *CNN News*, April 9, 2003, <www.cnn.com/2003/BUSINESS/04/09/bp.reut/>.

58. "US Pulls out of Saudi Arabia," *BBC News*, April 29, 2003, <news.bbc.co.uk/1/hi/world/middle_east/2984547.stm>.

59. PNAC, "Rebuilding America's Defenses: Strategies, Forces and Resources for a New Century," September 2000, <www.newamericancentury.org/RebuildingAmericasDefenses.pdf>.

60. "Saudi Arabia: A Balancing Act," *Stratfor*, January 30, 2004, www.stratfor.com.

61. Ibid.

62. Ibid.

63. Michael C. Ruppert, "Peak Oil Revisited: The Bill Collector Calls," *From The Wilderness*, June 21, 2004, <www.fromthewilderness.com/free/ww3/062104_berlin_peak.html>.

64. CIA Intelligence Memorandum (ER 77-10147), "The Impending Soviet Oil Crisis," March 1977, <www.foia.cia.gov>. In search field, type ER77-10147.

65. Heinberg, op. cit., p. 86.

66. Ibid. Includes a powerful, but fictitious, speech entitled: "What Should Have Been George W. Bush's Speech to the Nation, 9/11/01," pp. 76-77.

67. R. James Woolsey, "Defeating the Oil Weapon," *Commentator*, 114(2), September 2002.

68. Stan Goff, "The Infinite War and Its Roots," *From the Wilderness*, August 27, 2002, <www.fromthewilderness.com/free/ww3/082702_infinite_war.html>.

69. George Orwell, *Ninety Eighty Four: A Novel*, Harcourt Brace Jovanovich, 1949.
70. Barton Gellman, "Keeping the US First: Pentagon Would Preclude a Rival Superpower," *Washington Post*, March 11, 1992, A1.
71. Uppsala Hydrocarbon Depletion Study Group, UHDSG, Uppsala University, Sweden, <www.oilcrisis.com/uppsala/uppsalaProtocol.html>. The Uppsala Accord, <www.globalpublicmedia.com/DOCS/2004/05/RIMINI% 20PROTOCOL.pdf>.
72. Heinberg, op. cit., p. 168.
73. Adam Porter, "The Death of Cheap Crude," *Aljazeera.Net*, August 4, 2004, http://english.aljazeera.net/NR/exeres/416F7BA6-90FC-48E6-8F4C-CA30FDD6EB39.htm.
74. Michael Meacher, "Plan Now for a World without Oil," *Financial Times*, January 5, 2004, archived at <www.energycrisis.com/uk/planNow.htm>.
75. Richard Heinberg, "Beyond the Peak ," *Muse Letter*, 152, December 2004, <www.museletter.com/archive/152.html>.

Chapter 4. Manifest Subterfuge: Disguising the Macroeconomic and Geostrategic Rationales for War

1. US Department of State, press remarks of Secretary Powell with Egypt's Foreign Minister Amre Moussa, Cairo, Egypt (Ittihadiya Palace), February 24, 2001.
2. Vice President Cheney, remarks to the Veterans of Foreign Wars 103rd National Convention, August 26, 2002, <www.whitehouse.gov/news/releases/2002/08/20020826.html>.
3. Secretary Powell, remarks to the United Nations Security Council, New York, February 5, 2003, <www.state.gov/secretary/rm/2003/17300.htm>.
4. "Bush: 'Leave Iraq within 48 hours,'" transcript of Bush's televised speech to the nation, *CNN*, March 17, 2003, <www.cnn.com/2003/WORLD/meast/03/17/sprj.irq.bush.transcript/>.
5. Prime Minister Blair to House of Commons, March 18, 2003, *BBC News*, http://news.bbc.co.uk/nolpda/ukfs_news/hi/newsid_3054000/3054991.stm.
6. G. M. Gilbert, *Nurenberg Diary*, New York: Signet, 1947.
7. Ron Suskind, *The Price of Loyalty*, op. cit., pp. 75-76.
8. Glen Rangwala, "Claims and Evaluations of Iraq's Proscribed Weapons," *Middle East Reference*, February 25, 2003, http://middleeastreference.org.uk/iraqweapons.html#start
9. UNMOVIC Working Document, Unresolved Disarmament Issues: Iraq's Proscribed Weapons Programmes. March 6, 2003, p. 15, <www.un.org/Depts/unmovic/documents/6mar.pdf>.
10. IAEA Director General Mohamed ElBaradei, statement to the Security Council, March 7, 2003, <www.iaea.org/worldatom/Press/Statements/2003/ebsp2003n006.shtml>.
11. Tom Raum, "Cheney: Weapons Report Justifies Iraq War," *Associated Press*, October 7, 2004, <www.wjla.com/news/stories/1004/178314.html>.
12. Peter Beaumont and Faisal Islam, "Carve-up of Oil Riches Begins," *Observer* (UK), November 3, 2002, http://observer.guardian.co.uk/iraq/story/0,12239,825105,00.html.
13. "In Their Own Words: Iraq's Imminent Threat," Center for American Progress, January 29, 2004, <www.americanprogress.org/site/pp.asp?c=biJRJ8OVF&b=24970>.
14. "Plans for Iraq Attack Began on 9/11," *CBS News*, September 4, 2002, <www.cbsnews.com/stories/2002/09/04/september11/main520830.shtml>.

15. Michael Meacher, "This War on Terrorism Is Bogus," *Guardian* (UK), September 6, 2003.

16. Nafeez M. Ahmed, *The War on Freedom: How and Why America Was Attacked September 11, 2001*, Media Messenger Books; 3rd edition, 2002.

17. Michael Ruppert, *Crossing the Rubicon: The Decline of the American Empire at the End of the Age of Oil*, New Society Publishers, 2004.

18. Danny Postel, "Noble Lies and Perpetual War: Leo Strauss, the Neo-cons, and Iraq," October 16, 2003, <www.informationclearinghouse.info/article5010.htm>.

19. Niccolo Machiavelli, *The Prince*, written 1513, first published 1532.

20. Michael Ledeen, *Machiavelli on Modern Leadership: Why Machiavelli's Iron Rules Are As Timely and Important Today As Five Centuries Ago*, St. Martin's Press, 1999, p. 91.

21. "Wolfowitz: Iraq Intel Was 'Murky,'" *CBS News/Associated Press*, July 31, 2003, <www.cbsnews.com/stories/2003/07/31/iraq/main566000.shtml>.

22. Oliver Burkeman and Julian Borger, "War Critics Astonished as US Hawk Admits Invasion Was Illegal," *Guardian* (UK), November 20, 2003, <www.guardian.co.uk/Iraq/Story/0,2763,1089158,00.html>.

23. Danny Postel, op. cit.

24. Shadia Drury, *The Political Ideas of Leo Strauss*, Palgrave Macmillan, 1988.

25. Shadia Drury, *Leo Strauss and the American Right*, Palgrave Macmillan, 1997.

26. Danny Postel, op. cit.

27. Ibid.

28. Ibid.

29. Ibid.

30. Ibid.

31. Louis Dubose, "Bush's Hit Man: Karl Rove Wins...by Any Means Necessary," *Texas Observer*, March 16, 2001, <www.texasobserver.org/showArticle.asp?ArticleID=398>.

32. Glenn Kessler, "US Decision on Iraq Has Puzzling Past: Opponents of War Wonder When, How Policy Was Set," *Washington Post*, January 12, 2003, A01, <www.washingtonpost.com/ac2/wp-dyn/A43909-2003Jan11>.

33. Bob Woodward, *Plan of Attack*, Simon & Schuster, 2004, p. 30.

34. Ibid., p. 31.

35. Ibid., p. 137. Also see *CBS News* interview "Woodward Shares War Secrets," April 18, 2004, <www.cbsnews.com/stories/2004/04/15/60minutes/main612067.shtml>.

36. Seymour Hersh, "Selective Intelligence: Donald Rumsfeld Has His Own Special Sources. Are They Reliable?" *New Yorker*, May 12, 2003, <www.newyorker.com/fact/content/?030512fa_fact>.

37. Ibid.

38. Analysis by Jim Lobe, "War Critics Zero in on Pentagon Office," *Inter Press Service News Agency*, August 5, 2003, <www.ipsnews.net/interna.asp?idnews=19542>.

39. Hersh, op. cit.

40. Robert Dreyfuss and Jason Vest, "The Lie Factory," *Mother Jones Magazine*, January/February edition, 2004, <www.motherjones.com/news/feature/2004/01/12_405.html>.

41. Julian Coman, "Fury over Pentagon Cell That Briefed White House on Iraq's 'Imaginary' Al-Qaeda Links," *Telegraph* (UK), July 7, 2004, <www.telegraph.co.uk/news/main.jhtml?xml=/news/2004/07/11/wsept11.xml&sSheet=/news/2004/07/11/ixnewstop.html>.

42. Chris Strohm, "Rumsfeld: Pentagon Did Not Bypass Intelligence Community on Iraq," *govexec.com*, March 12, 2004, <www.govexec.com/dailyfed/0304/031204c1.htm>.

43. Dreyfuss and Vest, op. cit.

44. Hersh, op. cit.

45. Ibid.

46. Dreyfuss and Vest, op. cit.

47. Kim Sengupta, "Intelligence Agencies Doubt Al-Qaida Links," *UK Independent*, February 4, 2003, http://news.independent.co.uk/world/middle_east/story.jsp?story=375403.

48. Walter Pincus, "CIA Finds No Evidence Hussein Sought to Arm Terrorists," *Washington Post*, November 16, 2003, <www.washingtonpost.com/wp-dyn/articles/A46460-2003Nov15.html>.

49. Neil Mackey, "Revealed: The Secret Cabal Which Spun for Blair," *Sunday Herald*, June 8, 2003, <www.sundayherald.com/34491>.

50. Michael Meacher, "The Very Secret Service," *Guardian* (UK), November 21, 2003, <www.guardian.co.uk/comment/story/0,3604,1089931,00.html>.

51. Vice President Cheney, remarks, op. cit.

52. "Quotes: War of Words," *CBC News*, September 9, 2002, <www.cbc.ca/news/iraq/issues_analysis/quotes.html>.

53. "President Bush Outlines Iraqi Threat," White House press release, October 7, 2002, <www.whitehouse.gov/news/releases/2002/10/20021007-8.html>.

54. Jonathan Schell, "The Case against the War," *The Nation*, February 13, 2003, <www.thenation.com/doc.mhtml?i=20030303&c=6&s=schell>.

55. Wolf Blitzer, "Did the Bush Administration Exaggerate the Threat from Iraq?" *CNN News*, July 8, 2003, <www.cnn.com/2003/ALLPOLITICS/07/08/wbr.iraq.claims/>.

56. Timothy Noah, "Whopper of the Week: Donald Rumsfeld, Meet Dick Cheney," *slate.msn.com*, May 23, 2003, http://slate.msn.com/id/2083532/.

57. Vice President Cheney, transcript, Tim Russert, moderator, September 14, 2003, http://msnbc.msn.com/id/3080244/.

58. Postel, op. cit.

59. Schell, op. cit. Also see Srdja Trifkovic, "9-11 Commission: No Iraq Link to Al-Qaida," *choniclesmagazine.org*, June 18, 2004, <www.chroniclesmagazine.org/News/Trifkovic04/NewsST061804.html>.

60. Andrew Buncombe, "Official Verdict: White House Misled World over Saddam," *Independent*, June 17, 2004, http://news.independent.co.uk/world/americas/story.jsp?story=532341. Also see: Schell, op. cit.

61. G.M. Gilbert, *Nurenberg Diary*, New York: Signet, 1947.

62. Ian Traynor, "Pakistan's Nuclear Hero Throws open Pandora's Box: Investigators Have Uncovered a Sophisticated Black Market in Components with Islamabad at Its Centre," *Guardian* (UK), January 31,2004, <www.guardian.co.uk/pakistan/Story/0,2763,1135961,00.html>.

63. CRS Report for Congress, Received through the CRS Web: Order Code RS21293. "Terrorist Nuclear Attacks on Seaports: Threat and Response," August 23, 2002, Jonathan Medalia, Specialist in National Defense, Foreign Affairs, Defense, and Trade Division.

64. "Bush Continues to Insist on Link between bin Laden and Saddam," *CBC News*, June 18, 2004, <www.cbc.ca/stories/2004/06/17/world/bush040617>.

65. Bob Woodward, *Bush at War*, Simon & Schuster, 2002. Bush quoted in an interview by Bob Woodward in Crawford, Texas, August 20, 2002. Also see *CBS*

News, "A Rare Glimpse inside Bush's Cabinet," November 17, 2002, <www.cbsnews.com/stories/2002/11/17/60minutes/main529657.shtml>.

66. Al Karmen, "Road Map in the Back Seat?" *Washington Post,* June 27, 2003.

67. Ledeen, op. cit., p. 95.

68. Karen Kwiatkowski, "Career Officer Does Eye-opening Stint inside Pentagon," *Akron Beacon Journal,* July 30, 2003, <www.ohio.com/mld/beaconjournal/6424570.htm?1c>.

69. Hans Blix, *Disarming Iraq,* Pantheon Books, 1st edition, 2004.

70. Scott Ritter, *Frontier Justice: Weapons of Mass Destruction and the Bushwhacking of America,* Context Books, 2003.

71. Dilip Hiro, *Secrets and Lies: Operation "Iraqi Freedom" and After: A Prelude to the Fall of US Power in the Middle East?* , Nations Books, 2004, pp. 453–454, Appendix II.

72. Dreyfuss and Vest, op. cit.

73. Joseph Wilson, *The Politics of Truth: Inside the Lies that Led to War and Betrayed My Wife's CIA Identity: A Diplomat's Memoir,* Carroll & Graf, 2004.

74. John Dean, "The Bush Administration Adopts a Worse-than-Nixonian Tactic: The Deadly Serious Crime of Naming CIA Operatives," *FindLaw.com,* August 15, 2003, http://writ.news.findlaw.com/dean/20030815.html.

75. William Pitt, "Interview: 27-Year CIA Veteran," *www.truthout.org,* June 26, 2003, <www.truthout.org/docs_03/062603B.shtml>. McGovern was a CIA analyst during administrations from Kennedy to George H. W. Bush, chairing National Intelligence Estimates and briefing the President's Daily Brief (PDB). He co-founded Veteran Intelligence Professionals for Sanity (VIPS).

76. Ibid.

77. Ibid.

78. Mark Follman, "The White House War with the CIA," *Salon* interview with Thomas Powers, author of *Intelligence Wars: American Secret History from Hitler to Al Qaeda,* 2002, regarding the relationship between the Pentagon, OSP, and CIA, *salon.com,* November 8, 2003, <www.salon.com/news/feature/2003/11/08/powers/>.

79. Dreyfuss and Vest, op. cit.

80. Philip Sherwell, "The CIA 'Old Guard' Goes to War with Bush," *Telegraph* (UK), October 10, 2004, <www.telegraph.co.uk/news/main.jhtml?xml=/news/2004/10/10/wbush10.xml&sSheet=/news/2004/10/10/ixnewstop.html>.

81. Ibid.

82. "CIA Purge May Go Too Far," *Journal Sentinel,* editorial, November 18, 2004, <www.js.com/news/editorials/nov04/276355.asp>. Also see Knut Royce, "CIA Plans to Purge Its Agency," *Newsday,* Washington Bureau, November 15, 2004.

83. Barton Gellman, "Secret Unit Expands Rumsfeld's Domain: New Espionage Branch Delving Into CIA Territory," *Washington Post,* January 23, 2005, A01.

84. Marc Cooper, "Soldier for the Truth: Exposing Bush's Talking-points War," *LA Weekly,* February 20, 2004, <www.laweekly.com/ink/printme.php?eid=51202>.

85. "Spain, United Kingdom of Great Britain and Northern Ireland, and the United States United: Draft Resolution," UN Security Council Resolution #1483, passed May 21, 2003, <www.un.org/News/dh/iraq/iraq-blue-res-052103en.pdf>.

86. President Bush and President Alvaro Uribe of Colombia, White House press release, September 2002, <www.whitehouse.gov/news/releases/2002/09/20020925-1.html>.

87. Richard Benson, "Oil, the Dollar, and US Prosperity," August 11, 2003, <www.prudentbear.com>.

88. John Chapman, "The Real Reasons Bush Went to War," *Guardian* (UK), July 28, 2004, <www.guardian.co.uk/comment/story/0,3604,1270414,00.html>.
89. William Clark, "The Real Reasons for the Upcoming War in Iraq: A Macroeconomic and Geostrategic Analysis of the Unspoken Truth," January 2003 (updated January 2004), <www.ratical.org/ratville/CAH/RRiraqWar.html>.
90. Robert Dreyfuss, "The Thirty Year Itch," *Mother Jones Magazine*, March/April 2003, <www.motherjones.com/news/feature/2003/10/ma_273_01.html>.
91. "UN To Let Iraq Sell Oil for Euros, Not Dollars," *CNN News*, October 30, 2000, http://archives.cnn.com/2000/WORLD/meast/10/30/iraq.un.euro.reut/.
92. Charles Recknagel, "Iraq: Baghdad Moves to Euro," *Radio Free Europe*, November 1, 2000, <www.rferl.org/nca/features/2000/11/01112000160846.asp>.
93. Faisal Islam, "Iraq Nets Handsome Profit by Dumping Dollar for Euro," *Observer*, February 16, 2003, http://observer.guardian.co.uk/iraq/story/0,12239,896344,00.html.
94. Ibid.
95. Ibid.
96. Faisal Islam, "When Will We Buy Oil in Euros?" *Observer*, February 23, 2003, <www.observer.co.uk/business/story/0,6903,900867,00.html>.
97. Ibid.
98. Ibid.
99. Personal correspondence.
100. David E. Spiro, *The Hidden Hand of American Hegemony: Petrodollar Recycling and International Markets*, Cornell University Press, 1999, pp. 121–122.
101. Laurence Vance, "Eight Facts about Iraq." This addresses the history of covert CIA operations in Iraq, including involvement by the CIA and Saddam Hussein in the botched assassination attempt of Abd al-Karim Qasim. January 2, 2004, <www.lewrockwell.com/orig4/vance2.html>.
102. John S. Irons, "Beyond the Baseline: 10-year Deficits Likely to Reach $5.9 Trillion," *OMB Watch*, August 26, 2003, <www.ombwatch.org/article/articleview/1768/1/202/>.
103. Howard Fineman, "In Round 2, It's the Dollar versus the Euro," *msnbc.com*, April 23, 2003, <www.msnbc.com/news/904236.asp>.
104. Carol Hoyos and Kevin Morrison, "Iraq Returns to the International Oil Market," *Financial Times*, June 5, 2003, <www.thedossier.uk.co.uk/Web%20Pages/FINANCIAL%20TIMES_Iraq%20returns%20to%20international%20oil%20market.htm>.
105. Greg Palast, "OPEC on the March," *Harper's Magazine*, April 2005, pp. 74–76.
106. Nayyer Ali, "Iraq and Oil," *PakistanLink*, December 13, 2002, <www.pakistanlink.com/nayyer/12132002.html>.
107. "Albright acknowledges American responsability," *New York Times*, March 18, 2000.
108. Stephen Kinzer, *All the Shah's Men: An American Coup and the Roots of Middle East Terror*, John Wiley & Sons, 2003
109. Ibid., pp. 67–69, 79–80.
110. Ibid., p. 87.
111. Ibid.
112. Ibid., pp. 81–82.
113. Ibid., pp. 132–133.
114. Ibid., pp. 157–158.
115. Ibid., p. x.
116. Dan de Kuce, "The Spectre of Operation Ajax," *Guardian* (UK), August 20, 2003, <www.guardian.co.uk/comment/story/0,3604,1021997,00.html>.

117. Sun-tzu, *The Art of War*, Ralph D. Sawyer (trans.), Barnes and Nobles Books, 1994, p. 173.

118. General (Ret) Mohammad Yahya Nawroz, Army of Afghanistan, and LTC (Ret) Lester W. Grau, US Army, "The Soviet War in Afghanistan: History and Harbinger of Future War?"1996, United States Army, Foreign Military Studies Office, Fort Leavenworth, Kansas, http://fmso.leavenworth.army.mil/fmsopubs/issues/waraf.htm or <leav-www.army.mil/fmso.

119. Bob Woodward, *Plan of Attack*, op. cit., p. 150

120. Pepe Escobar, "Bremer a Quick Study in Colony Building," *Asia Times*, July 12, 2004, <www.atimes.com/atimes/Middle_East/EG12Ak02.html>.

121. "ECB Blasts Bush Economy," *Eupolitix.com*, October 30, 2003, <www.eupolitix.com/EN/News/1947cbee-bbfc-4804-aa90-46521fa785e8.htm>.

122. William Keegan, "Sinking US Dollar Could Drag World Under: The Bank of International Settlements Fears a Deflationary Crisis Because the Global Economy Is Too Tied to America," *Observer*, July 6, 2003, <www.guardian.co.uk/recession/story/0,7369,992277,00.html>.

123. "Russia Shifts to Euro as Foreign Currency Reserves Soar," AFP/Johnson's Russia List, June 8, 2003, <www.cdi.org/russia/johnson/7214-3.cfm>. Also see "Russia May Lift Euro Share of Reserves," *Bloomberg*, November 23, 2004.

124. "China to Diversify Foreign Exchange Reserves," *China Business Weekly*, May 8, 2004, <www.chinadaily.com.cn/english/doc/2004-05/08/content_328744.htm>.

125. Naomi Klein, "Baghdad Year Zero," *Harpers Magazine*, posted September 24, 2004, <www.harpers.org/BaghdadYearZero.html>.

126. Hannah Allam and Tom Lasseter, "Iraqi Whispers Mull Repeat of 1920s Revolt over Western Occupation," *Knight-Ridder Newspapers*, January 27, 2004: <www.realcities.com/mld/krwashington/7809559.htm>.

127. Klein, op. cit.

128. Henry Porter, "A History of Blood and Deception," *Guardian* (UK), August 17, 2004, <www.guardian.co.uk/Iraq/Story/0,2763,1284526,00.html>.

129. Ibid.

130. "100,000 Excess Iraqi Deaths Since War — Study," *Reuters*, October 28, 2004, <www.commondreams.org/headlines04/1028-08.htm>.

131. "The Fog of War," documentary film, directed by Errol Morris Film, Sony Classics Production, 2003. Robert McNamara quote from "Lesson #8: Be prepared to reexamine your reasoning."

132. Julian Coman, "CIA Plans New Secret Police to Fight Iraq Terrorism," *Telegraph* (UK), April 1, 2004, <www.telegraph.co.uk/news/main.jhtml?xml=/news/2004/01/04/wirq04.xml&sSheet=/news/2004/01/04/ixnewstop.html>.

133. Joshua Hammer, "Digging in: If the US Government Doesn't Plan to Occupy Iraq for Any Longer than Necessary, Why Is It Spending Billions of Dollars to Build 'Enduring' Bases?," *Mother Jones Magazine*, March/April 2005.

134. "Rebuilding America's Defenses: Strategies, Forces and Resources for a New Century," PNAC, September 2000, p. 14, <www.newamericancentury.org/RebuildingAmericasDefenses.pdf.420>.

135. Ibid., p. 17.

136. Sir Winston Churchill, 1874 – 1965, <www.quotationspage.com/quote/27333.html>.

137. Pepe Escobar, "The Shi'ites Faustian Pact," *Asia Times*, February 11, 2005, <www.atimes.com/atimes/Middle_East/GB11Ak02.html>.

138. Michael Hirsh, "Grim Numbers: A US-sponsored Poll Shows Iraqis Have Lost Confidence in the Occupying Authorities — and That the Majority of Iraqis

Want Coalition Troops out of the Country," *msnbc.com*, June 15, 2004 (updated June 16, 2004), <www.msnbc.msn.com/id/5217874/site/newsweek/>.

139. Escobar, op. cit.

140. Line Thomsen, "Privatising," *Baghdadbulletin.com*, March 28, 2005, <www.baghdadbulletin.com/pageArticle.php?article_id=146&cat_id=1>.

141. Dana Priest and Robin Wright, "Scowcroft Skeptical Vote Will Stabilize Iraq: Friend of Bush Family Joins Pessimists," *Washington Post*, January 7, 2005, A12.

142. Ibid.

Chapter 5. Dollar Dilemma: Why Petrodollar Hegemony is Unsustainable

1. "Euro Set to Be Currency of Oil Pricing?" *Scotsman*, June 17, 2003, http://thescotsman.scotsman.com/business.cfm?id=666132003.

2. "Iraq Wants to Stop Trading in US Dollars," *Reuters*, September 14, 2000, <www.arabia.com/business/article/english/0,,28727,00.html>.

3. Robert Block, "Some Muslim Nations Advocate Dumping the Dollar for the Euro," *Wall Street Journal*, April 15, 2003.

4. European Parliament resolution on the Communication from the Commission on the European Union's oil supply, COM(2000) 631 — C5-0739/2000 — 2000/2335(COS), June 14, 2001, <www.europarl.eu.int/plenary/default_en.htm>. Click on "words in title or text" under "Texts adopted by Parliament," and search for "oil supply."

5. Robin Newbold, "EU Urges Russia to Swap Dollar for Euro," *Asia Times*, May 19, 2001, <www.atimes.com/c-asia/CD19Ag01.html>.

6. Ibid.

7. "Economics Drive Iran Euro Oil Plan, Politics Also Key," *IranExpert*, August 23, 2002, <www.iranexpert.com/2002/economicsdriveiraneurooil23august.htm>.

8. Ibid.

9. "Should Oil Be Priced in Euros?" *Alexander's Oil and Gas Journal, 9* (4), February 25, 2004; Source, *Khaleej Times*, <www.gasandoil.com/goc/features/fex40825.htm>.

10. Larry Birms and Alex Volberding, "US Is the Primary Loser in Failed Venezuelan Coup," *Newsday*, April 21, 2002, <www.ratical.org/ratville/CAH/linkscopy/USprimaryL.html>. Also see "USA Intelligence Agencies Revealed in Plot to Oust Venezuela's President," *vheadline.com*, December 12, 2002, <www.ratical.org/ratville/CAH/linkscopy/USintelVen.html>.

11. "The Choice of Currency for the Denomination of the Oil Bill," speech by Javad Yarjani, head of OPEC's Petroleum Market Analysis Dept., on the International Role of the Euro, April 14, 2002, <www.opec.org/NewsInfo/Speeches/sp2002/spAraqueSpainApr14.htm>.

12. Ibid.

13. C. Shivkumar, "Iran Offers Oil to Asian Union on Easier Terms," *Hindu Business Line*, June 16, 2003, <www.thehindubusinessline.com/bline/2003/06/17/stories/2003061702380500.htm>.

14. Steve Johnson and Javier Blas, "OPEC Sharply Reduces Dollar Exposure," *Financial Times*, December 6, 2004.

15. James Turk, "OPEC Has Already Turned to the Euro," *GoldMoney*, February 18, 2004, <goldmoney.com/en/commentary/2004-02-18.html>.

16. Ibid.

17. Ibid.

18. Ron Suskind, *The Price of Loyalty: George W. Bush, the White House, and the Education of Paul O' Neill*, Simon & Schuster, 2004, p. 291.

19. Sam Fletcher, "Crude Futures Prices Rise in Shortened NYMEX Session," *Oil and Gas Exchange*, February 20, 2004.

20. Patrick Brethour, "OPEC Mulls Move to Euro for Pricing Crude Oil," *Globe and Mail*, January 12, 2004, <www.theglobeandmail.com/servlet/story/RTGAM.20040112.wopec0112/BNStory/Business/>.

21. United States Census: Imports of Energy Related Petroleum Products, including Crude Oil, Exhibit #17, <www.census.gov/foreign-trade/Press-Release/current_press_release/exh17.pdf>.

22. Christian E. Weller and Scott Lilly, "Oil Prices Up, Dollar Down: Coincidence?" *Center for American Progress}*, November 30, 2004, <www.americanprogress.org/site/pp.asp?c=biJRJ8OVF&b=258795>.

23. Faisal Islam, "When Will We Buy Oil in Euros?" *Observer*, February 23, 2003, <www.observer.co.uk/business/story/0,6903,900867,00.html>.

24. Ibid.

25. Allison Mitchell, "OPEC and the Euro," Tiscali UK Information, February 2, 2004, http://europe.tiscali.co.uk/index.jsp?section=Current%20Affairs&level=preview&content=169132.

26. Block, op. cit.

27. Martin Sieff, "Zogby: Iraq War a Mistake on Many Levels," Arab American Institute, March 18, 2003, <www.aaiusa.org/news/aainews031803.htm>.

28. John Garnaut, "US Dollar Losing Its Position As Asia's Reserve Currency," *www.rense.com*, July 17, 2002, <www.rense.com/general27/rec.htm>.

29. "US Dollar on Shaky Ground," *Associated Press*, 24 January 2003, <www.ratical.org/ratville/CAH/linkscopy/USDshakyGrnd.html>.

30. "Canada Sells Gold, Keeps Shift into Euro Reserves," *Forbes*, January 6, 2003, <www.forbes.com/newswire/2003/01/06/rtr838251.html>.

31. Grainne McCarthy, "Dollar's Decline Starting to Accelerate, Rattling Nerves," *Dow Jones Newswire*, January 25, 2003, <www.ratical.org/ratville/CAH/linkscopy/dollarDec.html>.

32. Personal correspondence.

33. William Pesek Jr., "Indonesia May Dump Dollar, Rest of Asia Too?" *Bloomberg News*, April 17, 2003.

34. Caroline Gluck, "North Korea Embraces the Euro," *BBC News*, December 2, 2002, http://news.bbc.co.uk/1/hi/world/asia-pacific/2531833.stm.

35. Block, op. cit.

36. Catherine Belton, "Putin: Why Not Price Oil in Euros?" *Moscow Times*, October 10, 2003, <www.moscowtimes.ru/stories/2003/10/10/001.html> or archived, <www.globalpolicy.org/socecon/crisis/2003/1010oilpriceeuro.htm>.

37. Ibid.

38. Ibid.

39. Ibid.

40. Ibid.

41. David E. Spiro, *The Hidden Hand of American Hegemony: Petrodollar Recycling and International Markets*, Cornell University Press, 1999, p. 121.

42. "Protest by Switching Oil Trade from Dollar to Euro," *Oil and Gas International*, April 15, 2002, <www.agitprop.org.au/nowar/20020415_ogi_switch_trade_currency.php>.

43. Jean-Charles Brisard and Guillaume Dasquie, *The Forbidden Truth: US-Taliban Secret Oil Diplomacy, Saudi Arabia and the Failed Search for bin Laden*, Nation Books, 2002, pp. 115–139.

44. Ibid, pp. 181–230.

45. Ibid, pp. xxvii–xxx.
46. Ibid, p. xxx.
47. Michael C. Ruppert, *Crossing the Rubicon: Decline of the American Empire at the End of the Age of Oil*, New Society Publishers, 2004, pp. 204–207, 220–222.
48. "Has Someone Been Sitting on the FBI?" *BBC 2*, November 6, 2001, http://news.bbc.co.uk/1/hi/events/newsnight/1645527.stm. Also see: Mosaddeq Ahmed Nafeez, *The War on Freedom: How and Why America Was Attacked September 11, 2001*, Media Messenger Books; 3rd edition, 2002, pp. 106–113, 176–202.
49. Spiro, op. cit., p. 121.
50. Islam, op. cit.
51. Johnson and Blas, op. cit.
52. James McInerney, "Saudi Sees Stronger Euro Role," *Middle East Finance and Economy, AME Info*, January 12, 2005, <www.ameinfo.com/news/Detailed/52008.html>.
53. Ibid.
54. Hazel Henderson, "Beyond Bush's Unilateralism: Another Bi-Polar World or a New Era of Win-Win?" *InterPress Service*, June 2002, <www.hazelhenderson.com/editorials/beyondBush'sUnilaterialism06-02.html>.
55. "Economics Drive Iran Euro Oil Plan, Politics Also Key," *Iran Expert*, August 23, 2002, <www.iranexpert.com/2002/economicsdriveiraneurooil23august.htm>.
56. Terry Macalister, "Iran Takes on West's Control of Oil Trading," *Guardian* (UK), June 16, 2004, <www.guardian.co.uk/business/story/0,3604,1239644,00.html>.
57. "War-Gaming the Mullahs: The US Weighs the Price of a Pre-emptive Strike," *Newsweek*, September 27, 2004, <www.msnbc.msn.com/id/6039135/site/newsweek/>.
58. Seymour Hersh, "The Coming Wars," *New Yorker*, January 24, 2005, pp. 40–47, <www.newyorker.com/fact/content/?050124fa_fact>.
59. "Iran Eyes Deal on Oil Bourse; IPE Chairman Visits Tehran," Rigzone.com, July 8, 2004.
60. Macalister, op. cit.
61. Shivkumar, op. cit.
62. Macalister, op. cit.
63. "Iran Eyes Deal" op. cit.
64. "Oil Bourse Closer to Reality," *IranMania.com*, December 28, 2004, <www.iranmania.com/News/ArticleView/Default.asp?ArchiveNews=Yes&NewsCode=28176&NewsKind=BusinessEconomy>.
65. "War-Gaming," op. cit.
66. "Terror and Regime Change: Any US Invasion of Iran Will Have Terrible Consequences," *News Insight: Public Affairs Magazine*, June 11, 2004, <www.indiareacts.com/archivedebates/nat2.asp?recno=908&ctg=World>.
67. Tactical analysis of Musa Island, <www.globalsecurity.org/wmd/world/iran/abu-musa.htm>.
68. James Fallows, "Will Iran Be Next?" *Atlantic Monthly*, December 2004, pp. 97–110.
69. Ibid.
70. Ibid.
71. "China, Iran Sign Biggest Oil and Gas Deal," *China Daily*, October 31, 2004, <www.chinadaily.com.cn/english/doc/2004-10/31/content_387140.htm>.
72. Michael C. Ruppert, "As the World Burns," *From the Wilderness*, December 1, 2004, <www.fromthewilderness.com/free/ww3/120104_world_burns.shtml>.

73. Sammy Salama and Karen Ruster, "A Preemptive Attack on Iran's Nuclear Facilities: Possible Consequences," Monterey Institute of International Studies, August 12, 2004, http://cns.miis.edu/pubs/week/040812.htm.

74. Robert Baer, "The Fall of the House of Saud," *Atlantic Monthly*, May, 2002.

75. Will Hutton, "Why Bush Is Sunk without Europe," *Observer*, January 26, 2003, http://observer.guardian.co.uk/print/0,3858,4591686-102273,00.html.

76. Peter Dale Scott, "Bush's Deep Reasons for War on Iraq: Oil, Petrodollars, and the OPEC Euro Question," updated May 27, 2003, http://ist-socrates.berkeley.edu/~pdscott/iraq.html

77. Johnson and Blas, op. cit.

78. Neil Mackey, "US Admits the War for 'Hearts and Minds' in Iraq Is Now Lost," *Sunday Herald*, December 5, 2004, <www.sundayherald.com/46389>.

79. Derek Brown, "Millennium in Review, Day 479, 1956-1957,"*Guardian Unlimited* (UK), <www.guardian.co.uk/Millennium/0,2833,246499,00.html>.

80. Ibid.

81. "Should Oil Be Priced in Euros?" op. cit.

82. Peter J. Cooper, "Forget the Oil Price, What About the Euro?" *Middle East Finance and Economy/AME Info*, October 14, 2000, <www.ameinfo.com/news/Detailed/16290.html>.

Chapter 6: Saving the American Experiment

1. Duncan Martell, "US: Ted Turner Calls Rival Media Mogul Murdoch 'Warmonger,'" *Reuters*, April 25, 2003, www.worldrevolution.org/article/875.

2. Miren Gutierrez, "World's Media: Fewer Players, Less Freedom," *Inter Press Service*, March 20, 2004, <www.ips.org/, <www.commondreams.org/headlines04/0320-01.htm>.

3. Sidney Blumenthal, "Reality Is Unraveling for Bush," *Guardian (UK)*, June 24, 2004, <www.guardian.co.uk/comment/story/0,3604,1245877,00.html>.

4. Sara Scavongelli, "Columnist Upset with White House: Helen Thomas Tells Indy Journalist, Bush Administration and Media Ignore Truth," *The Indianapolis Star*, July 8, 2004, <www.indystar.com/articles/9/160828-7329-009.html>.

5. George Monbiot, "The Newspapers Must Also Be Held to Account for the Decision to Invade Iraq," *Guardian (UK)*, July 20 2004, <www.monbiot.com/archives/2004/07/20/>.

6. Details about Operation Mockingbird, <www.disinfopedia.org/wiki.phtml?title=Operation_Mockingbird>.

7. "Media Conglomerates, Mergers, Concentration of Ownership," http://www.globalissues.org/HumanRights/Media/Corporations/Owners.asp.

8. Peter Phillips, *Censored 2004: The Top 25 Censored Stories*, Seven Stories Press, 2003, p. 171.

9. John R. Talbot, *America Went Wrong and How to Regain Her Democratic Ideas*, Financial Times Prentice Hall, 2004, p. 206.

10. "Reporters without Borders Publishes the First Worldwide Press Freedom Index," <www.rsf.fr, October 2002, <www.rsf.fr/article.php3?id_article=4116>.

11. Fraizer Moore, "Bill Moyers Retiring from TV Journalism," *AP News*, December 9, 2004, http://apnews.myway.com//article/20041209/D86SBTC80.html.

12. Chalmers Johnson, "The Military-Industrial Man: How Local Politics Works in America, or a 'Duke' in Every District," *www.tomdispatch.com.*, September 14, 2004, <www.tomdispatch.com/index.mhtml?pid=1818>.

13. "Winning Contractors: US Contractors Reap the Windfalls of Post-war Reconstruction," The Center for Public Integrity, October 30, 2003,

<www.publicintegrity.org/wow/report.aspx?aid=65>. Also see "Big Contracts Went to Big Donors," *CBS News/Associated Press*, October 30, 2003, <www.cbsnews.com/stories/2003/10/30/iraq/main580998.shtml>.

14. "What Did Eisenhower Mean When He Warned of a Military Industrial Complex? Take a Look at the Carlyle Group." June 23, 2003, *Buzzflash* interview with Dan Briody, author of *The Iron Triangle: Inside the Secret World of the Carlyle Group*, John Wiley & Sons, 2003, <www.buzzflash.com/interviews/03/06/23_briody.html>.

15. "The Full Cost of Ballistic Missile Defense." The Center for Arms Control and Non-Proliferation and Economists Allied for Arms Reduction, January 2, 2003.

16. "Straws in the Wind: The Terrorist Attacks and Missile Defense," Council for a Livable World, October 1, 2001, <www.clw.org/nmd/sept11.html>.

17. Chalmers Johnson, "Sorrows of Empire," Global Policy Forum, November 2003, <www.globalpolicy.org/empire/analysis/2003/11sorrow.htm>.

18. "The Real Price of Gas," International Center for Technology Assessment, 1998, <www.icta.org/projects/trans/rlprexsm.htm>.

19. "NDCF Report: The Hidden Cost of Imported Oil," Institute for the Analysis of Global Security, October 30, 2003, <www.iags.org/n1030034.htm>.

20. Thom Hartmann, *Unequal Protection: The Rise of Corporate Dominance and the Theft of Human Rights*, Rodale Books, 2002. Also see: Thom Hartmann and Neil Cohen (illustr.) *We the People: A Call to Take Back America*, Coreway Media, 2004

21. The concept of "corporate personhood" was evoked not by the Supreme Court justices, but by the court reporter in that Supreme Court case. Also see Cecil Adams, "How Can a Corporation Be Legally Considered a Person?" *thestraightdope.com*, September 19, 2003, <www.straightdope.com/columns/030919.html>.

22. "The Danger of American Fascism," by Henry A. Wallace, in *Henry A. Wallace, Democracy Reborn*, New York, 1944, Russell Lord (ed.), p. 259. Sunday April 9, 1944, <www.truthout.org/docs_03/082103F.shtml>.

23. "Record 2004 Lobby Expenditures to Exceed $2 Billion," Political Money Line, December 28, 2004, <www.tray.com/>.

24. CNN notes on exit polls: National Election Poll: Frequently Asked Questions, Edison Media Research / Mitofsky International, 2005, <www.exit-poll.net/faq.html>. Also see Stephen Freeman, "The Unexplained Exit Poll Discrepancy," http://center.grad.upenn.edu/center/get.cgi?item=exitpollp, to be published in Joel Bleifuss, *Was the 2004 Presidential Election Stolen?* Seven Stories Press, 2005, <www.appliedresearch.us/sf/epdiscrep.htm>.

25. Johns Hopkins University Information Security Institute Technical Report TR-2003, July 2003; principal researcher, Dr. Aviel D. Rubin: "Analysis of an Electronic Voting System," February 27, 2004, <http://avirubin.com/vote/analysis/>.

26. Report for Maryland's Department of Legislative Services, conducted by RABA Technologies. Michael A. Wertheimer, "Trust Agent Report: Diebold AccuVote-TS Voting System," RABA Innovative Solution Cell (RiSC), January 20, 2004, <www.raba.com/press/TA_Report_AccuVote.pdf>.

27. "For Those with a Flair for the Dramatic: How to SpeedHack the Vote, the FAST Version," Chuck Herrin, <www.chuckherrin.com/SpeedHackTheVote.htm>.

28. Johnson, op. cit., p. 310.

29. Ibid., p. 312.

30. G.G. Labelle, "Bush Speech Draws Cautious Reaction across Middle East," *The Olympian*, November 8, 2003, <www.theolympian.com/home/specialsections/War/20031108/144118.shtml>.

31. Ibid.

32. Ibid.
33. Ibid.
34. Ibid.
35. Terrorism Questions and Answers Facts Sheet, "Causes of 9/11: US Support for Repressive Regimes?" Council on Foreign Relations, <www.terrorismanswers.org/causes/regimes.html>.
36. Rory McCarthy, "We Will Fight until the End, until Each One of Them Dies." *Guardian* (UK), April 8, 2004, <www.guardian.co.uk/Iraq/Story/ 0,2763,1188156,00.html>.
37. Emmanuel Todd, *After the Empire: The Breakdown of the American Order*, Columbia University Press, 2004.
38. Ibid.
39. Bob Woodward, *Plan of Attack*, Simon & Schuster, 2004, p. 150.
40. Anonymous, *Imperial Hubris: The West Is Losing the War on Terror*, Brassey's, 2004, p. 17.
41. Donna Bryson, "Bin Laden Says He Wants to Bankrupt America," *Chicago Sun-Times*, November 2, 2004, <www.suntimes.com/output/terror/ cst-nws-laden02.html>.
42. Dan Eggen and John Mintz, "Seriousness of Threat Defended Despite Dated Intelligence," *Washington Post*, August 4, 2004, A11, <www.washingtonpost.com/wp-dyn/articles/A37954-2004Aug3.html>.
43. Ibid.
44. Anonymous, op. cit.
45. Ibid.
46. Ibid.
47. Ibid., p. 101.
48. Eric Margolis, "Anti-US militants showing up all over," *Toronto Star*, June 23, 2002, <www.ericmargolis.com/archives/2002/06/antius_militants_showing_ up_all_over.php>.
49. Rebecca Carr, "Only 200 Hard-Core Qaeda Members," *Palm Beach Post*, July 29, 2002, <www.why-war.com/news/2002/07/29/onlyhard.html>.
50. George Soros, "The Bubble of American Supremacy," *Atlantic*, December 2003, <www.theatlantic.com/issues/2003/12/soros.htm>.
51. Jack Kelley, "Al-Qaeda Fragmented, Smaller but Still Deadly," *USA TODAY*, September 9, 2002.
52. Adam Curtis, writer, producer and narrator of the three-part documentary series, *The Power of Nightmares*, BBC, http://news.bbc.co.uk/1/hi/magazine/ 4171213.stm.
53. Michael Mann, *Incoherent Empire*, Verso, 2003, pp. 165–170.
54. Anonymous, op. cit.
55. Ibid., p. 241.
56. "Fact Sheet on Counter-terrorism Operations," International Police/INTER-POL, <www.interpol.int/Public/Icpo/FactSheets/FS200102.asp>.
57. "What the World Thinks in 2002: How Global Publics View Their Lives, Their Countries, the World, and America," The Pew Charitable Trusts, 2002.
58. Oxfam GB/Oxfam International, <www.oxfam.org.uk/what_we_do/ fairtrade/ft_faq.htm#1>.
59. Universal Declaration of Human Rights, adopted and proclaimed by General Assembly of the United Nations, Resolution 217 A (III), 10 December 1948, <www.un.org/Overview/rights.html>.
60. International Court of Justice, <www.icj-cij.org/>.

61. Nat Hentoff, "Patriot Act Besieged: Justice Department Honcho Confesses: 'We Are Losing the Fight for the Patriot Act,'" *Village Voice*, May 28, 2004, <www.villagevoice.com/news/0422,hentoff,53938,6.html>.

62. Nat Hentoff, *The War on the Bill of Rights and the Gathering Resistance*, Seven Stories Press, 2003, p. 138.

63. Nat Hentoff, "Declarations of Independence: Since the Reign of King George III, Resistance Has Been Our Legacy — and to This Day Still Is," *Village Voice*, June 14, 2004, <www.villagevoice.com/news/0424,hentoff,54304,6.html>.

64. John W. Whitehead and Steven H. Aden, "Forfeiting 'Enduring Freedom' for 'Homeland Security': A Constitutional Analysis of the USA Patriot Act and the Justice Department's Anti-Terrorism Initiatives," *American University Law Review*, 51, 2002, pp. 1081–1133.

65. "Analysis of the USA Patriot Act," Electronic Privacy Information Center (EPIC), <www.epic.org/privacy/terrorism/usapatriot/>.

66. David Domke, *God Willing? Political Fundamentalism in the White House, the 'War on Terror' and the Echoing Press"*, Ann Arbor, MI: Pluto Press, 2004.

67. "Scholar Analyzes Religious Influence, Political Impact of Bush Administration's Strategic Communications in New Book," Press Release for lecture at Whitworth College September 22, 2004, <www.whitworth.edu/News/2004_2005/Fall/DomkeLecture.htm>.

68. Domke, op. cit., pp. ix–xii.

69. "Roosevelt in the Kansas City Star," May 7, 1918.

70. Richard C. Leone and Greg Anrig Jr., *The War on Our Freedoms: Civil Liberties in an Age of Terrorism*, Public Affairs, 2003.

71. Marvin R. Shanken, "Command Central," interview with General Franks, *Cigar Aficionado*, December 2003, p. 90.

72. House of Lords: Opinions of the Lords of Appeal for Judgment in the Cause, A (FC) and others (FC) (Appellants) vs. Secretary of State for the Home Department (Respondent), X (FC) and another (FC) (Appellants) vs. Secretary of State for the Home Department (Respondent), [2004] UKHL 56 on appeal from: 2002 *EWCA Civ 1502*, par. 96, <www.parliament.the-stationery-office.co.uk/pa/ld200405/ldjudgmt/jd041216/a&oth-1.htm>.

Chapter 7. Envisioning Progressive Global Reform in the New Century

1. Emmanuel Todd, *After the Empire: The Breakdown of the American Order*, Columbia University Press, 2004, p. 202.

2. "China Lays Into 'Bush Doctrine' ahead of US Poll," *Reuters*, October 31, 2004.

3. George Soros, "The Bubble of American Supremacy," *Atlantic*, December 2003, <www.theatlantic.com/issues/2003/12/soros.htm>.

4. Christopher Marquis, "US Image Abroad Will Take Years to Repair, Official Testifies," *New York Times*, February 5, 2004, <www.nytimes.com/2004/02/05/politics/05DIPL.html?pagewanted=print&position=>.

5. "Reckless Administration May Reap Disastrous Consequences," Senator Robert Byrd speech in the Senate, February 12, 2003.

6. Margo Kingston, "A Think Tank War: Why Old Europe Says No," *Sydney Morning Herald*, March 7, 2003, http://smh.com.au/articles/2003/03/07/1046826528748.html?oneclick=true.

7. Marquis, op. cit.

8. "Abu Ghraib Reports: Highest Echelon's Responsible for 'Sadism,'" Analysis of Foreign Media Reaction, Global Security, August 31, 2004, <www.globalsecurity.org/wmd/library/news/iraq/2004/08/wwwh40831.htm>.

9. "Anti-America Europe Would Be Dangerous: Blair," *Daily Times*, April 4, 2003, <www.dailytimes.com.pk/default.asp?page=story_29-4-2003_pg4_2>.

10. T.R. Reid, *The United States of Europe: The New Superpower and the End of American Supremacy*, Penguin Press, 2004, pp. 243–244.

11. Ibid., pp. 35–36.

12. Ibid., p. 63.

13. Ibid., pp. 1–6.

14. Ibid., pp. 227–244.

15. Zbigniew Brzezinski, *The Choice: Global Domination or Global Leadership*, Basic Books, 2004, pp. 220–221.

16. Novakeo, "Currency Wars: Euro versus Dollar," *Etherzone.com*, May 12, 2003, <www.etherzone.com/2003/nova051203.shtml>.

17. Ibid.

18. Ibid.

19. Paul Isbell, "The Shifting Geopolitics of the Euro," El Cano Institute, September 28, 2002, <www.realinstitutoelcano.org/analisis/70.asp>.

20. Germar Rudolf, "On the Brink of World War Three: Why the USA Must Wage War, But Cannot Wage It against the Country It Ought to." *Revisionist 1* (2), pp. 124–130.

21. Javad Yarjani, "The Choice of Currency for the Denomination of the Oil Bill," head of OPEC's Petroleum Market Analysis Dept., speech on the International Role of the Euro, April 14, 2002,

22. Michael Vatikiotis and Bertil Lintner, "The Renminbi Zone," *Asia Times*, May 29, 2003.

23. Allison Wiggin, "The Era of Fictitious Capitalism," *LewRockwell.com*, December 6, 2003, <www.lewrockwell.com/orig4/wiggin-addison1.html>.

24. Edith M. Lederer, "Economist: China Loses Faith in Dollar," *Associated Press*, January 26, 2005, as reported in the *Washington Post*, <www.washingtonpost.com/wp-dyn/articles/A39107-2005Jan26.html>.

25. Vatikiotis and Lintner, op. cit.

26. Ibid.

27. Wiggin, op. cit.

28. John M. Glionna, "China, US Each Hold Major War Exercises," *Global Policy Forum*, July 20, 2004, <www.globalpolicy.org/empire/intervention/2004/0721chinaus.htm>.

29. Todd Stein and Steven McIntyre, "China Dumps Dollars for Oil and Gold," *www.kitco.com*, October 18, 2004, <www.kitco.com/ind/Texashedge/oct182004.html>.

30. Brett Arends, "Economic 'Armageddon' Predicted," *Boston Herald*, November 23, 2004, http://business.bostonherald.com/businessNews/view.bg?articleid=55356.613.

31. Jephraim Gundzick, "Investor Demand to Push Gold Price Higher in 2004," *Middle East Finance and Economy, AME Info*, February 2004, <www.ameinfo.com/news/Detailed/35090.html>.

32. Jeffrey Sommers, "Dollar Crisis and American Empire," *Znet.com*, June 20, 2003, http://zmag.org/content/showarticle.cfm?SectionID=10&ItemID=3803.

33. Heather Stewart, "Japan Threatens Huge Dollar Sell-off," *Observer*, December 5, 2004, http://observer.guardian.co.uk/business/story/0,6903,1366578,00.html.

34. Isbell, op. cit.

35. Ibid.

36. Brzezinski, op. cit., pp. 220–221.

37. Carter Announcement Address for the 1976 Democratic Presidential Nomination, December 12, 1976.
38. President Bush, speech in Trenton, New Jersey, September 23, 2002.
39. Richard Heinberg, "The Choice of the Elites," *Powerdown: Options and Actions for a Post-Carbon World*, New Society Publishers, 2004, pp. 167–172.
40. Robert Freeman, "Will the End of Oil Mean the End of America?" *commondreams.org*, March 1, 2004, <www.commondreams.org/views04/0301-12.htm>.
41. Ibid.
42. Helon Altonn, "Pipeline Nourishes Ocean Tech Park," *starbulletoin.com*, January 2, 2002, http://starbulletin.com/2002/01/03/news/story8.html.
43. Michael Ventura, "Letters at 3 am - $4 a gallon," *Austin Chronicle*, April 29, 2005.
44. Kenneth S. Dreffeyes, *Hubbert's Peak: The Impending World Oil Shortage*, Princeton University Press, 2001, p. 149.
45. David E. Spiro, *The Hidden Hand of American Hegemony: Petrodollar Recycling and International Markets*, Cornell University Press, 1999, p. 157.
46. Bob Fitrakis and Harvey Wasserman, *Bush and America's Willing Executioners Would Be Guilty at Nuremburg*, Free Press, March 2, 2003, <www.commondreams.org/views03/0302-07.htm>.
47. *New Projects Cannot Meet World Demand This Decade*, ODAC/The Oil Depletion Analysis Centre, November 16, 2004.
48. Eamonn Fingleton, *In Praise of Hard Industries: Why Manufacturing, Not the Information Economy, Is the Key to Future Prosperity*, Buttonwood Press, 1999. Fingleton's website offers insightful articles on "why manufacturing still matters," <www.fingleton.net>.
49. Uppsala Hydrocarbon Depletion Study Group, Uppsala University, Sweden, <www.oilcrisis.com/uppsala/uppsalaProtocol.html>; Uppsala Accord, <www.globalpublicmedia.com/DOCS/2004/05/RIMINI%20PROTOCOL.pdf>.
50. Richard Heinberg, op. cit.
51. Duncan, *Dollar Crisis: Causes, Consequences, Cures*, John Wiley & Sons, 2003, p. 168.
52. Freeman, op. cit.
53. Danny Postel, "Noble Lies and Perpetual War: Leo Strauss, the Neo-cons, and Iraq," October 16, 2003, <www.informationclearinghouse.info/article5010.htm>.
54. Michael Hirsh, "Grim Numbers: A US-sponsored Poll Shows Iraqis Have Lost Confidence in the Occupying Authorities — and that the Majority of Iraqis Want Coalition Troops out of the Country," *msnbc.com*, June 15, 2004 (updated June 16, 2004), <www.msnbc.msn.com/id/5217874/site/newsweek/>.
55. "To Euro or Not: Should Oil Pricing Ditch the Dollar?" *EU Business*, February 4, 2004, <www.eubusiness.com/afp/040209030947.7x4cldn1>.
56. Zbigniew Brzezinski, speech at the New American Strategies for Security and Peace Conference, October 28–29, 2003, general website <www.newamericanstrategies.org/; speech>, <www.newamericanstrategies.org/transcripts/Brzezinski.asp>.
57. Richard Heinberg defined "Powerdown" in the opening page of his book. Power-down \\ n. 1. the energy famine that engulfed industrial nations in the early 21ˢᵗ century 2. the deliberate process of cooperation, contraction, and conversion that enabled humanity to survive, *Powerdown, Options and Actions for a Post-Carbon World*, New Society Publishers, 2004.

Epilogue

1. David Frum and Richard Perle, *An End to Evil: How to Win the War on Terror*, Random House, 2003.

2. Amy Svitak Klampe, "Former Iraq Administrator Sees Decades Long US Military Presence in Iraq," *Government Executive Magazine*, February 6, 2004, <www.govexec.com/dailyfed/0204/020604cdam3.htm>.

3. Dan Oberdorfer, *The Two Koreas*, Basic Books, 2001, p. 7.

Further Resources on Oil and Natural Gas Depletion

Campbell, Colin J. *The Coming Oil Crisis*, Multi-Science Publishing, 2004.

Campbell, Colin J. *The Essence of Oil and Gas Depletion*, Multi-Science Publishing, 2003.

Campbell, Colin J. *The Truth about Oil and the Looming Energy Crisis*, Post Carbon Books, 2005.

Darley, Julian. *High Noon for Natural Gas: The New Energy Crisis*, Chelsea Green, 2004.

Dreffeyes, Kenneth S. *Beyond Oil: The View from Hubbert's Peak*, Hill and Wang, 2005.

Dreffeyes, Kenneth S. *Hubbert's Peak: The Impending World Oil Shortage*, Princeton University Press, 2001.

Hamilton-Bergin, S. *The No 19 Bus: The Coming Global Energy Crisis*, <www.no19bus.org.uk/>, 2003.

Hartmann, Thomas. *The Last Hours of Ancient Sunlight: Waking up to Personal and Global Transformation*, Three Rivers Press, 2000.

Heinberg, Richard. *The Party's Over: Oil, War and the Fate of Industrial Societies, Revised and Updated Version*, Gabriola Island, BC: New Society Publishers, 2005.

Heinberg, Richard. *Powerdown: Options and Actions for a Post-Carbon World*, Gabriola Island, BC: New Society Publishers, 2004.

Klare, Michael T. *Blood and Oil: The Dangers and Consequences of America's Growing Petroleum Dependency*, Metropolitan Books, 2004.

Klare, Michael T. *Resource Wars: The New Landscape of Global Conflict*, Owl Books, 2002.

Kunstler, James Howard. *The Long Emergency: Surviving the End of the Oil Age, Climate Change, and Other Converging Catastrophes of the Twenty-first Century*, Atlantic Monthly Press, 2005.

Leeb, Stephen and Donna Leeb. *The Oil Factor: How Oil Controls the Economy and Your Financial Future*, Three Rivers Press, 2004.

Roberts, Paul. *The End of Oil: On the Edge of a Perilous New World*, Houghton Mifflin, 2004.

Ruppert, Michael C. *Crossing the Rubicon: The Decline of the American Empire at the End of the Age of Oil*, Gabriola Island, BC: New Society Publishers, 2004.

Simmons, Matthew R. *Twighlight in the Desert: The Coming Saudi Oil Shock and the World Economy*, Wiley, 2005.

Video (VHS or DVD)

The End of Suburbia: Oil Depletion and the Collapse of The American Dream. Hosted by Barrie Zwicker. Featuring James Howard Kunstler, Peter Calthorpe, Michael Klare, Richard Heinberg, Matthew Simmons, Michael C. Ruppert, Julian Darley, Colin Campbell, Kenneth Dreffeyes, Ali Samsam Bakhtiari, and Steve Andrews. Directed by Gregory Greene. Produced by Barry Silverthorn, www.endofsuburbia.com, 2004. Greene is working on a follow-up film, "Escape from Suburbia."

Additional Recommended Reading on US Media Censorship:

Borjesson, Kristina (ed.). *Into the Buzzsaw: Leading Journalist Exposes the Myth of a Free Press*, Promethesus Books, updated and expanded version, 2004.

Internet Resources

Post Carbon Institute,

Hubbert Peak of Oil Production,

Association for the Study of Peak Oil and Gas (ASPO), <www.peakoil.net>

Powerswitch (UK site),

Peak Oil Message Board, <www.peakoil.com>

Index

A

Afghanistan, XVI, 48, 49, 60, 71, 102, 114, 166, 179

Africa, 66-67, 72, 146, 181, 186. *See also* West Africa

Al Qaeda, 14, 70, 89, 98, 108-109, 148, 218
terrorism, 3, 15, 47, 88, 105, 176-181

Alaska, 31, 83

Alaska National Wildlife Refuge (ANWR), 82-83

Allawi, Ayad, 129

American Enterprise Institute (AEI), 99, 102

Annan, Kofi, 58

Anglo-Iranian Oil Company, 124. *See also* British Petroleum

anti-Americanism, 173, 182, 188

Association for the Study of Peak Oil (ASPO), 4, 64, 78-80, 88, 258

Austria, 20

Axis of Evil, 14, 117, 126, 137, 146

B

Baker Institute, 51, 52

Bank of International Settlement (BIS), 12, 20, 128, 149

Bilderberg Group, 19, 21, 28-30

Blair, Tony, 14, 68, 88, 96-97, 106, 156, 198-199

Blix, Hans, 97, 111, 114, 189

Blumenthal, Michael, 20

Bretton Woods Monetary Conferences, 17-22, 37, 143, 199

British Petroleum (BP), 31, 35, 39, 60, 88, 98, 152

Brzezinski, Zbigniew, 13, 40, 133, 199, 207, 219-220

Bush, George W., 45, 50, 95, 106, 109, 110, 115, 172, 188, 208
administration, 24, 25, 51, 56, 59, 111, 113-114, 144, 190. *See also* United States; Iraq War

Bush, H. W., 46, 52, 53

C

Campbell, Colin, XIII, 75, 82, 92

Canada, 20, 41, 51, 67, 79-83, 144, 164, 183

Caspian Sea region, 70-71, 184
oil, 27, 49, 51, 59-60, 152, 210, 224

Central Intelligence Agency (CIA), 80, 110-114, 123, 125, 150-151, 154, 218
and Afghanistan, xvi, 60, 98
and Al Qaeda, 3, 15, 177, 179
and Iraq, 3, 103-104, 109, 129-130, 189
and Russia, 48, 89
and Saudi Arabia, 30, 49, 147-148, 186
and Soviet Union, 13, 49

About the Author

William R. Clark's ground breaking
research on the Iraq War, oil currency
conflict, and U.S. geostrategy received
a 2003 Project Censored award, published in Censored 2004: The Top 25
Censored Stories. His research on Iran's
upcoming euro-dominated oil Bourse
received a 2005 Project Censored
award, to be published in the forth-
coming *Censored 2006*. William is an
Information Security Analyst at Argosy
Omnimedia, and he holds a Master of
Business Administration and Master of

Science in Information and Telecommunication Systems from Johns
Hopkins University. He lives in Rockville, Maryland.

If you have enjoyed *Petrodollar Warfare*,
you might also enjoy other

BOOKS TO BUILD A NEW SOCIETY

Our books provide positive solutions for people who want to
make a difference. We specialize in:

Environment and Justice • Conscientious Commerce
Sustainable Living • Ecological Design and Planning
Natural Building & Appropriate Technology • New Forestry
Educational and Parenting Resources • Nonviolence
Progressive Leadership • Resistance and Community

New Society Publishers

ENVIRONMENTAL BENEFITS STATEMENT

New Society Publishers has chosen to produce this book on Enviro 100, recycled
paper made with **100% post consumer waste**, processed chlorine free, and old
growth free.

For every 5,000 books printed, New Society saves the following resources:[1]

33	Trees
2,989	Pounds of Solid Waste
3,289	Gallons of Water
4,290	Kilowatt Hours of Electricity
5,434	Pounds of Greenhouse Gases
23	Pounds of HAPs, VOCs, and AOX Combined
8	Cubic Yards of Landfill Space

[1]Environmental benefits are calculated based on research done by the Environmental Defense Fund and
other members of the Paper Task Force who study the environmental impacts of the paper industry.
For more information on this environmental benefits statement, or to inquire about environmentally
friendly papers, please contact New Leaf Paper – info@newleafpaper.com Tel: 888 • 989 • 5323.

For a full list of NSP's titles, please call **1-800-567-6772** *or check out our website at:*

www.newsociety.com

NEW SOCIETY PUBLISHERS